In Search of Canine Justice

This book is part of the Peter Lang Political Science, Economics, and Law list.
Every volume is peer reviewed and meets
the highest quality standards for content and production.

PETER LANG
New York • Bern • Berlin
Brussels • Vienna • Oxford • Warsaw

Julie Walsh

In Search of Canine Justice

Law and Practice in the United States and European Union

PETER LANG
New York • Bern • Berlin
Brussels • Vienna • Oxford • Warsaw

Library of Congress Cataloging-in-Publication Data

Names: Walsh, Julie, author.
Title: In search of canine justice: law and practice
in the United States and European Union / Julie Walsh.
Description: New York: Peter Lang, 2019.
Includes bibliographical references and index.
Identifiers: LCCN 2018050129 | ISBN 978-1-4331-5901-5 (hardback: alk. paper)
ISBN 978-1-4331-6403-3 (ebook pdf) | ISBN 978-1-4331-6404-0 (epub)
ISBN 978-1-4331-6405-7 (mobi)
Subjects: LCSH: Dogs—Law and legislation—United States.
Dogs—Law and legislation—European Union countries.
Animal welfare—Law and legislation—United States.
Animal welfare—Law and legislation—European Union countries.
Classification: LCC K564.D64 W35 2019 | DDC 344.2404/9—dc23
LC record available at https://lccn.loc.gov/2018050129
DOI 10.3726/b15044

Bibliographic information published by **Die Deutsche Nationalbibliothek**.
Die Deutsche Nationalbibliothek lists this publication in the "Deutsche Nationalbibliografie"; detailed bibliographic data are available on the Internet at http://dnb.d-nb.de/.

29 Broadway, 18th floor, New York, NY 10006
www.peterlang.com

To Mike

TABLE OF CONTENTS

TABLES

ACKNOWLEDGMENTS

I am deeply indebted to many people who helped me to bring this project to completion. From the start, my colleagues at American International College have been supportive of this research. The College granted me a sabbatical in 2014, which helped me enormously to jumpstart the research and writing for the work. Otherwise, I am reliant on summers only to get writing done! While I was on sabbatical, Dean Susanne Swanker, and Professors Thomas Maulucci and Gary Jones covered my duties for me. In addition, Professors Debbi Anderson and Gary Jones encouraged me to present my early research findings to the campus community when I returned from sabbatical. The feedback from that presentation helped me to improve the manuscript. I am especially appreciative of the support of my colleagues given the inter-disciplinary nature of this work.

Kristin Purdy, Michelle Smith, Janell Harris, and the editorial team at Peter Lang have been enormously helpful and supportive of this project. Their enthusiasm for the project motivated me to work hard on the manuscript and their substantive recommendations helped to improve it. It has been a pleasure working with such a professional and competent team!

Special thanks, as always, are due to my husband, Mike, to whom this book is dedicated. Always incredibly supportive of all of my endeavors, including my research and writing, Mike traveled to England, where I presented some of my preliminary studies at a conference, with me. I cannot thank him enough for all of his support! My family too deserves thanks for the lifelong support that they have provided me. I can always count on Jim, Beth, Joan, Joe and Barbara McGivern, George and Mary Valentine, and Mary Walsh.

I also must acknowledge the support given to me by my canine friends and those human friends that have come into my life because of my canine connections. In the past year, Mike and I lost our two dogs, Devin and Sadie, to illness. Their presence and loss were constant reminders to me in the final stages of this project of how precious each canine life is. I hope that this work encourages readers to appreciate that fact if they do not already! It is so impressive to interact with those who care for animals and that experience also motivated me to write this work. When the dogs were ill, Lilly and Steve Feldman provided extraordinary care with compassion and love. They, my family, and other close friends also provided much needed emotional support. More recently, they have welcomed Keegan, our puppy, into their lives. Thank you more than words can say to Mike, my family, and close friends!

ABBREVIATIONS

AKC	American Kennel Club
APHIS	Animal and Plant Health Inspection Service
ASPCA	American Society for the Prevention of Cruelty to Animals
AVMA	American Veterinary Medical Association
AWA	Animal Welfare Act
BUAV	British Union for the Abolition of Vivisection
CARODog	Companion Animal Responsible Ownership
ECPPA	European Convention for the Protection of Pet Animals
ESDAW	European Society for Dog and Animal Welfare
EU	European Union
FEMA	Federal Emergency Management Agency
HSUS	Humane Society of the United States
ISPCA	Irish Society for the Prevention of Cruelty to Animals
NPS	National Park Service
PETS	Pets Evacuation and Transportation Standards
RSPCA	Royal Society for the Prevention of Cruelty to Animals
UK	United Kingdom
US	United States
USDA	United States Department of Agriculture

INTRODUCTION

CANINE WELFARE IN THE UNITED STATES AND EUROPEAN UNION

Are the Stereotypes True?

Americans and Europeans allegedly share a love for human's "best friend," the dog. Increasingly inclined to value their relationships with dogs, people are providing their canine companions with quality foods, veterinary care, and other services. Such people recognize dogs as sentient beings with needs and rights. Increasingly considered members of the family in fact, dogs accompany humans in their daily routines, share the same home, even bed, and make claim on human hearts. Undeniably, millions, on both sides of the Atlantic, love *their* dogs and act accordingly, treating *their own* dogs well. Yet it is equally clear that public policies do not extend this anecdotal love to all dogs. In both the European Union (EU) and the United States (US), there are several indicators of abysmal treatment of dogs, including overcrowded shelters, significant stray populations, and the routine euthanasia of healthy dogs. Despite these indicators, Europe is said to do a better job of "publicizing" all of this anecdotal love, per the conventional wisdom, with dogs more likely to be welcome in public places and accorded more protections in law. Strolling down the streets of Paris or many other European capitals, Americans cannot help but notice the warm welcome extended to canines. They sit in restaurants, tour castles, and walk off leash in parks. It seems obvious that Europe is a more dog-friendly place than the US. Does the evidence bear this stereotype out?

In fact, anecdotal experiences, true to their nature, tell conflicting tales. Surely, there are examples of canine paradise on the European side of the Atlantic with one extraordinarily fortunate Maltese poodle named Betty enjoying her own country farm, four-poster bed, and gourmet meals in the United Kingdom (UK). Yet in the same country, Peter the Chihuahua finds himself "trembling and terrified" in a shelter after being dumped twice, most likely a "handbag dog" who was a fashion accessory. As such, he was confined to a handbag with no opportunity for socialization. Fortunately, he has been adopted into a good home, but lots of other small dogs are in similar situations and the ending is not always a happy one. For a time, following the examples of celebrities, it became fashionable in the UK to have "handbag dogs," many of which are discarded after the novelty wears off.[1] Similarly in the US, there are conflicting stories. For example, there are multiple instances of people working to rescue dogs from perilous situations. When one dog, Boo, fell through an ice-covered pond, firefighters in Elsmere, Delaware used a boat to break through four inches of ice, get to Boo, and pull her to safety. The Fire Company spokesman said, "The way we look at it, it's a life."[2] Yet Snickers, a one-year old shar-pei mix who singed her paws to wake her caretakers "as they slept…in a burning motor home," finds herself at an animal shelter running out of time. "If someone doesn't adopt her soon, …'we'll be forced to do what we have to do' and euthanize Snickers."[3] Given such mixed messages in both the US and EU, it is necessary to probe beyond the anecdotes to determine which is the more dog-friendly place.

American and European Differences?

Scholars have long posited significant differences in American and European policies. In particular, per the conventional wisdom, European countries are likely to have stronger social safety nets, stricter environmental regulations, more comprehensive regulation of businesses, and more worker-friendly policies than the US. With its strong traditions of individualism and property rights, the US is less likely to rely on government and more likely to trust the free market to address social problems. Given these differences, one would expect Europe to regulate human activities toward animals more diligently. In contrast, one would suspect the US likely to legislate few regulations and to place the onus on individuals to care for their own dogs. Based on these distinct approaches, the US would be inclined to privatize dog ownership and responsibility, while Europe would accept some public responsibility for the care of dogs.

After sketching these two approaches, "American" and "European," in detail, they will be used to develop expectations for canine policies in the form of hypotheses. Actual policies in the US and EU will then be compared to these hypotheses to assess whether, in fact, the policy stereotypes ring true. There is debate among scholars about the very existence of distinct "American" and "European" approaches to public policy. This study will contribute to this debate. If European and American public policies do not match their respective expectations, then there is evidence in this one policy area against their existence. On the other hand, if European and American canine policies match expectations, there is some vindication of the existence of distinct approaches.

In the area of canine welfare, it is not sufficient to compare "European" and "American" policies per se. Indeed, most of the responsibility for legislation in this area is at the national and/or local levels in Europe and at the state and local levels in the US. An examination of policy at these sub-levels is critical to the overall picture. Its results, we will see, will somewhat "muddy" the proverbial waters in terms of identifying the more "dog-friendly" place. Some states in the US conform more to a "European" approach, as it is defined by conventional wisdom, in the area of canine policy, while some EU member states apply a more quintessentially "American" approach. Yet, particularly at the *supra*-national level in Europe and the national level in the US, there is evidence of these distinct approaches to canine policy. It is only the actions of sub-units that challenge the monolithic nature of these categories, and even there, it is a minority of states that consistently *legislate* contrary to expectations. In fact, there is evidence, particularly in Europe, of increasing homogenization in this policy area, perhaps attributable to central governmental influence over constituent units. In the US, even without that central leadership, there is some movement away from the American stereotype thanks largely to the work of animal advocacy groups and changes in public opinion. However, in most of the policy areas examined, the majority of American states will conform to expectations.

Policy Indicators of Canine Welfare

What public policies would best extend the private attitudes of love and compassion for companion dogs, so common in the US and EU, to *all dogs* in society? The five basic "freedoms" of dogs are often invoked in assessing their welfare. These freedoms are 1) freedom from hunger and thirst, 2) freedom from pain, injury and disease, 3) freedom from discomfort, 4) freedom from fear and distress, and 5) freedom to express natural behaviors.[4] Public policies should ensure the satisfaction of these freedoms to the greatest extent possible. While certain public policies simultaneously protect more than one of these freedoms, it is nonetheless possible to identify critical policies for each freedom. To be free from hunger and thirst, dogs rely on their caretakers to provide them with an adequate supply of food and water. The law should criminalize the failure to do so in the form of neglect and/or anti-cruelty statutes, ideally supplemented with a list of affirmative obligations for those caring for dogs. In addition, there should be quality dog food available readily, which would require a well-regulated food supply. Dogs most at risk for hunger and thirst are strays. A dog-friendly society would therefore not have a "stray problem." Nor would it have significant numbers of dogs in shelters. There are different means to achieve this goal. If universally practiced, responsible ethics of canine care can result in a society with virtually no "unwanted" dogs. Other societies, where people commonly allow dogs to roam freely or abandon them, require public policies and practices, such as incentives for spay/neuter programs, to prevent a significant "stray problem."

Several policies help to protect dogs from "pain, injury, and disease." General anti-cruelty and animal welfare statutes, with enforcement, are essential, particularly if they affirm the sentience of animals and the value of their lives. Given their generality, such statutes cover unforeseen forms of cruelty. It is desirable as well to legislate in specific areas of known cruelty so as to prevent legal "loopholes" and assist with law enforcement. In light of the history with canines, at a minimum, legislation should specifically address dogfighting, commercial greyhound racing, commercial breeding, scientific experimentation, medically unnecessary surgeries, and the sale of dog fur and meat. Optimally, the law would impose an affirmative duty on the caretakers of dogs to provide veterinary care to maintain good health. Additionally, there should be regulations covering the provision of medical care to dogs, including requirements to use anesthesia for surgeries and to allow only licensed veterinarians to perform surgeries and other necessary procedures.

Discomfort implies mild physical pain or psychological unease of some kind. It is distinguished only by degree from pain or distress. There is accordingly some overlap with the indicators for pain, injury, and disease and those for fear and distress. For all dogs to be free from discomfort, there would be need for shelters with adequate space, humane conditions, and staffing to ensure that attention and exercise be provided to all canine guests. Public policies that regulate and/or subsidize shelters would help to achieve this goal. To protect dogs in private homes, governments could publicize or legislate the responsibilities of caretakers of dogs and criminalize certain behaviors, such as tethering or crating dogs inhumanely or for unreasonable amounts of time. The criminalization of hoarding animals would be critical in protecting this freedom as well. Public oversight of kennels and other services caring for dogs might also be helpful in maximizing this freedom.

Because a loss of home and human protectors would undoubtedly result in high levels of "fear and distress," policies that minimize the likelihood of that outcome are critically important. The mandatory registration and identification of dogs with microchips or other permanent markers would assist their quick return if lost and therefore help to facilitate this freedom. Enforced and hefty penalties for the abandonment of dogs would be useful as well. Regulations on the use of dogs in advertisements and entertainment would also help to prevent fear and distress. Since dogs can develop fears in the absence of abuse, other markers for this freedom might be availability of both veterinary services for anti-anxiety medications and trainers to assist with reconditioning. Although the latter remedies would not be a matter of public policy necessarily, an affirmative duty to provide medical care would surely help to increase the likelihood that caretakers would avail themselves of such remedies for their dogs.

Finally, dogs should be free *to* express natural behaviors. At a minimum, such a freedom must include the right to live. Dog-friendly societies would therefore not routinely euthanize healthy animals. Public policies would forbid that practice. Outright prohibitions on the keeping of certain "dangerous breeds," resulting in their death or confinement solely on the basis of breed, would violate this freedom as well. To be sure, policies could certainly deem individual dogs dangerous but that judgment would be based on the behavior of a particular dog. Dog parks and/or trails that allow dogs off-leash exercise would also be important in fulfilling this freedom. As social animals, dogs would be more likely to satisfy their need for companionship if such public spaces were ample. Caretakers' responsibility codes, which serve to educate people about dogs' natural behaviors and might include the duty to walk a dog daily, would also be helpful in the achievement of this freedom.

There is no claim that this listing of the legislative needs of canines is a comprehensive one. Given its length, it is nonetheless necessary for the purposes of this study to narrow the scope of the review. With goals of including at least one policy for each freedom and covering several of those policies aimed at preventing common abuses of canines, the study will test US and EU policies for their conformity with their respective approaches in the following areas: codes of caretakers' responsibilities, commercial breeding, mandatory identification, euthanasia of healthy dogs, commercial greyhound racing, scientific experimentation, and unnecessary medical procedures. For these seven policy areas, information will be provided for the US and EU, where applicable, and all US states and EU member states. While the UK has voted to exit the EU, it is included in this analysis since the formal process of disassociation is not yet complete. In addition, any comprehensive assessment of canine welfare in the US and EU arguably must also include a discussion of population management, dogfighting, and the social acceptance of canines in public places. Given that there is a variety of ways to manage canine population levels effectively, legal prohibitions against dogfighting throughout the US and EU, and too great a variety of private, local, and state actors involved in determining social acceptance, these policies are not formally tested for adherence to US and EU approaches, but their inclusion contributes to the overall picture of canine welfare.

Dogs, Labels, and Inconsistencies in the US and EU

The review of policies is grouped thematically. More specifically, policies directed toward those with companion animals, such as those defining the status of canines as property or sentient beings, stipulating the responsibilities of canine caretakers, and ensuring the likelihood of the fulfillment of those responsibilities via public acceptance and accommodation, are reviewed together. The human conception of canines is the driver of public policies. Companion animals, by definition friends of humans, are afforded the strongest protections. The public accommodation of these canines, after all, serves human needs. In the case of companion animals, humans observe for themselves sentience and indeed, did so long before "scientific experts" recognized the emotional capacities of dogs.[5] The status of "companion" to a human places these dogs in the most privileged position.

One of the challenges for canine advocates is to elevate the status of all dogs to this position. The treatment of dogs before they join human families, whether in breeding facilities or shelters, and potentially after they leave such families is addressed separately. For these dogs, protective policies include the regulation of commercial breeding, requirements to permanently identify dogs so as to reduce abandonment and reunite lost dogs with their human caretakers, and a prohibition on the routine euthanasia of healthy but "unwanted" dogs. While these policies will be formally compared, strategies to manage population levels, including public education and/or sterilization, will also be reviewed, as their ineffectiveness greatly increases the numbers of dogs in this category or without human caretakers.

Finally, policies to prevent and mitigate common cruelties against canines, such as commercial greyhound racing, scientific experimentation, unnecessary surgeries, and dogfighting, are addressed together. Once again, the conceptualization of the dog matters. A lab or racing dog, after all, could have been a human companion. Assigned a different "use," these dogs are not given the same protection or status in law. To imagine one's companion in these roles is to recoil in horror, but cognitive dissonance applies when the animal is re-labeled. In other words, people hold two contradictory beliefs about the same species of animal. Indeed, the EU almost universally deems unnecessary surgeries, such as ear cropping and tail docking, unacceptable for companions, but experimentation on lab dogs is still permitted. In both the US and EU, racing dogs are increasingly viewed as friends and the "sport" is legal in fewer places and losing its popularity even in those areas. Dogfighting is now fully recognized, in law at least, as socially deviant. The more that people see dogs as one species, whatever the role assigned to them, the more likely these common abuses will be regulated or prohibited. The challenge for canine advocates is to break through the cognitive dissonance. There is more evidence of such a breakthrough in the EU than US. Yet policies in both places remain inconsistent, reflecting contradictory beliefs about the capacities and sentience of dogs.

These three broad policy areas, impacting companion animals, animals without human caretakers, and commonly accepted and deviant "uses" of dogs, will not necessarily provide a complete portrait of canine welfare, but they cover enough of a range to trigger "American" and "European" approaches to policy, if existent, and to provide a sense of how seriously canine protection is taken in public policy. A study of these canine policies will provide *much* vindication of distinct American and European approaches, but some fodder for critics as well. Because policies do not in and of themselves determine canine welfare, the study will incorporate discussion of practices and use factual indicators, such as the existence of inhumane breeding facilities, the numbers of dogs euthanized, the existence of race tracks and the size of stray populations, whenever possible to enhance the depiction of canine welfare.

To be clear, though, it is the policies, not the practices, which will be tested for conformity with American and European approaches, which will be detailed in the following chapter. Yet practices complicate the assessment of canine justice and expose outposts of both canine distress and joy in both the US and EU.

Notes

1. Hannah Gilman, "5 of the Most Pampered Pets in the World," *Daily Treat*, August 11, 2015. https://www.rover.com/blog/most-pampered-pets/, accessed June 1, 2016. For dogs dumped, see Lorraine Fisher, "Heartache of the Dumped Handbag Dogs: Celebs made them oh-so Fashionable—but now Rescue Centers are filling up with Tiny Abandoned Pets," *Daily Mail*, April 28, 2016. http://www.dailymail.co.uk/femail/article-3562186/Heartache-dumped-handbag-dogs-Celebs-oh-fashionable-rescue-centres-filling-tiny-abandoned-pets.html, accessed June 1, 2016.
2. Esteban Parra, "Viral: Millions See Delaware Dog Rescue Video," *The News Journal Delaware Online*, December 17, 2015. http://www.delawareonline.com/story/news/local/2015/12/17/viral-millions-see-delaware-dog-rescue-video/7747466, accessed June 1, 2016.
3. Hudson Hongo, "Time Running Out for Shelter Dog Who Saved Family from Fire (Update)," *The Dodo*, February 5, 2016. https://www.thedodo.com/time-running-out-1588080914.html, accessed June 1, 2016.
4. Katherine Albro Houpt, et al., "Proceedings of a Workshop to Identify Dog Welfare Issues in the U.S, Czech Republic, Spain and the United Kingdom," *Applied Animal Behavior Science* 106 (2007): 222.
5. Jeffrey Moussaieff Masson, *When Elephants Weep: The Emotional Lives of Animals* (Delta, 1996).

· 1 ·

DOGS FOR DEMOCRATIC SOCIALISM

US and EU Approaches to Canine Welfare

Laissez-faire and individualist tendencies, allegedly hallmarks of an American approach, would yield very different canine policies than would one with a regulatory emphasis, which is associated with the European approach. Arguably, dogs would prefer the regulatory or democratic socialist model, especially in light of their status as property in the individualist one! Scholars disagree about the very existence of distinct persuasions. Some cite unique American and European persuasions, while others dispute those claims. One way to add evidence to this scholarly debate about the existence of such approaches is to investigate to what extent these persuasions inform canine policies at the macro or national/*supra*-national and micro or state/national levels. Before turning to that task in subsequent chapters, it is necessary to develop hypotheses for expected policies if in fact American and European approaches were applied in their pure forms. To do so, not only must the contours of each approach be detailed, but it is additionally important to gain a basic understanding of the governmental systems in the US and EU. Those systems impact the formulation and enforcement of policy.

Governmental Systems

Federalism and Protection from Governmental Tyranny in the US

The US has a federal system, with both states and the national government sovereign. The US Constitution endows the national government with enumerated or stated, implied, and inherent powers. In all cases in which the national government has a constitutional power to legislate or act, it is supreme and therefore would override or take precedence over any state law in conflict with its will. States can and do legislate in areas that overlap with national power, but they could override national laws only if the national government lacked the constitutional power to legislate on the topic. For this reason, state powers are said to be residual, or exclusively sovereign only in those areas not under national jurisdiction.

Until the 1930s, states and the national government acted mainly in separate spheres, with the national government responsible for areas such as foreign policy, trade and monetary policy and states in charge of areas such as public health, most crime, and education. Facing the crisis of the Great Depression, the national government became much more active. Although the Supreme Court initially rebuffed such intervention as unconstitutional, it significantly relaxed its reading of national powers in 1937. In particular, the commerce clause, which states that Congress has the power to regulate "Commerce with foreign Nations, and among the several States, and with the Indian tribes," became the constitutional rationale for the national government to assume a substantial role in economic matters.[1] In the 1960s, the national government additionally took advantage of empowering clauses in the 1868 or Civil War amendments to pass civil rights legislation and thereby insert itself into both social and economic policy. The Bill of Rights, or first ten amendments of the Constitution, restricts state powers as well, as there are specific prohibitions now applicable to all governmental levels. Today there would be few areas indeed in which the national government could make no *legal* claim to legislate. That is not to say, however, that the national government takes full advantage of this capability. To the contrary, states retain the leading role in many areas, such as education, and legislate concurrently with the national government in others, such as drug crimes. As long as state laws do not conflict with the US Constitution or national laws, there is no legal problem. Historically, public policies for canines have been a state matter, but the national government has the legal power to legislate on some important issues impacting canine welfare. For example, the sale of puppies across state lines allows the national government to regulate the conditions under which dogs are bred. As we will see, the national government has passed some legislation in the area of canine welfare, though the states are the primary actors in this policy area.

There are significant differences between the American national government and those of most states. A creation of the eighteenth century, the American national government is designed to protect against tyranny of the majority and the abuse of governmental power. A system of separation of powers and checks and balances combine to make legislative accomplishments extremely difficult. Individuals who answer to separate constituencies at different times must come to agreement. What is more, the checks and balances allow a minority, sometimes of one person, to block initiatives. Distinguishing "temporary" from "permanent" majorities, Alexander Hamilton, one of the American founders, expected the Constitution to prevent the former from legislative success.[2] As a result, the system is heavily biased toward inaction, intentionally structured to frustrate the majority's will. Most often, major and sometimes minor legislative initiatives require persistent efforts, perhaps even a social movement, for any chance of success.

Indeed, the national lawmaking process is filled with multiple veto points, both formal and informal. Since Congress is bicameral, both the House of Representatives and the Senate must pass bills in identical form. Senators can filibuster a bill to prevent a vote on it and a *supra*-majority of sixty percent is required to stop the filibuster, thereby allowing only for a vote on the bill! With the exception of those few times in contemporary history when one political party had sixty percent of the Senate seats, the minority party effectively has an informal veto over legislation because of these rules. In both chambers of Congress, committee chairs can delay or squash bills as well. It is also common in the US for different political parties to control one of the chambers of Congress and the Presidency. Since 1968, such periods, known as divided government, have occurred in fourteen of the last eighteen Congresses. The President can thus formally veto the legislative products of the other political party in such times. Finally, the US Supreme Court has the power of judicial review, allowing it to strike down any challenged law that conflicts with the Constitution. Given the ambiguous nature of the Constitution, the Court's ideology can play a role in such decisions. While speaking about foreign policy, Edward S. Corwin, a scholar, referred to the Constitution as "an invitation to struggle."[3] That famous description is apt for other areas as well. What is more, the Court often lags behind the other two branches in its reflection of the public mood, as its nine appointed members have lifetime tenure. As a result, it can and has struck down popular bills. In short, the legislative process presents ample opportunities, via lobbying, contributions, and litigation, for well financed interest groups, such as Big Agriculture or the scientific community, to derail regulatory efforts on behalf of labor, consumers, animals, and/or the environment. The *structure* of American government is thus biased toward laissez-faire policies.

While there is great variety in the structure and systems of state governments, they are generally more responsive to majority will than the national government. State senators, for example, represent roughly equal numbers of people, unlike US Senators who represent states. Each state has two US Senators regardless of its population. Unlike the national government, many states have elected judiciaries or fixed terms for judicial appointees. Additionally, states can allow for the recall of elected officials and referendums. With the latter, citizens can vote directly on policy. At the national level, there is no possibility of a referendum and elected officials can be removed only for criminal acts. Given these differences, one would expect public policies to be more consistent with majority preferences at the state rather than national level. However, the influence of money on the political process is as much of a problem (or more of one) at the state level as the national, a factor that increases minority influence or that of the wealthy over the majority. Still, particularly in the area of canine welfare, there is more potential at the state level for an ambitious legislative agenda.

Governance in the EU and Its Member States

Europe, of course, refers to the continent itself, but also includes countries detached from the mainland, such as Ireland, Malta, and the United Kingdom. While there is no real governing body for Europe as a whole, there is a Council of Europe. Established via the Treaty of London in 1949, the Council currently includes 47 member states, all of which have signed the European Convention on Human Rights. All 28 of the EU member states belong to it. Describing itself as "the continent's leading human rights organization," the Council is an "inter-parliamentary body that negotiates treaties on various issues," including animal welfare.[4] While there is a Parliamentary Assembly in the Council, the decision-making body is the Committee of Ministers, which is formally comprised of each member state's minister of foreign affairs. In practice, permanent diplomatic representatives from each member state fulfill this role in Strasbourg, France, the headquarters of the Council.[5]

The Council is designed to foster international cooperation or more specifically, greater European unity. Aside from the European Convention on Human Rights, which all member states have signed, member states need not sign conventions adopted or may sign them with exceptions to various provisions stipulated. Even if a member state has signed a Convention, responsibility for its enforcement and implementation are in its own hands. The Committee of Ministers can pressure a member state to comply, but it has no enforcement power. Should one of the members openly disregard its conventions and procedures, the Committee could suspend or expel it. However, that has never been done. In short, the Council provides a forum for European countries to negotiate treaties or conventions intended to advance democracy, further human rights, improve living conditions, and ensure human values.

In contrast, the EU is more akin to a *supra*-national government. Originally called the European Economic Community, the EU traces its origins to the Treaty of Rome in 1957. In that year, it had six founding members, namely, Belgium, France, Germany, Italy, Luxembourg, and the Netherlands. It has since expanded to 28 members as of 2018, though the UK is in the process of withdrawing from it. For many countries, the draw for EU membership is still economic in nature. Member states benefit at a minimum from inclusion in the "common market" of the EU, but can also receive substantial economic subsidies and investments. Because the economic incentives to join the EU are so strong, some countries might join it for those reasons alone and retain reluctance to surrender national powers in other areas to the EU. The United Kingdom (UK) is a classic example of a member state that consistently expressed concerns about the extension of the EU's power into non-economic areas until it finally voted to withdraw from the EU in 2016. As the reader may recall, it is included in this analysis nonetheless since the process of withdrawal is not yet complete. Despite the UK's exit and concerns about the expansion of the EU's powers, it had attracted fifteen member states by 1995. Added to the original six were Denmark (1973), Ireland (1973), the UK (1973), Greece (1981), Portugal (1986), Spain (1986), Austria (1995), Finland (1995), and Sweden (1995). In 2004 and 2007, the EU expanded dramatically when several former Communist countries, including Bulgaria, Croatia, the Czech Republic, Estonia, Hungary, Latvia, Lithuania, Poland,

Romania, Slovakia, and Slovenia joined. These countries stood to gain much from membership given the economic disparities between eastern and western Europe. Cyprus and Malta also joined in 2004. States seeking membership in the EU must have a functioning and stable democratic regime, and a market-oriented, capitalist economy, as well as accept all of the laws and regulations of the EU, with the ability to implement the obligations of membership.[6] Prior to a state's admission, the EU has some leverage to ensure compliance with these criteria. Once admitted, however, a state would not have the same incentive to accommodate the EU's concerns. The expansion of the EU, which is now more than four times its original size, is referred to as "widening." There are concerns that such widening weakens the ties or sense of community within the EU, as boundaries are in flux.

Over the course of its history, the EU has also "deepened" or extended its jurisdiction into more policy areas and accordingly, impacted more directly the lives of its citizens. The 1992 Treaty on the European Union or Maastricht Treaty was of critical significance on this front, as it put the EU on the path to a single currency (the euro), which was introduced in 1999. It also asserted three "pillars" of policy relevance: trade, common foreign and security policy, and justice/home affairs. As McCormick notes, "It was only with the passage in 1992 of the Treaty on the European Union ... that the debate moved into a higher gear with concerns that new efforts were being made to build a federal United States of Europe,...."[7] This Treaty, however, additionally embraced the principle of subsidiarity, which holds that the EU should only act in areas in which policy goals cannot be achieved by national or subnational governments and are more likely to be reached at the supranational level. Abandoning the three pillar approach, the Treaty of Lisbon, which became effective in 2009, deepened further the reach of the EU into multiple areas. Agricultural policy, which encompasses food and animal welfare, is one of the key areas of EU authority. In addition, the Lisbon Treaty introduced several institutional reforms intended to make the EU more democratically accountable and bureaucratically efficient.

Based in Brussels, the EU is comprised of several institutions. Reflective of its unique nature as a government with sovereign nation-states in its membership, the EU has both an elected Parliament, representing the European people, and a Council of the EU, which represents the member states comprised as it is with officials from those national governments. In the ordinary legislative procedure, both the European Parliament and Council of the EU must approve bills. A "qualified majority" or a vote covering 55 percent of member states, comprising at least 15 of them and representing at least 65 percent of the population of the EU, is required for a bill to pass. Even if obtained, a minority with at least four member states, representing at least 35 percent of the population, can potentially block legislation. There are certain areas for which "special legislative procedure" can apply in which case the Council of the EU is the sole authority.[8] This option provides indication that the EU continues to favor nation-states over popular representation, though more areas are now subject to ordinary legislative procedure. Policy for canine welfare would almost certainly fall under ordinary, not special procedure.

The European Commission initiates all legislation. Responsible for the implementation of EU policies and the spending of funds, the Commission is headed by a President selected by the Council of the EU for a four-year term. As the permanent bureaucracy, the Commission is the public face of the EU. Before proposing new legislation, whether at its own behest, at the request of another EU institution, or based on a citizens' initiative, the Commission prepares an "impact assessments," which summarizes the advantages and disadvantages of policy options and evaluates potential consequences of proposed legislation. At this early stage of the drafting process, citizens can provide input into the process and national Parliaments can state objections if they deem it preferable to deal with the policy matter at the national level.

There is also a European Court of Justice, which has issued rulings establishing both the individual rights of EU citizens and the supremacy of EU law, and a European Council, which consists of both national and EU leaders and sets the overall priorities for the EU but has no lawmaking power. For states within the EU, then, there is a centralized policy-making body with executive and judicial bodies even if responsibility to implement and comply with EU legislation rests primarily with the member states themselves. What is more, there are some markers of a single governmental identity, such as a common currency and open borders. Twenty-two EU member states as well as Norway, Iceland, and Switzerland have removed internal border controls (Schengen) and 18 member states have adopted the euro in place of national currency.[9] Citizens of the EU can work and live in any EU member state, though they have rights to participate in local and EU elections only, not national ones. There can be and has been a delay in granting these full rights to the citizens in newly admitted states pursuant to the terms of accession. Nonetheless, there is clearly a governmental structure with tangible benefits for its citizens.

Compared to US states, there is a great deal more variation among the governmental systems in EU member states. According to Sakwa and Stevens, 15 member states have pure parliamentary systems, with the chief executive elected by the legislative body or Parliament and subject to a vote of confidence by that body. Only one member state, Cyprus, has a Presidential system, which like the US, has a separation of powers between the legislature and executive. The remaining 12 member states have hybrid systems, with a popularly elected President with varying degrees of power and a separate head of government subject to election by and a confidence relationship with Parliament.[10] Parliamentary systems tend to be more responsive to majoritarian wishes, while Presidential systems make legislative action more difficult given the need for separately elected branches to agree on a course of action. Among the EU member states, there are three federal systems, Austria, Belgium, and Germany. In those systems, like in the US, subnational governments have more control over local policy than in unitary systems, where the central government has claim to all sovereign power. At least three additional member states, Italy, Spain, and the UK, delegate power to regions and autonomous communities to make policy for local matters. Delegation in the area of canine policies to subnational governments is likely to result in variable levels of protection. Finally, party systems are nationally distinct in the EU. The Republican and Democratic parties dominate in the US at both the national and state levels. There is no such two-party dominance in the EU. In some member states, with multi-party systems, the Green party, which would be inclined to advocate for animal welfare, has a legislative presence. In short, there are diverse forms of government and politics in the EU, which undoubtedly yield varying degrees of responsiveness to public opinion and quite possibly, unique renditions of any "European consensus" on policy.

Oceans Apart: US and EU Values?

The American Creed

Despite their skepticism toward governmental activity, Americans are said to believe in the superiority of *their system* of governance. Indeed, belief in a constitutional form of government is a vital part of the American creed. Absent the domination of one ethnic group, the US, it is claimed, is the "only nation in the world that is founded on a creed."[11] To be "American," in other words, is to share a set of political beliefs that support a particular way of life. As Warshawsky explains, this thinking is "rooted in the ideals proclaimed in the Declaration of Independence; in the system of personal liberty and limited government established by the Constitution; in our traditions of self-reliance, personal responsibility, and entrepreneurism; in our emphasis on private property, freedom of contract, and merit-based achievement; in our respect for the rule of law; and in our commitment to affording equal justice to all. Perhaps, above all, it is marked by our abiding belief that, as Americans, we have been called to a higher duty in American history."[12] The latter belief that Americans are uniquely charged with a "higher" duty to lead or set an example via adherence to this creed is known as American exceptionalism.

The very notion of American exceptionalism implies superiority, as the US is distinguished from other countries in a positive way. Indeed, the label of "exceptional" indicates top placement in a hierarchy. As Ceaser explains, one element of the notion, an American mission, is grounded in both "the religion of the Puritans and the political science of some of the Founders."[13] To the Puritans, God was the source of the American task to set an example of pious living. According to the Founders, Americans were to demonstrate by their example that "societies of men" are capable of "establishing good government from reflection and choice."[14] In both the secular and sacred versions, there is a clear implication that America alone is to set the example for the world to follow. Alternatively, the US is cast as a "redeemer nation," either bringing democracy to other lands and/or saving the souls of others. In both scenarios, the US has a special role to play in the world.

As Heclo elaborates, American exceptionalism refers not only to a mission, but also to conditions and character. Separated from Europe via the Atlantic Ocean, the US has a favorable geographic location. What is more, its European founding and development occurred at a point in historical time that allowed the ideals of the Enlightenment, particularly the notion of universal rights, to take root unchallenged.[15] In Louis Hartz's seminal account of the domination of such liberal ideals in American thought, much weight is attached to geographic conditions, especially the widespread availability of land and the lack of a feudal tradition. In his view, the absence of feudalism explained the absence of socialism later in American history.[16] With land widely available, Americans of the middling classes came to value property rights. Life on the frontier or in the wilderness additionally cultivated self-reliance. The unusual conditions of the US, then, account for such political values as property rights, equality, individualism, and limited government. Whether or not cultivated from the particular conditions in the US, American exceptionalism also refers at times to a unique character. Americans, in this view, display a character containing "dynamic tensions." They are individual yet public-spirited, skeptical yet optimistic, patriotic yet distrustful of government, and religious yet materialistic.[17] There is, in other words, an American outlook and perspective distinguishable from that of other countries and evident in a unique approach to domestic and foreign policies.

Compared to that of EU member states, the American social safety net is less generous. Prone to hold individuals accountable for their own plight, Americans are less likely to ensure their economic well-being in hard times. That view is grounded in both a distrust of government and the remnants of the Protestant work ethic, according to which those who work hard reap material benefits and those who do not get what they deserve. Americans are entitled only to opportunity, not results. Skeptical of government, Americans are leery of public programs, initiatives, and regulation. Reflexively, Americans prefer market-based solutions to problems with the government playing a minimal role. As a result, there are fewer governmental investments in public goods and any such investments are channeled through private contractors. In the area of environmental policy, the US has been slow to respond to threats, such as climate change. The American public's preference for private solutions and its reluctance to regulate business hinder governmental solutions to environmental problems. As Rifkin has highlighted, Americans are more inclined to accept risk in this area and place material concerns above environmental ones.[18] The strong American belief in God perhaps serves to tame any fear of environmental catastrophe as well, as there is divine guidance and possibly even divine protection of the US in this thinking.

Because animals are conceptualized legally as property, they are deprived of effective protection in US policies. As Wagman and Liebman explain, "in countries such as the United States, which tends to exalt individual property rights as inviolable, one may find greater resistance to government regulation of how individuals use their property."[19] Indeed, criminal anti-cruelty laws were originally intended to protect property, as they applied only to *non-owners*. Owners could do as they pleased with their animals. That is no longer the case, a development that implies animals are now distinguished somewhat from property at least. Still, though, state anti-cruelty laws apply only to deviant behavior and exempt in most instances "conduct that occurs in modern animal agricultural practices, entertainment activities, sporting events using animals, and scientific research."[20] The national government has gone even further to criminalize travel in interstate or foreign commerce and the use of the mails for purposes of disrupting the operations of animal enterprises. Passed in 2006, this Animal Enterprise Terrorism Act protects commercial and academic entities that use or sell animals, including commercial dog breeders, animal shelters, and pet stores.[21] American policy is especially notorious for its very weak protection of laboratory and farm animals. For example, the Humane Slaughter Act exempts fowl, or over 95 percent of the animals killed for food. The US is the creator of the factory farming model, which turns animals into complete commodities with all sentience denied. Likewise, the Animal Welfare Act (AWA), which is the "principal source of regulation for animals used in research," excludes mice, rats, and birds or over 90 percent of the relevant animals.[22]

The tensions in American ideals manifest themselves in controversies over select social issues. For example, the American preference for laissez-faire policies and individualism leads to support of abortion rights, while religiosity, at least of some faiths, yields strident opposition to those rights. In the area of criminal justice, there is harmony between the values of individual responsibility and moral accountability. As a result, there are harsh penalties in the US for breaking the law, with astronomical rates of imprisonment and the death penalty operative in 32 states and the national government. Gun rights are widely supported in the US as well, reflecting the value of self-reliance and a mistrust of government. In short, the American creed yields economic and environmental policies that lean toward laissez faire, a conception of animals as private property, and social policies that embody the tension between individualism and communal morality.

European Consensus?

If McCormick is correct in asserting that "the assumptions Europeans make, the way they see the world around them and the way they live their lives and relate to others—is distinctive from the experience of others," then how is it so?[23] What substantively defines the "European" perspective? In common with all constitutional democracies, Europeans value equality and individual rights. However, they strike a unique balance between these two values. One scholar associates the very quest to realize *both* principles as specifically European.[24] While Americans are more inclined to prioritize individual rights and emphasize equality of opportunity only, Europeans are more likely to insist on some equality of results. In Europe, democracy takes precedence over individualism. As McCormick explains, "Most Europeans would argue that society can sometimes be a better judge of what is good for individuals than vice versa, and that there may sometimes be good reason for the state to limit individual rights in the interests of the greater good of the community."[25] This persuasion manifests itself in a distinctly European approach to domestic and foreign policies, though the concern here is with the former.

It is perhaps most strikingly evident in the area of social welfare policy. Committed to some equality of results, Europe, as the reader may recall, has more generous social welfare programs and as a result, is more economically egalitarian than the US.[26] Europeans do not blame the poor for their plight, instead attributing it to "the inevitable ups and downs of a cyclical economy." Given that assumption, Europeans, Hill observes, allow unemployed individuals "to retain their dignity—as well as sufficient income, health care, child care, housing subsidies, skills retraining, job counseling, and more…."[27] Compared to the US, Europe spends "three times more per capita on families."[28] To be sure, there are differences among European member states, with the UK for example, less generous than the Scandinavian member states but "variation within the 'states' of Europe [in economic equality] is about the same as variation within the American states."[29] The commitment to a social safety net among Europeans is so strong that it has led to concerns about the EU itself, as membership could lead to some loss of national control over this policy.[30] The values of equality and social welfare, in other words, are strongly grounded in the grassroots of Europe.

The governmental role in the economy is not limited to providing social welfare or income redistribution. According to Hill, European governments are more likely than their American counterpart to employ public-private partnerships and a policy of co-determination or works councils, which are "elected councils at individual companies through which workers gain significant input into their working conditions at the shop-floor level."[31] Hill argues that such councils provide Europe with a "distinct advantage" because they are "one of the keys" to harnessing the "wealth-generating capacity" of capitalism "for the good of the many instead of the enrichment of the few."[32] With a greater willingness to regulate individual behavior for the benefit of the community, Europeans are supportive of a strong governmental role in the economy and are likely to advocate the "precautionary principle" as a means to evaluate the need for governmental regulation. "When there is sufficient evidence to suggest a potential deleterious impact but not enough evidence to know for sure, [this principle allows] … regulatory authorities to err on the side of safety by either suspending the activity altogether, modifying it, employing alternative scenarios, monitoring the activity to assess causal impacts, or creating experimental protocols to better understand its effects."[33] In contrast, less risk-adverse Americans might place the onus on the governmental regulator to prove a negative effect before justifying any intervention. Here again, a European preference for the public good wins over an individual's interest to be free of regulatory burdens.

Not surprisingly, this way of thinking has resulted in stronger environmental regulations and investments in Europe. Indeed, Europe has been a world leader in investments in alternative energy sources. "Perhaps no single horizon better illustrates Europe's technological advances, combined with political will and future-thinking, than its leadership in launching the world into a new era of renewable energy, conservation, and low greenhouse gas economies," argues Hill.[34] Compared to the US, Europe has also invested more money into state-of-the-art systems of public transportation.[35] What is more, Europeans, according to Rifkin, are more comfortable living in close proximity to one another, versus Americans who prefer space and distance from neighbors. He writes, "Americans covet exclusive space. Each person strives to be self-contained and autonomous.... Europeans seek inclusive space—being part of extended communities, including family, kin, ethnic, and class affiliation."[36] Given higher gasoline taxes, heavily subsidized public transportation, and a developmental model that favors smaller cities over suburban sprawl, governmental incentives promote this thinking as well.[37]

Despite its Christian heritage, Europe today is marked by a strong sense of secular identity. McCormick goes as far as to say that "secularism has become...a defining part of what it means to be European."[38] Secular attitudes might partly account for a greater amount of compassion for animals, as some denominations of western religion posit stark dichotomies between human and other animals that are now questioned in science. Whether for that reason or not, Europe, according to scholars, is the "world leader in animal protection."[39] In law, animals are recognized as "sentient" beings with interests of their own. According to Article 13 of the Lisbon Treaty, which became effective in December 2009, the EU and its member states are to "pay full regard to the welfare requirements of animals, while respecting the legal or administrative provisions and customs of the member states relating in particular to religious rites, cultural traditions and regional heritage."[40] Even prior to the Lisbon Treaty, Tomaselli commented, "The most significant difference between the laws in Europe and the laws in the United States is the desire to protect an animal for the sake of the animal."[41] As a result, there are more regulations in Europe protecting farm and laboratory animals. For example, there is a ban on the use of animals in testing cosmetics. Additionally, common practices used in factory farming in the US, such as veal crates, battery cages for hens, and gestation crates for pigs, are illegal in the EU.[42]

Secular attitudes are evident in other social policies as well. For example, in their approach to criminal justice, European countries tend to be less punitive than the US. Indeed, capital punishment is almost universally condemned in Europe.[43] Indicative of secular views, costs, deterrence, public safety and individual rights weigh more heavily than the need for retributive punishments. In sum, the European approach has been marked by secularism, welfarism, economic regulation, environmentalism, and concern for animal welfare.[44]

Questioning the Stereotypes

Many scholars question the universal acceptance and applicability to policy of the "European" approach throughout the EU and the "American" one in all US states. Indeed, these approaches have been challenged in multiple ways, such as via the exposure of regional differences in values, partisan disagreements on policy, and demographic and historical changes undermining favorable conditions for these beliefs. Despite these myriad critiques, the contrasting poles of the two distinct approaches retain a hold on the imagination.

The very idea of "American exceptionalism" is controversial. Most relevant to this study, some criticize the "unique" nature of an American creed or persuasion. Indisputably, these critics highlight, the underlying American ideals, such as individual rights and laissez-faire capitalism, are of European origin. Ironically, the Declaration of Independence has very British roots.[45] The claim to exceptionalism, then, is not supported by the originality of American ideals themselves. In early American history, these ideals were able to take firm hold given American conditions, particularly the widespread availability of land. Today, however, such unusual conditions are no longer in place. Property is not available for the taking and the state, following the Great Depression in the 1930s, plays a significant role in the management of the American economy. Laissez faire, if it ever existed, is dead. Additionally, several other countries share similar ideals to those of the US. As a result, concludes Gordon, "the difference between us [US] and others is not as stark as exceptionalism suggests."[46] According to this line of thinking, it is a fallacy to posit a common American creed, at least one of any substantive meaning. Similar to Europe, the US can claim unity only in the value and acceptance of diversity itself. There are "distinctive ways of belonging to America" given the particular histories of the myriad groups comprising it.[47] Even if common ideals, such as equality and freedom, are universally valued, there are substantial differences in their meanings to Americans. There is not one American persuasion, then, but countless persuasions all with the common thread of the toleration of others' views. In the Trump era, even that thread is in question.

Scholars additionally highlight increasing levels of partisan voting and greater intensity of ideological conflict in the US. The contemporary party system in the US has been described as one in which Democrats and Republicans are at relatively equal levels of strength in the national electorate.[48] With its base of support in rural areas, the Republican party's policy positions tend to be more consistent with the American creed's emphasis on de-regulation or laissez faire and strong protections for property rights, inclusive of animals. The Democrats, with a larger urban base, are more likely to advocate policies in tension with the American creed, such as environmental regulations and more generous social welfare policies. Skeptics of an "American" approach could highlight this basic philosophical division. Why should one expect consistency in American policy when there are fundamental disagreements about its desirability? In fact, Republicans have at times dubbed their Democratic opponents as "Europeanists." Such disagreement among groups of roughly equal size casts doubt on the notion of an American "consensus," say the critics. However, there is scholarly debate over just how ideologically polarized Americans are.[49]

Likewise, some scholars and political actors question the existence of such a uniform "European" approach. While the EU does not include all member states of Europe, a European persuasion, if it exists, should be most evident and strongest within the EU itself, where a central body can serve to reinforce it, even if its origins have application beyond EU borders to all of Europe. Critics highlight the ideological diversity within and among EU member states as a means to question a single European persuasion. While Risse argues that a European community exists, he depicts two major alternative options for a European world view, the secular and cosmopolitan one previously described and "a Europe of white Christian peoples that sees itself as a distinct civilization ... less open to strangers….."[50] The tenets of this latter conception of Europeanization would challenge the alleged consensus on welfare, particularly for non-nationals, and secularization. The popularity of far right parties is one indicator of the spread of this more nationalist vision. However, there are moderate supporters of it as well. The rising popularity of this nationalist approach, even if held by a significant minority, would cast doubt on the very existence of a single European persuasion. A nationalist vision of Europe is undoubtedly more popular in some countries rather than others. In Hungary, for example, a far right party has taken power. While defenders of a European persuasion, such as Martinelli, argue that national and regional differences in Europe, though existent, "are often no greater than those within other great countries…," others consider such divisions to undermine the notion of a European consensus.[51]

The Anglo-Saxon—Continental split might be the most potent such division, as the UK has consistently embraced an alternate and weaker vision for the EU. Opting out of the common currency and borderless traffic, the UK has accepted only a "Europe a la carte" and as a result, is the "least Europeanized" of the member states.[52] Given this persuasion, it is perhaps not all that surprising that the British opted to leave the EU. Indicative of this difference, the British model of social welfare is less generous than continental ones. At times, the UK has also positioned itself between the US and the "Continent" on foreign policies, most notoriously supporting the 2003 Iraq War and thereby rejecting European preferences for multilateralism.

Historically, there has been a North-South division in the EU as well. The Scandinavian countries, the Netherlands and a few other northern countries, for example, spend higher amounts on social welfare compared to southern Europe, where poverty is more prevalent.[53] The embrace of secularization varies somewhat along this fault line as well. Arguing this point, Forse and Parodi write, "…a gap appears that pits religiously skeptical France and the Nordic countries against Southern Europe and Ireland [a geographical exception], more devoted to Christianity and the Church of Rome."[54] However, even in Ireland, the Church's influence has waned, with gay marriage and abortion made legal in referendums. Given the "widening" of the EU to include the former Communist countries, an East-West division has also emerged. As newly formed democracies, these states have had to build popular support for constitutional values, while simultaneously creating capitalist economies.[55] Recently, right-wing governments, which have emerged in Hungary and Poland, have put such constitutional values under great strain. Compared to the West, the eastern members are poorer. That economic disparity could possibly lead to differing perspectives on social welfare, environmental issues, and animal welfare.

In addition, millions of people from eastern member states have migrated to western states in search of economic opportunities.[56] Internal immigrants, or those from other EU member states, range from two-to-five percent of the total population, with Spain at the high end.[57] The number of these internal migrants, however, is small compared to the number of immigrants from outside of Europe. Spain and Germany have the highest percentage of external immigrant populations or 7.4 and 5.7 percent of their total, respectively, while Sweden is on the lower end for western countries with 3.2 percent.[58] Compared to western Europe, there are very few immigrants in the East. In the wealthier western countries, the growth in immigration has provoked concerns about the sustainability of generous social welfare benefits, a tenet of the alleged European creed. Additionally, the immigrants themselves are less likely to embrace secularization and therefore they might reduce the level of consensus on that value.

Do these divisions, within and among member states, undermine the case for a distinctly "European" approach to public policy? Alternatively are the common points of a European approach, namely social welfare, secularism, economic regulation, environmentalism, and animal welfare, prevalent *enough* to be the hallmarks of a single persuasion? Several other large countries, including the US, have regional and ideological divisions but retain a common and overarching persuasion, according to some scholars. In contrast, skeptics of a European persuasion point to the persistence of national, regional, ideological, ethnic, and even generational diversity.

Impact of "Consensus" Approaches on Canine Welfare

The issue of canine welfare has certainly engaged the citizenry and national legislatures of several EU member states over the last two decades. As a matter of fact, the European Commission held its first conference on the welfare of dogs and cats, entitled "Building A Europe that cares for Companion Animals," in 2013. There has not only been a flurry of legislative activity in this area, but public debates and controversies over such matters as the handling of stray populations, breed bans, and many other issues. Likewise, in the US, several state governments and localities have addressed canine issues, legislating on matters such as breed bans, leash laws, limitations on tethering, and several others. In some cases, there have been heated debates over these issues with much public involvement. If in fact, the EU and US legislated on canine welfare consistently with their hallmark approaches, they would produce policies in polar opposition.

US: Dogs as Property?

What type of policies would an American approach yield for canines? Arguably, the American aversion to governmental regulation, strong individualist strain, and defense of property rights, in particular, would result in less protective legislation than found in Europe. Defined as property in the law, dogs are bound to be at the mercy of their "owners'" treatment. Dogs might be valued for their uses, such as companionship or search and rescue, but not for their own sake. There might be regulations concerning the treatment of animals, but their purpose would be to ensure the moral development and health of human beings. For example, cruelty, such as fighting dogs, is arguably degrading and corrupting to those humans who partake in it. If the American approach was implemented, the following hypothesis should be sustained:

> 1) *American states are likely to ban extreme cruelty and neglect, but are not likely to legislate affirmative obligations for the caretakers of animals.*

Because dog ownership is privatized in the American model, public spaces, including parks, are also less likely to be welcoming to canines. Dog "owners" would be expected to exercise their dogs on their own property, with little public accommodations made for them. As a result, there will likely not only be no legislative enticements to ensure the welfare of animals, beyond prohibitions on abuse, but an unhelpful social context.

If the American "consensus" prevailed in policy areas impacting the management of canine populations, including the treatment of dogs before they join and after they leave human families, there would most likely be a "stray problem." Because Americans are reluctant to rely on the government and to provide subsidies to individuals, there are not likely to be public programs and monies for spaying/neutering and/or education. Instead, an individual would bear responsibility for his or her "own" dog. Coupled with a lack of codes of caretakers' responsibilities, such an approach would possibly yield "unwanted" populations. The mandatory microchipping of dogs so as to prevent abandonment or loss would provoke American fears of government and elicit a popular outcry. Thus, it is additionally hypothesized that

> 2) *Neither the US government nor the states will require permanent markers, such as microchips, on dogs.*

Given the American aversion to regulation, there is likely to be weak standards in the area of commercial breeding as well. Any regulations over the breeding industry would primarily be for the benefit of human consumers who purchase puppies, not for the benefit of the dogs. It is therefore hypothesized that:

3) *The US government and American states will have lax regulations on commercial breeders for the benefit of consumers only.*

In the event of an "unwanted" population of dogs, it is highly unlikely that the euthanasia of healthy dogs would be banned in the US. Defined in law as property and valued for their use to humans, dogs' lives would probably not be protected for their own sake. Accordingly, it is hypothesized that

4) *Neither the US government nor American states will prohibit the euthanasia of healthy dogs, instead leaving that prerogative to individual owners and shelters.*

While acts of cruelty would be illegal in the US, the definition of cruelty would be inclined to be limited to socially deviant activities, such as dogfighting. Of course, what is deemed socially acceptable can change over time. That appears to be the case for commercial dog racing. However, if the American model is followed, it is hypothesized that

5) *The US government and American states will not prohibit commercial greyhound racing.*

For activities that are not considered cruel by their very definition, the American model, biased as it is against governmental regulation, would be inclined to rely upon industries to police themselves and would have government only minimally oversee that process. As a result, it is hypothesized that

6) *The US government and American states will not prohibit scientific experiments on dogs and will have lax regulations over any such experiments; and*
7) *The US government and American states will not prohibit unnecessary surgeries, such as ear cropping and tail docking, on dogs.*

The American model would likely give the power to the dog "owner" to make such a decision about his/her dog, considered to be property.

EU: Socialism for Dogs?

The EU has endorsed the view that animals are sentient beings and entitled to consideration of their interests. That assumption should influence canine policies. Indeed, the overarching values of the European approach hint of an active role for the government in protecting canine welfare, as it values the lives of animals and is predisposed to use the government in pursuit of the public good. What is more, individuals are inclined to yield to collective judgment over individual prerogatives. In light of this orientation, it is hypothesized that

8) *EU member states will legislate affirmative and demanding obligations for the caretakers of companion animals.*

In other words, the standards of care are not likely to be "minimalist," but to accommodate animals' status as sentient beings. It is anticipated as well that EU member states will be more likely to facilitate the fulfillment of these obligations via the acceptance of canines in parks and other public spaces. Indeed, the European value on environmentalism should yield more park or open space, cutting down on the potential for conflict with other users and ensuring that dogs can express natural behaviors, such as running and interaction with other dogs.

Given the obligations of the caretakers of dogs, there should not be a significant problem with the management of the canine population. If confronted with problems in this area, it is expected that EU member states would actively address the problem via publicly subsidized spay/neuter programs, public education, and/or enforcement of caretakers' responsibilities. To prevent abandonment and ensure the fulfillment of individual responsibilities, it is hypothesized that

9) *The EU and its member states will mandate both the permanent identification and registration of dogs.*

Given the value of animal lives for their own sake, it is also hypothesized that

10) *The EU and its member states will strictly regulate the commercial breeding of dogs and sale of puppies for purposes of protecting both the animals and prospective human caretakers; and*
11) *The EU and its member states will prohibit the euthanasia of healthy dogs.*

Likewise, one would expect EU member states to have strict laws against cruelty, including those commonly perpetuated against dogs. As a result, the following hypotheses are expected:

12) *The EU, to the extent it has jurisdiction, and its member states will prohibit commercial greyhound racing;*

13) *The EU and its member states will either outrightly ban the use of dogs in scientific experiments or heavily regulate their use for the animals' benefit; and*
14) *The EU, to the extent it has jurisdiction, and its member states will prohibit unnecessary surgeries, such as tail docking and ear cropping, done for the sake of appearance or human preference.*

Conclusion

These expectations establish "pure" models, the epitome of "European" and "American" approaches. In reality of course, US and EU policies and those of their member states demonstrate diversity and do not match the models in their purity or all of their particulars. However, if there are European and American approaches, then their respective policies should lean in the proper direction. In other words, the member states of the EU should cluster toward the European approach, not the American one; and US states should lean toward the American, not European, end of the spectrum. Of course, if the doubters of such homogeneous approaches are correct, there will not be such a pattern at all. We turn now to evaluating the conformity of policies for companion dogs with these respective approaches. Do these macro approaches hold water at the micro-level? Or for that matter, do they hold up at the macro-level?

Notes

1. Article I, Section 8, United States Constitution.
2. Alexander Hamilton, "The Judiciary Department," Federalist #78, 1788, *The Federalist Papers* (Library of Congress). http://thomas.loc.gov/home/histdox/fedpapers.html, accessed June 22, 2015. For goal of preventing tyranny of the majority, also see James Madison, Federalist # 10, 1788, *The Federalist Papers*.
3. Edward S. Corwin, *The President: Office and Powers*, Second Ed., revised (New York: New York University Press, 1941), Chapter VI.
4. For its own characterization, see Council of Europe, "The Council of Europe in Brief," 2014. http://www.coe.int/en/web/about-us/who-we-are, accessed July 20, 2014. For definition, see V. Caporale, B. Alessandrini, P. Dalla Villa, and S. Del Papa, "Global Perspectives on Animal Welfare: Europe," *Revue Scientifique et Technique (International Office of Epizootics)*, 24:2 (2005): 567.
5. Council of Europe, "Structure." (2014) http://coe.ent/en/web/about-us/structure;jsessionid=8338AE38BF119C09582C6C37C99C8D61, accessed July 21, 2014.

6. European Commission, "Conditions for Membership, Enlargement," November 28, 2013. http://www.ec.europa.eu/enlargement/policy/conditions-membership/index_en.htm, accessed July 21, 2014.
7. John McCormick, *Why Europe Matters: The Case for the European Union* (New York: Palgrave Macmillan, 2013), 11–12.
8. Europa, "The Union's Decision-Making Procedures: The New System of Qualified Majority Voting." http://europa.eu/scadplus/constitution/doublemajority_en.htm, accessed June 22, 2015. For more information about the history, institutions and policy-making procedures of the EU, see Michelle Cini and Nieves Pérez-Solórzano Borragán, *European Union Politics*, Fourth Ed. (Oxford: Oxford University Press, 2013); Helen Wallace, Mark A. Pollack, and Alasdair R. Young, *Policy-Making in the European Union*, Sixth Ed. (New York: Oxford University Press, 2010); and Ian Bache, Stephen George, and Simon Bulmer, *Politics in the European Union*, Third Ed. (New York: Oxford University Press, 2011).
9. For statistics on the euro, see European Commission, "The Euro, Economic and Financial Affairs," March 27, 2014. http://www.ec.europa.eu/economy_finance/euro/index_en.htm (accessed July 21, 2014). For information about internal border controls, see European Commission, "Schengen Area, Home Affairs," July 1, 2013. http://www.ec.europa.eu/dgs/home-affairs/what-we-do/policies/borders-and-visas/schengen/index_en.htm, accessed July 21, 2014. The six EU member states currently not included are Bulgaria, Croatia, Cyprus, Ireland, Romania and the UK.
10. Richard Sakwa and Anne Stevens, eds., *Contemporary Europe* (Palgrave Macmillan, 2012), 109.
11. Charles W. Dunn, "Introduction: The Magnetism of American Exceptionalism," in Charles W. Dunn, ed., *American Exceptionalism: The Origins, History, and Future of the Nation's Greatest Strength* (New York: Rowman & Littlefield Publishers, Inc., 2013), 2.
12. Steven M. Warshawsky, "What Does It Mean to Be an American?" in David T. Canon, John J. Coleman, and Kenneth R. Mayer, eds., *Fault Lines: Debating the Issues in American Politics*, Third Ed. (New York: W.W. Norton & Company, 2011), 12.
13. James W. Ceaser, "The Origins and Character of American Exceptionalism," in Dunn, *American Exceptionalism*, 21.
14. Quoted in *Ibid*., 22. The original quotation comes from *The Federalist Papers* (Essay #1).
15. Hugh Heclo, "Varieties of American Exceptionalism," in Dunn, *American Exceptionalism*, 29–31.
16. Louis Hartz, *The Liberal Tradition in America: The Classic on the Causes and Effects of Liberal Thought in the U.S., with a New Introduction by Tom Wicker* (New York: A Harvest/HBJ Book, Harcourt Brace Jovanovich, Publishers, 1991). Original version published in 1955.
17. See Heclo, "Varieties of American Exceptionalism," 39.
18. Jeremy Rifkin, *The European Dream: How Europe's Vision of the Future Is Quietly Eclipsing the American Dream* (New York: Jeremy P. Tarcher/Penguin, a member of Penguin Group, USA, Inc., 2004), 320–334.
19. Bruce A. Wagman and Matthew Liebman, *A Worldview of Animal Law* (Durham, North Carolina: Carolina Academic Press, 2011), 26.
20. *Ibid*., 151.

21. Susan Hunter and Richard A. Brisbin, Jr., *Pet Politics: The Political and Legal Lives of Cats, Dogs, and Horses in Canada and the United States* (West Lafayette, Indiana: Purdue University Press, 2016), 177.
22. Pamela D. Frasch, Katherine M. Hessler, Sarah M. Kutil, and Sonia S. Waisman, *Animal Law in a Nutshell* (St. Paul, Minnesota: Thomas Reuters, 2011), 328. For exclusions, see Wagman and Liebman, 38.
23. McCormick, *Why Europe Matters*, 86.
24. Alberto Martinelli, "The European Union and the United States as two variants of Western modernity," in Alberto Martinelli, ed., *Transatlantic Divide: Comparing American and European Society* (New York: Oxford University Press, 2007), 11.
25. McCormick, *Why Europe Matters*, 103.
26. Paul W. Kingston and Laura M. Holian, "Inequality," in Martinelli, *Transatlantic Divide*, 72.
27. Steven Hill, *Europe's Promise: Why the European Way Is the Best Hope in an Insecure Age* (Berkeley: University of California Press, 2010), 89.
28. *Ibid.*, 75.
29. For quotation, see Kingston and Holian, "Inequality," 73. Also see Gerard Cornilleau, "Welfare," in Martinelli, *Transatlantic Divide*, 150.
30. *Ibid.*, 143.
31. Hill, *Europe's Promise*, 55.
32. *Ibid.*, 54.
33. Rifkin, *The European Dream*, 327–328. Not all agree that there is a difference between the US and Europe in terms of precaution. See Jonathan B. Wiener and Michael D. Rogers, "Comparing Precaution in the United States and Europe," *Journal of Risk Research* 5:4 (2002): 317–349. Contrary to the conventional wisdom, they argue that the level of caution varies enormously by issue and they cite the handling of mad cow disease as one example for which the US is more cautious.
34. Hill, *Europe's Promise*, 157.
35. *Ibid.*, 179–182.
36. Rifkin, *The European Dream*, 91.
37. On latter point, see Patrick Le Galés and Mathieu Zagrodzki, "Cities," in Martinell, *Transatlantic Divide*, 224–229.
38. McCormick, *Why Europe Matters*, 86.
39. Stephanie Engelsman, "'World Leader'—At What Price? A Look at Lagging American Animal Protection Laws," *Pace Environmental Law Review* 22 (Fall 2005): 331. Also see Wagman and Liebman, *A Worldview*, 41.
40. European Commission, "The EU and Animal Welfare: Policy, Objectives." http://ec.europe.eu/food/animal/welfare/policy/index_en.htm, accessed 16 September 2014. Even prior to the enactment of this Treaty, there was a legally binding protocol to recognize animals as sentient beings, see Engelsman, "World Leader," 347.
41. Paige M. Tomaselli, "International Comparative Animal Cruelty Laws," Animal Legal and Historical Center (Michigan State University College of Law, 2003). http://www.animallaw.info/articles/art_details/print.htm, accessed 22 July 2010.

42. Peter Stevenson, "European and International Legislation: A Way Forward for the Protection of Farm Animals," in Peter Sankoff and Steven White, eds., *Animal Law in Australasia* (Sydney: Federation Press, 2009), 308.
43. McCormick, *Why Europe Matters*, 86.
44. Alberto Martinelli, "Politics and institutional architectures," in Martinelli, *Transatlantic Divide*, 134.
45. See T. David Gordon, "Taking Exception to American Exceptionalism," in Dunn, *American Exceptionalism*, 87. In addition to John Locke whose *Second Treatise on Government* is assumed to have influenced the Declaration of Independence, Gordon cites Adam Smith, whose *Wealth of Nations*, originally published in 1776, provided a defense of laissez-faire capitalism.
46. Gordon, "Taking Exception to American Exceptionalism," 92.
47. Sarah Song, "What Does It Mean to Be an American?," in Canon, Coleman and Mayer, *Fault Lines*, 9.
48. James A. Morone and Rogan Kersh, *By the People: Debating American Government*, Brief Third Ed. (New York: Oxford University Press, 2018), 309.
49. See Morris P. Fiorina, "*What* Culture Wars? Debunking the Myth of a Polarized America," in Canon, Coleman and Mayer, *Fault Lines*, 232; John Kenneth White, *The Values Divide: American Politics and Culture in Transition* (New York: Chatham House Publishers, Seven Bridges Press, LLC, 2003), 163; Morris P. Fiorina with Samuel J. Adams and Jeremy C. Pope, *Culture War? The Myth of a Polarized America*, Second Ed. (New York: Pearson Longman, 2006); Matthew S. Levendusky and Jeremy C. Pope, "Red States vs. Blue States: Going Beyond the Mean," *Public Opinion Quarterly* 75:2 (2011), 227–248; and James Q. Wilson, "How Divided Are We?" in Canon, Coleman and Mayer, *Fault Lines*, 238.
50. Thomas Risse, *A Community of Europeans? Transnational Identities and Public Spheres* (Ithaca: Cornell University Press, 2010), 6. For an example of a skeptic's view about a common European culture and the lack of public support for one, see, respectively, Gerard Delanty, *Inventing Europe: Idea, Identity, Reality* (New York: St. Martin's Press, 1995); and John Gillingham, *Design for a New Europe* (New York: Cambridge University Press, 2006).
51. Martinelli, "The European Union and the United States," 21.
52. For opt out, see Risse, *A Community*, 251; for a la carte, see *Ibid.*, 83; and for least Europeanized, see *Ibid.*, 160.
53. Cornilleau, "Welfare," 151.
54. Michel Forsé and Maxime Parodi, "Value Change," in Martinelli, *Transatlantic Divide*, 180.
55. For an elaboration of the difficulties confronting eastern states in building popular support for constitutional values and making this transition, see Tina Rosenberg, *The Haunted Land: Facing Europe's Ghosts After Communism* (Vintage, 1996). She discusses case studies of the Czech Republic, Poland and East Germany after unification. For more recent difficulties, see Timothy Snyder, *The Road To Unfreedom: Russia, Europe, America* (Tim Duggan Books, 2018).

56. Berthold Forssman, "Labour Migration from East to West," *Euro Topics* 2007. http://www.eurotopics.net/en/home/presseschau/archiv/magazin/gesellschaft-verteilerseite/migration_2007_11/debatte_migration_2007_11/, accessed June 23, 2015.
57. "Immigration to Europe: How many foreign citizens live in each country?" *The Guardian*, September 7, 2010. http://www.theguardian.com/news/datablog/2010/sep/07/immigration-europe-foreign-citizens, accessed June 22, 2015.
58. *Ibid.*

Bibliography

Bache, Ian, Stephen George, and Simon Bulmer, *Politics in the European Union*. 3rd ed. New York: Oxford University Press, 2011.

Canon, David T., John J. Coleman, and Kenneth R. Mayer, eds. *Fault Lines: Debating the Issues in American Politics*. 3rd ed. New York: W.W. Norton & Company, 2011.

Cini, Michelle and Nieves Pérez-Solórzano Borragán. *European Union Politics*. 4th ed. Oxford: Oxford University Press, 2013.

Delanty, Gerard. *Inventing Europe: Idea, Identity, Reality*. New York: St. Martin's Press, 1995.

Dunn, Charles W., ed. *American Exceptionalism: The Origins, History, and Future of the Nation's Greatest Strength*. New York: Rowman & Littlefield Publishers, Inc., 2013.

Fiorina, Morris P., with Samuel J. Adams, and Jeremy C. Pope. *Culture War? The Myth of a Polarized America*. 2nd ed. New York: Pearson Longman, 2006.

Frasch, Pamela D., et al. *Animal Law in a Nutshell*. St. Paul, Minnesota: Thomas Reuters, 2011.

Gillingham, John. *Design for a New Europe*. New York: Cambridge University Press, 2006.

Hartz, Louis. *The Liberal Tradition in America: The Classic on the Causes and Effects of Liberal Thought in the U.S., with a New Introduction by Tom Wicker*. New York: A Harvest/HBJ Book, Harcourt Brace Jovanovich, Publishers, 1991.

Hill, Steven. *Europe's Promise: Why the European Way Is the Best Hope in an Insecure Age*. Berkeley: University of California Press, 2010.

Hunter, Susan and Richard A. Brisbin, Jr. *Pet Politics: The Political and Legal Lives of Cats, Dogs, and Horses in Canada and the United States*. West Lafayette, Indiana: Purdue University Press, 2016.

Levendusky, Matthew S. and Jeremy C. Pope. "Red States vs. Blue States: Going Beyond the Mean." *Public Opinion Quarterly* 75:2 (2011): 227–248.

Martinelli, Alberto, ed. *Transatlantic Divide: Comparing American and European Society*. New York: Oxford University Press, 2007.

McCormick, John. *Why Europe Matters: The Case for the European Union*. New York: Palgrave MacMillan, 2013.

Rifkin, Jeremy. *The European Dream: How Europe's Vision of the Future is Quietly Eclipsing the American Dream*. New York: Jeremy P. Tarcher/Penguin, a member of Penguin Group, USA, Inc., 2004.

Risse, Thomas. *A Community of Europeans? Transitional Identities and Public Spheres*. Ithaca: Cornell University Press, 2010.

Rosenberg, Tina. *The Haunted Land: Facing Europe's Ghosts After Communism*. Vintage, 1996.

Sakwa, Richard and Anne Stevens, eds. *Contemporary Europe*. New York: Palgrave Macmillan, 2012.

Snyder, Timothy. *The Road to Unfreedom: Russia, Europe, America.* Tim Duggan Books, 2018.

Wagman, Bruce A. and Matthew Liebman. *A Worldview of Animal Law*. Durham, North Carolina: Carolina Academic Press, 2011.

Wallace, Helen, Mark A. Pollack, and Alasdair R. Young. *Policy-Making in the European Union*. 6th ed. New York: Oxford University Press, 2010.

White, John Kenneth. *The Values Divide: American Politics and Culture in Transition*. New York: Chatham House Publishers, Seven Bridges Press, LLC, 2003.

Wiener, Jonathan B. and Michael D. Rogers. "Comparing Precaution in the United States and Europe." *Journal of Risk Research* 5:4 (2002): 317–349.

· 2 ·

CARING FOR BEST FRIENDS

Public Policies to Protect Companions

In the US and EU, there are approximately 138 million dogs who are companion animals.[1] While millions of these dogs most likely have the good fortune to live in loving homes, public policies are nonetheless essential to secure their well-being. In defining and criminalizing abuse and neglect, such policies establish a "floor," below which standards of care are not to go. There is also potential for public policy to state the duties of canine caretakers affirmatively and thereby to elevate the requirements of care. In other words, policies can demand not only that caretakers refrain from abusing and neglecting their dogs but that they provide decent care. Because dogs require exercise and socialization, public policies also impact the ability of caretakers to satisfy canine needs. For instance, policies grant or deny access to parks and recreational trails as well as other public spaces.

While EU member states are more likely to have legislated affirmative duties of care or "codes of responsibilities," such duties are not entirely absent in US states. What is more, in several EU member states, caretakers do not universally abide by these duties. Especially in the East and South, practices do not necessarily match legal requirements. In the US, there are norms of quality care in select parts of every region despite the absence of legislative mandates. Yet only some US municipalities have created "dog-friendly" space in the form of off-leash parks and outdoor restaurants, making the fulfillment of responsibilities to exercise and socialize dogs easier. In contrast, EU member states tend to have supportive policies with canines allowed in more public spaces. Despite any exceptions and the realities of non-compliance with legislation in many places, hypotheses that American states are not likely to *legislate* affirmative obligations for the caretakers of animals while EU member states are likely to do so are validated.

What Are Dogs? Philosophical Disagreements

Implicit in the codification of responsibilities to canines is an assumption that dogs are sentient beings. They are not things or machines, as Descartes once proclaimed. Yet in law, dogs are often conceptualized as the property of individuals and they are bought and sold. Their status is not consistently defined in either the EU or US and is indeed evolving at this time. However, EU member states are closer to the acceptance of dogs as sentient beings than the US, which clings to the notion of canine property despite passing enactments that assume sentience.

Indeed, because Article 13 of the Lisbon Treaty recognizes the sentience of animals and demands that the EU and its member states pay full regard to their welfare requirements, dogs have a claim to such treatment. In law, they *are* sentient animals. Several member states reflect this assumption in their national laws. Germany, for example, amended its constitution or Basic Law in 2002, well before the Lisbon Treaty was negotiated, to read that the "environment 'and the animals' were to be afforded protection…on a level with the basic rights of humans."[2] In 2016, Luxembourg proposed a law recognizing that animals are "'living non-human sentient beings with a nervous system scientifically capable of feeling pain and experiencing emotions' like 'suffering and anguish.'"[3] Most other countries affirm the sentience of animals in their welfare or protection acts. For example, Latvia's law asserts that "every unique being is in itself of value," and Poland's law stipulates that an animal is not a "thing," but a living creature entitled to respect, protection, and the care of humans.[4] What is more, Müllerová argues that in the Czech Republic, there is wide popular acceptance of the sentience of animals, which since 2014 are no longer "objects" in the legal sense.[5] To be sure, there are inconsistencies in national laws, with animals treated as objects in the Italian civil system but sentient beings in its criminal code. In Spain, there is a similar inconsistency in the conception of animals, but France changed its Civil Code in 2014 to eliminate that duality.[6] More problematically, Slovakia has no comprehensive animal welfare laws and therefore no philosophical assertions about their entitlements.[7] However, that country is in the process of developing such a law as of 2018. Despite this delay and any inconsistencies, the trend in the laws of EU member states is toward the recognition of sentience.

The European Convention for the Protection of Pet Animals (ECPPA), a product of the Council of Europe, not the EU, reflects this assumption as well. Its preamble asserts that "man has a moral obligation to respect all living creatures" and then notes the "special relationship" with pets. As we will see, the Convention, signed by 18 EU member states and ratified by 17, establishes several protective guidelines for pets. Croatia, Estonia, Hungary, Ireland, Malta, Poland, Slovakia, Slovenia, Spain, and the UK have *not* signed this Convention. The Netherlands has yet to ratify it. It specifically demands that "nobody shall cause a pet animal unnecessary suffering or distress."[8] Similarly, EU Directive #63, which stipulates *supra*-national guidelines in the area of scientific experimentation on animals, states that "animals have an intrinsic value which must be respected" in its opening statements.[9] Even laboratory dogs, in this mindset, are sentient beings, a status that demands some consideration of their interests.

In contrast, the US does not recognize the sentience of animals in its Constitution. Animals are, for the most part, conceptualized as property. At the national level, there is not a comprehensive anti-cruelty law dealing with all species of animals. Instead, the AWA focuses on specific activities, which are interstate in nature and have been rife with abuse in the past. The Act seeks to ensure the "humane" treatment of animals in these activities, but does not allude to the value or sentience of animal life. Nor do state anti-cruelty statutes, which are general in nature, assert the sentience of animals. They typically omit an introductory statement and begin with definitions. Usually, animals are "living creatures" and "not human," with common categories, such as livestock, sometimes excluded from the definition entirely. The language is succinct, with no philosophical assertions about the capacities and/or claims of animals.

Most US state anti-cruelty laws originally were intended to protect "property" of economic value, such as horses, and omitted dogs and pets. However, they now criminalize acts against all animals, including one's own property, and are even more favorable toward companion animals than livestock. As Wagman and Liebman explain, "While animals remain property under the law, the presence of animal welfare and anticruelty laws represents a tacit rejection of animals' pure property status."[10] Indeed, there has been a concerted effort to change the status of dogs and cats from "property" to living beings with rights. Since language matters, animal advocates have pushed for the use of the word "guardian" instead of "owner" for those who care for dogs and cats. According to Grimm, "nineteen cities—from San Jose to St. Louis—two counties, and the state of Rhode Island have added 'guardian' language to their animal laws." Not all have eliminated the word "owner," placing the new term as an alternative to it.[11] This shift in terminology signals more than a change in semantics, as the scientific research community and the American Veterinary Medical Association (AVMA) strongly oppose it. Once animals are spoken of as sentient beings, their lives acquire more value. Veterinarians fear lawsuits for malpractice, while the scientific research community worries that people will realize that other animals are sentient too. Per this thinking, there will be more opposition to the use of not only dogs and cats, but all animals in experimentation. The reasoning is somewhat analogous to the domino theory, once one animal has a claim to sentience, others will follow.

Despite the opposition in the US, there have been some advancements in the legal status of canines. In Tennessee, Connecticut, and Illinois, people can recover non-economic damages up to specified limits for the loss of a pet in the case of negligent or intentional acts. Prior to the enactment of these laws, the only economic compensation for the loss of a dog or cat was "replacement" cost. Several other states are considering similar legislation.[12] What is more, animals can now inherit money themselves, a clear sign that they are not just "property." Since 2000, people can leave money to a trustee for their care. If the trustee does not discharge the duties properly, "a judge can appoint someone to advocate for the animal's right to inherit its money…." This code has now been adopted in 42 states.[13] Evincing the propensity to think of animals as more than "property," the US Congress declared that "The federal government and the states have a compelling interest in preventing intentional acts of extreme animal cruelty" in the Animal Crush Video Prohibition Act of 2010. If accepted by the Supreme Court, such a declaration has much significance because laws advancing compelling interests, if narrowly construed to those purposes, can take precedence over claims of individual rights. While there has been progress in the US in protecting animals, especially companion ones, for their own sake, the legal terrain is more challenging than in the EU given the formal status of animals as property and the lack of constitutional commitment to their interests.[14]

Caretakers' Basic Duties

US: Prohibition of Abuse

In the US, any affirmative duties of caretakers of companion animals are generally woven into state laws via the definitions of cruelty and neglect. There is no national statement or law about caretakers' responsibilities. Every state criminalizes the denial of food and water to animals under the charge of a human. With the exception of only six states, all others explicitly require adequate shelter as well, often with directives to protect animals from the elements and to provide sanitary conditions. The denial of shelter would almost certainly violate general cruelty prohibitions anyway, but the statement of the need for shelter and specifications about its adequacy strengthen the protections for animals.

Requirements for the level of health care vary. All states require rabies vaccinations for the protection of public health. However, do states legislate medical care for the sake of the dog? A large minority of states, 23, indeed mandate that caretakers provide medical care for the sake of the dog. In most of those states, or 17, caretakers must provide medical care to prevent unnecessary or unjustifiable pain or suffering. This language seems to imply a need for veterinary intervention in cases of accidents or serious illness, but not necessarily as a routine matter. Indeed, some states, such as Montana, qualify the mandate to apply only to cases of "immediate, obvious and serious illness or injury."[15] Arguably, the denial of care in such cases could constitute a violation of the general prohibition of cruelty applicable in all states anyway. When states invoke such qualifying language in their statutes, they are considered to be requiring minimal care. If such qualifying language is absent or a clear directive is stated, then states are classified as requiring medical care to ensure the health of the dog. Six states impose an affirmative duty on caretakers to provide veterinary care to maintain the health of animals. For example, West Virginia demands "medical treatment necessary to sustain normal health and fitness." Other states, such as Maryland, lack qualifying language and define the failure to give veterinary care as cruelty.[16] While six states constitute a very small minority, the trend is in the direction of a stronger duty of care in this area with an affirmative duty to provide veterinary care "increasingly common."[17]

In addition, there are four states that posit the duties of caretakers affirmatively. In Illinois, Michigan, and Virginia, there are clear instances of caretakers' codes, with sections headed "Owners' Duties," "Duty to Provide Care," and "Care of Companion Animals by Owner," respectively. Alaska's law simply notes "Minimum Standards of Care."[18] While the duties are not at all inconsistent with those required in other anti-cruelty laws, they are stated affirmatively and in Illinois, include a requirement to provide animals with "humane care and treatment."[19] Virginia demands "adequate exercise, care, treatment and transportation." Three other states deem the failure to provide exercise a form of neglect as well. Minnesota requires exercise if animals are enclosed. In a similar vein, several states have legislated restrictions on the practice of tethering dogs[20] (see Table 2.1).

Table 2.1: US Caretakers' Responsibilities.

	Duties: Affirmative or Negative	**Shelter—Sanitary Conditions (SC)**	**Medical Care: Not explicit, Minimal, for Health**	**Other**
Alabama	N	Shelter	Not explicit	
Alaska	A	Shelter, SC	Health	
Arkansas	N	Shelter	Not explicit	
Arizona	N	Shelter	Minimal	
California	N	Shelter	Not explicit	
Colorado	N	Shelter	Not explicit	
Connecticut	N	Shelter	Not explicit	
Delaware	N	Shelter	Minimal	
Florida	N	Not explicit	Not explicit	
Georgia	N	Not explicit but SC	Not explicit	
Hawaii	N	Shelter	Not explicit	
Iowa	N	Shelter	Not explicit	
Idaho	N	Shelter	Not explicit	
Illinois	A	Shelter	Minimal	"Humane care and treatment"
Indiana	N	Shelter	Minimal	
Kansas	N	Shelter	Health	*Exercise*
Kentucky	N	Not explicit	Minimal	Space
Louisiana	N	Shelter	Minimal	
Maine	N	Shelter, SC	Minimal	

	Duties: Affirmative or Negative	**Shelter—Sanitary Conditions (SC)**	**Medical Care: Not explicit, Minimal, for Health**	**Other**
Maryland	N	Shelter, SC	Health	
Massachusetts	N	Shelter, SC	Not explicit	
Michigan	A	Shelter, SC	Minimal	*Exercise*
Minnesota	N	Shelter	Not explicit	Exercise if enclosed
Mississippi	N	Shelter	Not explicit	
Missouri	N	Shelter	Health	
Montana	N	Minimum protection from adverse weather	Minimal	
Nebraska	N	Not explicit	Health	
Nevada	N	Restrictions on outdoor enclosures	Not explicit	
N. Hampshire	N	Shelter	Not explicit	
New Jersey	N	Shelter	Not explicit	
New Mexico	N	Not explicit	Not explicit	
New York	N	Shelter	Not explicit	
N. Carolina	N	Not explicit	Not explicit	
North Dakota	N	Shelter, SC	Minimal	
Ohio	N	Shelter	Not explicit	
Oklahoma	N	Shelter	Minimal	
Oregon	N	Shelter, SC	Minimal	*Exercise*
Pennsylvania	N	Shelter, SC	Minimal	
Rhode Island	N	Shelter, SC	Not explicit	
S. Carolina	N	Shelter	Not explicit	
South Dakota	N	Shelter, SC	Not explicit	
Tennessee	N	Shelter	Not explicit	"care"
Texas	N	Shelter	Not explicit	
Utah	N	Shelter	Not explicit	"essential care"
Virginia	A	Shelter, SC	Minimal	Adequate *exercise*, care, treatment and transportation

	Duties: Affirmative or Negative	Shelter—Sanitary Conditions (SC)	Medical Care: Not explicit, Minimal, for Health	Other
Vermont	N	Shelter, SC	Minimal	Rest
Washington	N	Shelter, SC	Minimal	Rest
Wisconsin	N	Shelter, SC	Not explicit	
W. Virginia	N	Shelter	Health	
Wyoming	N	Protection from weather	Minimal	

Source: Laws accessed from "Anti-Cruelty Related Statutes," (Animal Legal and Historical Center, Michigan State University College of Law). https://www.animallaw.info/statutes/topic/anti-cruelty, accessed June 15, 2018.

Despite examples of select states with a more "European" approach, the basic standards of care are minimalist in most states, with the care only in need of rising to a level slightly above cruelty or neglect. Hypothesis #1 that *American states are likely to ban extreme cruelty and neglect, but are not likely to legislate affirmative obligations for the caretakers of animals* is therefore validated. However, there are a few exceptions and the trend, though early, appears to be in the other direction. Indeed, it should be stipulated that US states have not only imposed harsher penalties for animal cruelty, with all states now considering it a felony, but most have also stepped up enforcement efforts.[21] There are animal police programs on television and special units of police forces now dedicated to these more serious crimes. The American model is more likely to treat socially deviant activities, such as egregious forms of animal cruelty, harshly in the law, but less inclined to impose affirmative obligations on the caretakers of animals.

EU: Affirmative Duties

Like the US, the EU delegates the legislation for the duties of animal caretakers to its member states. However, the ECPPA asserts responsibilities for the keepers of animals. What is more, the language is affirmative, imposing duties and not simply preventing neglect and cruelty. Keepers are responsible for their animals' "health and welfare." To that end, keepers are to "provide accommodation, care and attention," and are specifically tasked with providing sufficient food and water, "adequate opportunities for exercise," and taking "all reasonable measures to prevent escape."[22] This statement is in keeping with expectations for the European model. For the 17 EU member states that have ratified this Convention, caretakers' duties are therefore affirmative. Nine other EU member states posit the duties affirmatively as well. Only 2/28 EU member states frame caretakers' responsibilities negatively or via definitions of cruelty or neglect. In one of those states, Spain, there are 17 autonomous communities, each with its own law. There is simply not a national statement of affirmative duties.

While the provision of shelter is not explicitly required in two EU member states, general statements would almost certainly cover that requirement in the Netherlands where keepers must take "sufficient care of animals" and in Malta where keepers are "responsible for health and welfare of animals."[23] Four of the signatories of the ECPPA, namely Bulgaria, Cyprus, Greece, and Latvia, have exceeded the minimum guarantee of responsibility for health in that Convention. Bulgaria calls for "regular preventative veterinary care and immediate treatment in the case of disease or injury," while Cyprus stipulates that "a person must ensure an animal's health and welfare." Greece also requires medical care, and Latvia obliges caretakers to "take care of health, welfare and use in accordance with species, age and physiology."[24] For those countries that have not signed and ratified the ECPPA, seven nonetheless require minimal medical care but four do not state anything explicitly.

Because the ECPPA requires "adequate opportunity for exercise," 17 EU member states consider this a caretaker's responsibility. Bulgaria goes further to require that dogs in apartments be walked and that caretakers have sufficient indoor space in relation to the dog's size.[25] In its 2013 law, Ireland, which is not a signatory of the ECPPA, includes an exercise requirement as well."[26] While not explicitly requiring exercise, The Netherlands and the UK demand that natural behaviors not be limited and that normal behavior patterns be exhibited, respectively. Those edicts could be interpreted as requiring exercise.[27] It should be noted that England and Wales, Scotland, and Northern Ireland have separate Animal Welfare Acts, but all require the exhibition of normal behavior patterns and that animals be protected from pain, suffering, injury, and disease."[28] Six of the remaining eight EU member states have general language requiring "care" or "responsibility for welfare." Only two member states, Poland and Slovakia, make no specific or general reference to a dog's need for exercise. It should be stipulated that exercise is distinguished from "movement," which is typically included in anti-cruelty statutes. A caretaker's responsibility to exercise a dog would include a walk or off-leash play and running (see Table 2.2).

Table 2.2: EU Caretakers' Responsibilities.

	Duties: Affirmative or Negative	Shelter, Sanitary Conditions (SC)	Medical Care: Not Explicit, Minimal, for Health	Adequate Opportunity for Exercise	Other
Austria*	A	Shelter	Minimal	Yes	Social contact
Belgium*	A	Shelter, SC	Minimal	Yes	
Bulgaria*	A	Shelter	Health	Yes	
Croatia	N	Shelter	Minimal	Not explicit	"care"
Cyprus*	A	Shelter, SC	Health	Yes	"care," welfare
Czech Rep.*	A	Shelter	Minimal	Yes	"well-being"
Denmark*	A	Shelter	Minimal	Yes	"care"
Estonia	A	Shelter, SC	Minimal	Not explicit	"adequate care"
Finland*	A	Shelter, SC	Minimal	Yes	"treated well," "needs met"
France*	A	Shelter	Minimal	Yes	
Germany*	A	Shelter, SC	Minimal	Yes	Natural daylight if kept indoors; education of caretaker
Greece*	A	Shelter, SC	Health	Yes	
Hungary	A	Shelter, SC	Not explicit	Not explicit	Care for demands at least 1x/day
Ireland	A	Shelter	Minimal	Yes	"safeguards the health and welfare of the animal"
Italy*	A	Shelter, SC	Minimal	Yes	
Latvia*	A	Shelter, SC	Health	Yes	Ensure society has favorable attitude toward animal
Lithuania*	A	Shelter, SC	Minimal	Yes	Rest; ensure welfare
Luxembourg*	A	Shelter, SC	Minimal	Yes	
Malta	A	Not explicit	Not explicit	Not explicit	"responsible for health and welfare"

	Duties: Affirmative or Negative	Shelter, Sanitary Conditions (SC)	Medical Care: Not Explicit, Minimal, for Health	Adequate Opportunity for Exercise	Other
Netherlands	A	Not explicit	Minimal	Not explicit	"sufficient care of animals;" natural behaviors not limited
Poland	A	Shelter	Not explicit	Not explicit	Access to daylight
Portugal*	A	Shelter, SC	Minimal	Yes	
Romania*	A	Shelter	Minimal	Yes	
Slovakia	A	Shelter	Minimal	Not explicit	
Slovenia	A	Shelter, SC	Not explicit	Not explicit	Checked at least 1x/day
Spain	N	Shelter, SC	Minimal	Not explicit	"Welfare and safety"
Sweden*	A	Shelter, SC	Minimal	Yes	
UK	A	Shelter, SC	Minimal	Not explicit	Exhibit normal behavior patterns

*signed and ratified ECPPA

Sources: European Convention for the Protection of Pet Animals (effective date May 1, 1992), http://conventions.coe.int/treaty/en/treaties/html/125.htm, accessed September 17, 2014; European Enforcement Network of Animal Welfare Lawyers and Commissioners, "National Animal Welfare Legislation." http://www.lawyersforanimalprotection.eu/national-animal-welfare-legislation (accessed May 28, 2018); and EU Dog and Cat Alliance, "The welfare of dogs and cats involved in commercial practices: a review of the legislation across EU countries," 102. https://s3-eu-west-1.amazonaws.com/assets.dogandcatwelfare.eu/live/media/filer_public/f3/c4/f3c44506-728a-4b38-a05e-bc4909214db6/all.pdf, accessed June 3, 2018.

In general, EU member states are likely to state the duties of caretakers affirmatively, include exercise requirements and use more compassionate language, such as Finland's imperative to "treat animals well."[29] Given that 26/28 EU member states posit affirmative duties, 24/28 require at least minimal health care, and 18/28 assert the need for adequate exercise, it is reasonable to conclude that hypothesis #9, *EU member states will legislate affirmative and demanding obligations for the caretakers of companion animals*, is confirmed. However, there are limited exceptions with at least one member state weaving responsibilities into definitions of cruelty and neglect, similarly to American states, and the obligations themselves are not so very different from American ones in substantive content. In fact, requirements for shelter and veterinary care are quite alike. About the same percentage of EU member states as US states require veterinary care to maintain the health of the dog, 4/28 or 14 percent in the EU and 6/50 or 12 percent in the US. Yet 86 percent of EU member states and only 46% of US states explicitly state a requirement of medical care. Even if the substantive requirements are not so starkly different, the language matters. Over time, the use of affirmative language has the potential to socialize humans to fulfill the responsibilities they have to animals in their care. The prohibition of "neglect" and "abuse" has less of an educative effect on caretakers, as it asks them to refrain from behaviors most consider deviant. In contrast to affirmative language, there is no invitation to consider the extent of one's duties to animals. However, there are indicators of changing mores in the US with more states imposing duties on caretakers of animals and many local governments referring to these caretakers as "guardians," not "owners."

Acceptance of Individual Responsibilities?

The best legislation is meaningless unless it is enforced and accepted by the population. In this area of provision of care to companion animals, penalties for the violation of standards are typically not as severe as they would be in the case of egregious cruelty. Fines, not prison, are more commonly applied. Because sub-standard care is also difficult for outsiders to identify, the implementation of codes of responsibility is heavily reliant upon their popular acceptance. In both the US and EU, there is wide variability in the individual acceptance of duties of care.

EU: Absolute Acceptance or Rejection?

In the EU, with approximately 60 million companion dogs, there are overall indicators of quality care and human attachment to canine friends. People in EU member states spend 24 billion annually on pet food and related supplies and there are an estimated 550,000 direct and indirect jobs related to pet care, such as veterinarians and breeders.[30] Indeed, Europeans pay the most per dog for food. Norway, which is not in the EU, tops the list, but the EU average is $14.81 per month compared to $13.81 in the US.[31] What is more, there are at least eight EU member states that report virtually no problem with abandonment, a strong indicator of a norm of responsible care.[32] These countries are clustered in north-central Europe. In Sweden, one of those countries, dogs "occupy a high status in society" and are "considered members of the family."[33] According to Tasker's Report on Stray Practices in Europe, there is "an impressive degree of social responsibility where dog ownership is concerned" in Sweden.[34] Likewise, Germans take the responsibilities of care seriously, adhering to requirements.

Indeed, crating or even a leaving a dog alone for a typical workday is not socially acceptable in Germany.[35] Some, in fact, might say that dogs are cherished to the point of pampering in these north-central member states. Particularly in high-income areas, some businesses have gone to new lengths to cater to dogs and their caretakers. In Germany, for example, the first restaurant for cats and dogs opened in one of Berlin's upscale neighborhoods in 2013.[36] Sweden claimed the world's first gourmet food truck for dogs in 2015. The owner noted that the "same high demands we put on our food is now placed on the food we feed our dogs."[37] The eastern section of Berlin is home to the Hundemuseum, a museum with over 20,000 canine-related items testifying to the German love for dogs. It is worth noting as well that the former GDR or East Germany does not have the same problem with stray dogs found elsewhere in the old Communist bloc.

According to Euromonitor International, the trend among pet caretakers throughout north-central and northwestern Europe is toward the "humanization" of companion animals. Increasingly considering these animals to be members of the family, caretakers have demonstrated a willingness to pay for premium foods and to attend to health and wellness. In France, for example, caretakers "are becoming generally more concerned about their pets' well-being." The dog-friendly Swedes "are increasingly looking at their pets through parental eyes." Such loving attitudes toward pets are not limited to the Northwest. "Pet humanization," as Euromonitor calls it, is present in the South and trending in the East as well. About Italy, a report on pet care notes, caretakers "increasingly consider their pets to be part of their families, to the point that their presence influences several aspects of their lives…." As a result, Italians "are willing to purchase for their pets the best they can afford to improve their lives and health." Likewise, in Spain and Portugal, growing numbers of people consider companion animals to be family members. Despite the economic downturn in Portugal, there was "robust growth" in spending on companion animals in 2013. Given the dire economic circumstances,

Greece is an exception, with only ten percent of caretakers willing to spend "lavishly" on companion animals.[38]

In eastern member states, there are signs that companion animals are also becoming family members or in the words of Euromonitor's Reports, "humanized." During the Communist era, people in several eastern countries had dogs. They were generally fed table scraps, not commercial dog food. While a majority in the region continue to feed scraps to dogs, "a growing number are purchasing prepared products…." In Poland, according to Pregowski and Wlodarczyk, "The practice of feeding dogs table scraps is long gone—particularly in urban areas…."[39] Compared to markets in the West, household expenditures on pet care in the East are low but they are steadily rising. Indeed, there is demand for higher quality foods for dogs in several eastern member states, including Poland, Slovakia, the Czech Republic, Hungary, and Bulgaria. In these member states, there is polarization, with wealthy caretakers opting for the same premium foods available in the West but also increasing numbers of people with fewer resources still willing to spend money for economy dog foods. In the Czech Republic, one study found that while attitudes toward dogs are polarized, caretakers often consider them members of the family, talk to them, and love them. Urban dogs, in particular, are "taken on vacation,…allowed to use furniture and sleep on beds…."[40] Eastern Europe is slowly trending closer to convergence with Western views about companion animals.[41] In their study about the changing relationship between Polish citizens and dogs, Pregowski and Wlodarczyk argue that even in training "value is now placed on the dogs' enjoyment." While people once obtained dogs for their use value as hunters or defenders, they now seek to cultivate the human-canine bond and opt for gentle and social dogs who serve as companions for children and "buddies for outdoor pursuits."[42]

Yet such norms of responsible and loving care are not in place throughout all of the South and East. While southern attitudes and cultures are changing to the benefit of animals, there are still significant problems with abuse and sub-standard care. In southern Spain, especially Andulucia, it remains too common for hunting dogs, most frequently Galgos and Podencos, to be treated as objects, not sentient beings. Galgos are sight hounds somewhat similar in appearance to greyhounds, while Podencos resemble Pharoah hounds and are multi-sensory hunters. In rural Spain, these dogs often live in very poor conditions, sometimes near starvation, and they are kept in small, dark spaces or tied to short chains.[43] There is a prevailing myth that starving dogs will prove to be better hunters. Training methods are also inhumane, with dogs at times tied to vehicles and forced to run. Often, these dogs are either abandoned to fend for themselves or killed after one hunting season. The Madrid Federation of Animal Shelters estimates that 300,000 pets are abandoned in Spain each year.[44] Since it is cheaper to buy a new dog each season than it is to care for one throughout the year, hunters "dispose" of dogs and "replace" them with new ones the following year. The methods by which the dogs are killed are also brutal, as they are shot, drowned, hanged, or beaten to death.[45] Most notoriously, those dogs who have not performed up to expectations in the hunt and therefore "embarrassed" their keepers are subjected to the "pianist" or "typewriter death." With this torturous method of hanging, the noose is placed so that the dog's front paws cannot touch the ground and the back paws barely do so. To survive, the dog tries to stay on his back paws until he succumbs to fatigue and dies. Before that point, for many hours and even days, the dog's back paws "scrabble against the ground and make the clicking sound of a typewriter" and the front paws sway back and forth similar to the playing of a piano.[46] Nor is it uncommon to see dogs tied in the sun, without food or water, for hours or days waiting for owners to return to country homes.[47] To be sure, attitudes about these practices are changing, with one poll reporting that 98 percent of Spaniards believe that people who abuse animals should go to jail and a "plethora of animal charities springing up across the country, with over 50 in Andalucia alone."[48] As late as 2013, though, the killing of dogs via hanging was allegedly a "regular occurrence in rural hunting areas," with "few" willing to "break the code of silence and actually denounce it."[49]

Unfortunately, the abuse and abandonment of dogs is not limited to Spain, but occurs in France and other southern regions including parts of Cyprus, Greece, Italy, and Portugal. In Italy, for example, approximately 25 percent of pets are abandoned every year.[50] Likewise, in Cyprus, "dozens of stray dogs" are found every day, most abandoned. According to a rehoming association in Cyprus, people are reluctant to take the responsibilities of dog ownership seriously and simply dispense with dogs when no longer wanted.[51] In some of these areas, like in Spain, hunters treat dogs as tools, not beings, and subject them to cruel training and abandonment. In many countries across Europe, including Spain and Italy, vacationers abandon their domestic animals before embarking on month-long trips in the summer. In France, approximately 100,000 domestic animals are dumped at shelters for this reason each year.[52] On an optimistic note, there are many animal charities and growing support for animal welfare and protection in these southern countries.

In the eastern member states, there are significant and ongoing problems with stray dogs in all but Slovenia. This "unwanted" population is partly the result of poor adherence to duties of care. In particular, dogs are not sterilized and are allowed to roam unsupervised. Abandonment is also a major problem. In Romania, the loss of housing units exacerbated this problem when the former Communist regime, under Ceausescu, ordered the demolition of large numbers of houses in Bucharest and other cities and their replacement with apartments. At that time, many owners were forced to abandon their dogs.[53] According to a 2011 Report, there is still no promotion of sterilization to manage population levels.[54] There is poor enforcement of abandonment laws in many eastern member states as well.[55] In Romania, per Arsene, "owned dogs continue to be kept for years in chains, beaten, starved," deprived of veterinary care and "abandoned and sometimes brutally killed by their owners."[56] In parts of Poland and other places in the East, dogs are sometimes also considered to be communal property and therefore individual responsibility for them does not attach. To be sure, there are efforts afoot to increase adherence to codes of responsibility and there are segments of the population who take duties of care seriously. In Poland, for example, canine advocates host an annual event "aimed at educating society about the welfare of dogs" in rural areas of the country. It is still common in those areas to allow unsterilized dogs to run free and myths about the need for females to have a litter remain.[57] While public policies in the East and South are undoubtedly helping to spread more responsible practices, there is not yet compliance with those policies, especially in rural areas. On the ground, in other words, the European model is not universally in place even if legislation reflects its assumptions.

US: Growing Acceptance?

In the US, on the one hand, there are many indications of the acceptance of caretaking responsibilities. Caring for approximately 78 million companion dogs, Americans spend over 50 billion dollars annually on their companion animals. What is more, the US is the leader in offering innovative services for dogs, such as daycare for working caretakers, organic foods and treats, and alternative forms of medicine.[58] According to one survey, 94 percent of American pet owners regularly take their companion animals to a veterinarian. By 2007, according to Schaffer, there were almost 9,000 veterinary specialists who held board certifications compared to 1,981 in 1980.[59] Availing themselves of these services, Americans spent 1.32 billion dollars on knee surgeries for dogs in one year alone. This willingness to spend money to ensure the health and well-being of dogs is strong evidence of their high status. Indeed, per one survey, ninety percent consider their companion animals to be family members.[60] While survey results vary, anywhere from half to "93 percent of pet owners would risk their lives to save their animals."[61] In their study of American and Canadian perceptions of animal welfare and rights, Hunter and Brisbin found that over 70 percent of Americans believe that animals have a right to sufficient food, water and shelter for safety, comfort, and freedom from pain. In addition, over 60 percent of Americans believed that animals had a right to companionship and socialization as well as the right to exercise and freedom of movement sufficient to sustain mental and physical health.[62] A large majority therefore accept the legitimacy of the requirements typically legislated in codes of responsibility for canine caretakers. With their need to be walked, dogs also bring people out into the community, where they are likely to interact with and befriend others.[63] Dogs are not only family members, then, but also facilitators of social connection, an important role in an individualist culture. In short, in the eyes of many, dogs have a high social status.

Yet, on the other hand, each year in the US, approximately 3.9 million dogs enter shelters, where 1.2 million of them will be euthanized.[64] Of the dogs surrendered to shelters, according to one study, 46.4 percent had been with their caretakers for less than one year.[65] Based on this statistic, it is fair to say that there are substantial numbers of people who do not commit to the care of the animal and/or do not do the appropriate research about care requirements before adoption. While dogs are surrendered to shelters in all parts of the US, the chances of rehoming such dogs differ significantly by region. In the South and Plains, there is a problem with the management of canine population and more evidence of irresponsible care. As Caufield and Gazzola note, there are "low spay/neuter rates" in the South and "a large number of animals [are] allowed to roam…." As a result of that and the relinquishment of dogs, shelters are crowded with high euthanasia rates. In some cases, overcrowding is so bad that some dogs only last a few days before workers euthanize them to make room for the constant influx.[66] In other parts of the US, specifically the Northeast, Pacific Northwest, and Upper Midwest, there are high spay/neuter rates, few dogs roaming unsupervised, and minimal problems with large shelter populations. As Strand explains, "what the US has today is a dog distribution problem, not a dog overpopulation problem—a situation that has led to a practice labeled humane relocation."[67] While over 1,400 groups have worked to relocate rescue dogs to the Northeast and Upper Midwest, where they will be adopted, many are left behind to be euthanized in shelters.[68] At the urging of animal welfare organizations, both legislative and educational efforts are being made to change the ethic of pet care in areas of the rural South and Plains. Although the situation is improving, the fact remains that thousands of dogs are betrayed and fail to receive adequate care.

However, a norm of responsible care, especially in the provision of sustenance, shelter, and veterinary services despite the absence of legal obligations to provide the latter, coexists with this reality of an "unwanted" population. Problematically, though, there are strong indications that Americans fail to provide proper exercise to their companion animals. Whether as a result of a lack of exercise or overfeeding, approximately 53 percent of American dogs are overweight, with 17 percent obese. Two of the three most popular breeds, Labrador and golden retrievers both of which are sporting dogs in need of exercise, are even more likely to be overweight. This condition causes dogs to be susceptible to pain, injury and disease, with countless surgical procedures, for example, performed for weight-related conditions.[69] The sheer numbers of overweight dogs denotes a problem in the provision of adequate food and exercise.

Law and Practice in the EU and US

In sum, with a few exceptions, the EU member states have more protective laws in place than the US states to ensure that the keepers of companion animals provide adequate care. However, there is not full adherence to these policies in EU member states, particularly in the South and East. There have been increasing efforts, though, to educate citizens about caretaking responsibilities and to change practices. For example, in 2013, as the reader may recall, the EU Commission, under the Belgian Presidency, hosted a conference entitled, "The Welfare of Dogs and Cats in the EU: Building a Europe that Cares for Companion Animals." There are additionally greater numbers of animal welfare organizations working in problematic areas to educate the public and to assist the victimized dogs. While the US can boast of fewer protective laws in the area of caretaker responsibilities, there are nonetheless practices of individual responsibility in several areas of the country. Yet there are some rural pockets where irresponsible care is the norm and a generalized blindness to the exercise and dietary needs of dogs. Similarly to the EU, state legislative bodies and animal welfare organizations are actively trying to address these problems. For their efforts, they can already claim some legislative successes.

Social Acceptance of Canines

While caretakers bear the primary responsibility for fulfilling the needs of canine companions, public policies, cultural mores, and popular attitudes can either help or hinder the fulfillment of that obligation. It is more difficult to meet the exercise requirements of dogs, for example, if they are not allowed in public parks! Housing policies can also impact a family's ability to have a dog at all or retain one. The more that dogs are legally allowed and culturally accepted in public spaces, the easier it is for their caretakers to fulfill their individual responsibilities.

A Warming but Still Cool Reception in the US

There are undeniably pockets of dog-friendly places, mainly select cities, in the US. San Francisco, for example, caters to the caretakers of dogs with outdoor restaurants, dog-friendly accommodations, and lots of "dog" events, such as walks. Several other cities, especially on the west and east coasts, are similarly dog-friendly. However, even in these places, dogs are not legally allowed *inside* restaurants or any eating establishments. In the winter, such a policy translates into their banishment in the colder climates. What is more, they are often prohibited from public transportation or subject to stringent regulations, such as crating or travel at unusual hours. In short, businesses in upscale areas have courted "dog people" with more welcoming treatment, but public policies in the US are generally hostile to the presence of canines, at least indoors.

In housing, owners of property typically can make the determination to allow pets or not and many have blanket exclusions. In fact, per one survey, the primary reason for the surrender of dogs to a shelter in the US is relocation or moving.[70] Presumably, in some such cases, people were unable to find housing willing to accommodate their dogs. Applicable national laws in this area relate only to specific categories of people, such as the disabled, and allow people so categorized to retain animals despite the wishes of landlords if there is a relationship between the animal and the disability. Congress has also passed legislation that allows elderly and handicapped residents of federally-assisted housing to have common household pets subject to "reasonable requirements."[71] While state policies vary, none unequivocally forbids landlords from excluding pets. Condominiums, which are owned not rented, also can exclude or limit pets in purchase agreements. Some municipalities also place restrictions on households, for example, limiting the number of dogs or banning certain breeds. In short, with the exception for limited categories of people, public policy does not facilitate the "ownership" of dogs in the US.

However, the US nonetheless has the world's largest companion dog population in "both absolute and per capita terms."[72] In the aftermath of Hurricane Katrina in 2005, policymakers started to grasp the breadth and depth of the bond between companion animals and people. Tragically, countless persons failed to evacuate during that devastating storm because either shelters and/or public transportation refused to accept their companion animals. Recognizing the negative ramifications for people in such circumstances, the national government passed the Pets Evacuation and Transportation Standards (PETS) Act in 2006. Incorporating pets into federal disaster plans, the bill requires Red Cross shelters and hotels to ensure the safekeeping of pets. Additionally, it allows the Federal Emergency Management Agency (FEMA) to "reimburse state and local governments for transporting, housing, and caring for pets during disasters."[73] According to HSUS, 17 states now require state emergency response plans to include pets and that number is sure to increase.[74] In a sense, the governments had to change laws for disasters because there was cultural rejection of their original anti-animal versions. People, true to surveys, risked their lives to stay with and protect their companion animals. Facing that reality, lawmakers had to conform to the cultural sea change.

In recent years, state governments have also been responsive to people's concerns about breed-specific legislation. Beginning in the 1980s, more than 700 municipalities passed bans and other restrictions to keep "pit-bulls" out of their communities. Ironically, as we will later see, a "pit-bull" is not a specific breed, but refers to several terrier breeds and crosses of those breeds favored for use in illegal dogfighting rings. Such bans forced people to surrender dogs, who had no indication of aggressive tendencies, to shelters. According to animal welfare groups, only individual dogs can be accurately classified as dangerous or not. Blanket bans are not only unjust, but ineffective. Finally responding to these points, at least 12 states have passed legislation in the last few years to prevent local governments from enacting breed-specific legislation. In addition, more than 100 local governments have overturned such bans.[75] Only one state, namely Ohio, previously placed restrictions on pit bulls, requiring caretakers to obtain liability insurance, muzzle the dogs in public, and confine and leash them according to stringent regulations. That state too has now removed the "vicious" classification on the breed.[76]

In the absence of public pressure, governments have been less inclined to create dog-friendly spaces. Perhaps of greatest importance to canines are parks. To exercise and interact with members of their own species, dogs need open space in the form of parks, woodland trails, or beaches. For many breeds, off-leash exercise is essential to their well-being. In the US, local governments are primarily responsible for legislating leash laws and park rules but the national and state governments have jurisdiction in some areas. National law is applicable in national parks, recreation areas, forests, and other lands managed by that level of government. National forests, which tend to be in rural areas, ask that dogs be under control only, though they are to be leashed in developed areas and in areas with known wildlife. At national parks, however, dogs are to be leashed when allowed at all.[77] Because the National Park Service (NPS) manages recreation areas and parks in urban settings, such as San Francisco and Washington, D.C., there has been concern with this policy. In those areas, national land comprises a large percentage of park area available for recreational use. The leashing policy therefore deprives people of the opportunity to exercise their dogs and in the case of San Francisco, is a dramatic break from past practice.[78] In that City, after a very lengthy political and legal struggle, the NPS has dropped its efforts to impose stringent leashing restrictions for now at least. However, in most cases, in keeping with the American model, the NPS does not consider the needs of canines and puts the onus on individuals to find outlets to exercise their dogs.

Most state laws do not mandate leashing, but prohibit dogs running at large without supervision.[79] However, states manage parklands and it is commonly the policy to leash dogs at state parks, beaches (when they are allowed at all), and recreation areas. There are exceptions to this rule, with designated off-leash areas at select parks and much variation in enforcement. However, it is primarily at the local level that public areas have been established for off-leash play. Particularly in urban areas, such as New York City, there are off-leash hours at parks and dog runs. Indeed, the establishment of dog parks has spread across the country, with an estimated 1,200 such parks now in existence and the number is growing. According to a 2010 study by the Trust for Public Land, the growth rate for dog parks over the previous five years was 34 percent, with 569 in the 100 largest cities in the US.[80] This trend continues, with many municipalities now touting dog parks on their websites. In short, while some localities, particularly large urban areas, provide public space for the exercise and socialization of dogs, the national government, most state governments, and the majority of localities do not. With that said, there are multiple efforts underway to establish off-leash areas across the country and several websites available to provide information to people about places to walk dogs.

In sum, there are many canine advocates in the US. These advocates have made some inroads in establishing more dog-friendly public spaces, such as dog parks, hotels, and outdoor restaurants. To understate the matter greatly, public policymakers have not led the way in making these changes but have relented to demands for the establishment of off-leash parks in *some* areas. In others, they have not only refused to accommodate dog owners but have depicted them as a troublesome group.[81] There have been some inroads, with federal housing now more welcoming of dogs and the inclusion of pets in disaster planning. Yet overall, public *policies* remain decidedly cool to the acceptance of dogs, but private businesses have warmed up to the idea and the consequent opportunity to make money.

The Banality of Dogs in the European Public Sphere

Perhaps more than any other factor, the general acceptance of dogs in public spaces distinguishes the EU from the US and accounts for the conventional wisdom that the EU is more dog-friendly. Visiting Americans immediately notice this distinction. Dogs are, in fact, commonly accepted inside pubs; restaurants, including fancy ones; many hotels; public transportation; and public sites. Tourists can spot the occasional golden retriever touring a French castle. In Germany, there are few places *closed* to canines. They even have their own public swimming pools.[82] Likewise, in the Netherlands and the UK, dogs permeate public spaces and are simply part of the landscape. There is, of course, variation in the degree of dog-friendliness in the public sphere of EU member states, but the default is toward a canine presence.

There are, however, a couple of qualifications to this public acceptance. Several countries in the EU ban certain dog breeds, typically those used in fighting, such as ones associated with "pitbulls," but often others as well. Additionally, more public regulations are placed on "guarding" and "attack" breeds. For example, in Germany, certain breeds must be muzzled in public unless they have been individually evaluated for safety.[83] Likewise, in France, "guard" dogs must be leashed and muzzled in public, while "fighting" breeds are not to be imported. Compared to the US, there have been more national regulations and breed-specific bans. At least 16 EU member states ban or treat differently select breeds.[84] In the US, as the reader may recall, hundreds of localities enacted breed-specific regulations and bans though only one state, Ohio, did so and it has subsequently been retracted. The trend in the US is away from breed-specific legislation. To be sure, the EU bans vary in their requirements with some forbidding only the reproduction of certain breeds. What is more, Italy and the Netherlands have retracted breed-specific bans, actions perhaps signaling the beginning of a trend away from them. However, it is fair to say that the warm welcome of dogs in European society does not extend to all breeds.

There are also those in EU member states who decidedly do not welcome *any* dogs in the public sphere. In particular, Muslims, *some* of whom consider dogs unclean, have complained about the presence of dogs on public transportation, claiming a violation of religious rights. There have been controversies over this issue in several EU member states, including the UK, the Netherlands, and Spain. In the UK, there have been multiple examples of bus and taxi drivers refusing to transport service dogs for people with disabilities. Some people have also voiced discontent over their harassment when taking their dogs into public spaces.[85] Despite minority calls for more limitations on dogs in public places, the EU has largely remained open to them.

This canine tolerance extends to housing policy in select areas as well. In France, for example, landlords cannot prohibit companion animals, "even for a summer rent."[86] Nor can German landlords forbid the keeping of an animal in advance of a rental agreement, though they can later restrict or regulate ownership if the animal disturbs others.[87] In Greece as well, dogs must be allowed in apartments unless they are a "public nuisance."[88] Such protective policies facilitate relocation for the caretakers of companion animals. While these policies are by no means found in all EU member states, their presence in a few is emblematic of a greater acceptance of dogs in public life. The "no pets" clause, so standard in American rental agreements, is decidedly less so in the EU.

Not surprisingly, dogs generally find more freedom in parks in EU member states as well. Similarly to the US, local governments frequently dictate leashing policies. There are off-leash parks in large cities, such as Amsterdam, London, and Paris. According to Robertson, "dogs can choose from 72 gardens to walk in—from formal palace grounds to tiny urban squares" in Paris. They can run sans leash at the Jardin de Tuileries.[89] In Germany, the default is off-leash, with on-leash areas typically marked. Even on the crowded sidewalks of Berlin, dogs can be spotted off-leash.[90] There is an expectation, though, of controlled behavior. In other words, off-leash freedom goes hand-in-hand with the acceptance of caretakers' responsibilities.

According to Euro-camp, approximately 60 percent of campsites in Europe accept dogs and dogs are also allowed on several beaches, though there can be restrictions during high seasons. In many places, dogs are allowed off leash in rural areas provided that they are under control and do not disturb farm animals or wildlife. In the UK, as one example, dogs are welcome to run in the national parks of Scotland and all but four of the beaches. Even for those four exceptions, there are "dog-friendly" sections.[91] Great Britain's famed lake district is also open to dogs, with lots of hiking trails where they must be under control and not disturb farm animals. In a very telling complaint about Wales, a guidebook questions, "So if Rhossili is Britain's dog-friendliest beach, why are we [dogs] not welcome to use its amenities," such as the café and pub nearby?[92] It is somewhat inconceivable that such a complaint would be found in an American guide to dog-friendly places. Americans, in contrast, would be ecstatic over the leash-free access to the beach! Such access is a "given" in the UK and many other EU member states. The British find it annoying in those instances when they cannot take the dog into the pub after the walk.

In the past, Ireland was less dog-friendly and had leashing restrictions as an "American-style" default on its walking trails. But even there, dog-friendly changes are gaining ground. In December 2017, a law was passed that will allow dogs in cafes and pubs at the choice of business owners.[93] There is a dog-friendly association in Ireland that is aimed at opening more businesses to dogs. What is more, there are Facebook groups identifying hikes and parks where dogs can now play off leash.

To be sure, there are leashing restrictions at several national parks in the EU, such as those in Hungary and Slovenia, to protect ecosystems and to prevent wildlife encounters. Similarly, the UK's Environmental Protection Act empowers local authorities to ban dogs from certain areas and to require leashing in others.[94] In contrast to the US, such restrictions are not invoked indiscriminately or as a default setting, but rather with more discretion. If in an area with a fragile environment or farm animals, for example, keepers are expected to leash their dogs but can release them when out of that area. Luxembourg has leashing restrictions in cities and towns, including fitness trails and all public areas. In rural areas, though, dogs must remain under supervision and control only.[95] In some eastern countries, where dogs are too often allowed to roam unsupervised, there are calls for regulations. Ideally, such regulations will take the form of supervision and control, not just leashing.

Conclusion

In general, US states act consistently with expectations in codifying the responsibilities of the caretakers of animals. They are reluctant to specify affirmative obligations and instead criminalize only cases of neglect and abuse. However, there are exceptions with four US states now stating the duties of animal caretakers affirmatively. Six states are requiring the provision of routine veterinary care for an animal's health as well. In many parts of the US, there is a norm of responsible caretaking and ample evidence of some behaviors, such as spending on veterinary care and food, which intimate a high status for dogs. In the EU member states, there is overwhelming consistency with the European model in legislation of caretakers' responsibilities, but practices have yet to catch up to those standards in several member states especially in the rural areas of the South and East. However, the establishment of legislation in the East and South should help to improve the ethic of care over time. The EU itself, with its constitutional statement about the sentience of animals, has arguably helped to encourage this national legislation.

The greater social acceptance of canines in public spaces in the EU arguably facilitates the fulfillment of caretakers' responsibilities. Yet there are unfriendly outposts in the EU. In the US, there have been hundreds of off-leash areas established over the last decade and many businesses, mainly in upscale and resort areas, are recognizing the financial benefits of welcoming dogs. The strengthening relationship between companion animals and people in the US has spawned some protective legislation even at the national level and could mark the beginning of a trend in the US. Yet compared to Europe, the US more often delegates responsibility to individuals to care for their "own" dogs with default leash laws and bans on dogs in many public places. As a result, American caretakers would more often find the fulfillment of the exercise and social needs of canines more challenging than would European caretakers.

Notes

1. In the EU, there are estimated to be about 60 million owned dogs. See Eurogroup for Animals, "Pets," http://www.eurogroupforanimals.org/pets, accessed May 29, 2018. In the US, the total population is about 78 million. About 44 percent of American households have at least one dog. See American Society for the Prevention of Cruelty to Animals (ASPCA), "Pet Statistics," https://www.aspca.org/animal-homelessness/shelter-intake-and-surrender/pet-statistics, accessed May 29, 2018.

2. Erin Evans, "Constitutional Inclusion of Animal Rights in Germany and Switzerland: How Did Animal Protection Become an Issue of National Importance?" *Society and Animals* 18 (2010): 238–239.
3. John Dye, "Luxembourg Set to become Most Animal Friendly Country in the World," *Vice News*, May 13, 2016. https://news.vice.com/article/luxembourg-is-set-to-become-the-most-animal-friendly-country-in-the-world, accessed June 1, 2016.
4. Animal Protection Law, Latvia, 2010, available at European Enforcement Network of Animal Welfare Lawyers and Commissioners, "National Animal Welfare Legislation." http://www.lawyersforanimalprotection.eu/national-animal-welfare-legislation (accessed May 28, 2018); and Chapter 1, Article 1, Polish Animal Protection Act (1997/1998), available at Animal Legal and Historical Center, "Anti-Cruelty: Related Statutes" (Michigan State University College of Law). https://www.animallaw.info/statutes/topic/anti-cruelty, accessed May 29, 2018.
5. Hana Müllerová, "Animals Finally Above Objects and Stricter Criminalization of Cruelty: Some Insights in Czech Animal Legislation," *da Derecho Animal* (March 2012). http://wwwderechoanimal.info/images/pdf/mullerova-legal-protection-of-animals-in-the-Czech-republic.pdf, accessed November 19, 2014.
6. Docs4Dogs, European Network, "Comment on the Italian Animal Welfare Act." http://www.aerztefuertiere.de/index.php?option=com_content&view=article&id=121:italy&catid=136&itemid=586&showall=&limitstart=2&lang=en, accessed November 19, 2014; "National Legislation and Standards, France" Carodog Responsible Ownership. http://wwwcarodog.eu/?p=3&s=5, accessed September 17, 2014; and Lois Laimene Lelanchon, "Detailed Discussion of Anti-maltreatment Laws in France and Spain," Animal Legal and Historical Center (Michigan State University College of Law, 2013). http://www.animallaw.info.articles/ddfrancespaincruelty.htm, accessed June 16, 2014.
7. European Enforcement Network of Animal Welfare Lawyers and Commissioners, "Animal Protection in World Constitutions." http://lawyersforanimalprotection.eu/national-animal-welfare-legislation/#AWleg-Slovakia, accessed June 4, 2016.
8. "Preamble" and Article 3—"Basic Principles for Animal Welfare," European Convention for the Protection of Pet Animals, Council of Europe (effective date May 1, 1992). http://conventions.coe.int/treaty/en/treaties/html/125.htm, accessed September 17, 2014.
9. "Directive 2010/63/EU of the European Parliament and of the Council on the Protection of Animals Used for Scientific Purposes," 22 September 2010. http://eur-lex.europa.eu/legal-content/EN/TXT/?uri=CELEX:32010L0063, accessed December 22, 2014.
10. Bruce A. Wagman and Matthew Liebman, A *Worldview of Animal Law* (Durham, North Carolina: Carolina Academic Press, 2011), 144.
11. David Grimm, *Citizen Canine: Our Evolving Relationship with Cats and Dogs* (New York: Public Affairs, 2014), 150.
12. *Ibid.*, 144.
13. For quote, see *Ibid.*, 153. For number of states, see HSUS, "Humane State Rankings" (2017). https://blog.humanesociety.org/wp-content/uploads/2018/01/State-Rank-2017-MT-WY-1.pdf and https://blog.humanesociety.org/wp-content/uploads/2018/01/State-Rank-2017-AL-MO-2.pdf, accessed May 29, 2018.

14. Some argue that companion animals are moving toward a status of more than mere property. See Elizabeth Ann Overcash, "Unwarranted Discrepancies in the Advancement of Animal Law: The Growing Disparity in Protection between Companion Animals and Agricultural Animals," *North Carolina Law Review* 90 (March 2012): 854.
15. MCA 45–8-211—"Cruelty to Animals—Exceptions," Montana's Anti-Cruelty Law, available at Animal Legal and Historical Center, "Anti-Cruelty Related Statutes."
16. WV 61–8-19, "Cruelty to Animals; Penalties; Exclusions;" West Virginia Consolidated Anti-Cruelty Laws; and MD 10–604—"Abuse or Neglect of Animal, Code, Criminal Law," Maryland Consolidated Anti-Cruelty Laws. Both available at Animal Legal and Historical Center, "Anti-Cruelty: Related Statutes."
17. Susan J. Hankin, "What Is the Scope of the Duty to Provide Veterinary Care?" *Maryland Bar Journal* 43:2 (March 5, 2010): 18. http://digitalcommons.law.umaryland.edu/cgi/viewcontent.cgi?article=1919&context=fac_pubs, accessed September 16, 2014. For example one statute requires "necessary veterinary care," but does not define what that is.
18. For Alaska, see AS Section 03.55.100—"Minimum Standards of Care for Animals," Alaska Consolidated Anti-Cruelty Statutes; for Illinois, see ILCS 70/3—"Owner's Duties," Human Care for Animals Act; for Virginia, see VA Code Ann. 3.2–6503—"Care of Companion Animals by Owner," Virginia Comprehensive Animal Care Laws; and for Michigan, see MCL 750.50—"Duty to Provide Adequate Care Provision," Michigan Consolidated Anti-Cruelty Laws, all available at Animal Legal and Historical Center, "Anti-Cruelty: Related Statutes."
19. See Overcash, "Unwarranted Discrepancies," 858; and ILCS 70/3—"Owner's Duties."
20. For Virginia, see VA Code Ann. 3.2–6503—"Care of Companion Animals by Owner." For Minnesota, see 343.21—"Overworking or Mistreating Animals; Penalty," Pet and Companion Animal Welfare Act, available at Animal Legal and Historical Center, "Anti-Cruelty: Related Statutes." For information about tethering laws, see Rebecca F. Wisch, "Table of State Dog Tether Laws," Animal Legal and Historical Center (Michigan State University College of Law, 2009 with 2013 update). http://www.animallaw.info/articles/State Tables/&bustetherlaws.htm, accessed November 19, 2014; and Susan Hunter and Richard A. Brisbin, Jr., *Pet Politics: The Political and Legal Lives of Cats, Dogs, and Horses in Canada and the United States* (West Lafayette, Indiana: Purdue University Press, 2016), 188–191.
21. HSUS, "Humane State Rankings."
22. Article 4—"Keeping," European Convention for the Protection of Pet Animals.
23. Article 1.4—General Duty of Care, "Act of 19 May 2011 containing an integral framework for rules on kept animals and related subjects," The Netherlands, available at European Enforcement Network of Animal Welfare Lawyers and Commissioners, "National Animal Welfare Legislation"; and Part IV—Caring of Animals, "Animal Welfare Act," Chapter 439, ACT XXV, Malta, available at Animal Legal and Historical Center, "Anti-Cruelty: Related Statutes."
24. EU Dog and Cat Alliance, "The welfare of dogs and cats involved in commercial practices: a review of the legislation across EU countries," 19, https://s3-eu-west-1.amazonaws.com/assets.dogandcatwelfare.eu/live/media/filer_public/f3/c4/f3c44506-728a-4b38-a05e-bc4909214db6/all.pdf, accessed June 3, 2018; Part II—General Provisions, "Law for the

Protection, Health and Welfare of Animals," 1994, Cyprus, available at "Laws and Regulations," Animal Party Cyprus, http://animalpartycyprus.com/wp-content/uploads/2016/10/Animal-Welfare-Law.pdf, accessed May 28, 2018; Article 5—"Responsibilities of a Companion Animal's Owner," "Animal Welfare Act," Greece, available at European Enforcement Network of Animal Welfare Lawyers and Commissioners, "National Animal Welfare Legislation;" Animal Protection Law, Latvia.

25. Chapter 2—"Animal Keeping and Care," and Chapter 4—"Pet Animals." Animal Welfare Act, 2008, Bulgaria, available at European Enforcement Network of Animal Welfare Lawyers and Commissioners, "National Animal Welfare Legislation."
26. Section 14—"Prohibition on Abandonment of Animals," Animal Health and Welfare Act 2013, Ireland. http://www.irishstatutebook.ie/eli/2013/act/15/enacted/en/html, accessed June 3, 2018.
27. Article 1.3—Intrinsic Value, "Act of 19 May 2011," The Netherlands; and Section 9 -Duty of Person Responsible for Animal to ensure Welfare, Animal Welfare Act, 2006, UK, available at European Enforcement Network of Animal Welfare Lawyers and Commissioners, "National Animal Welfare Legislation."
28. EU Dog and Cat Alliance, "The welfare of dogs and cats involved in commercial practices," 102.
29. Chapter 2—"Keeping of Animals," Animal Welfare Act, 1996, with amendments up to 2006, Finland, available at European Enforcement Network of Animal Welfare Lawyers and Commissioners, "National Animal Welfare Legislation."
30. FEDIAF, European Pet Food Industry, "Facts and Figures" (Brussels, 2012). http://www.fediaf.org/facts-figures/, accessed June 24, 2015.
31. Theresa Bradley, "The Dog Index: What Man's Best Friend Tells Us about Global Economic Development," *Quartz*, November 13, 2012. http://qz.com/26579/the-dog-index-what-mans-best-friend-tells-us-about-global-economic-development/, accessed July 9, 2015.
32. The eight EU member states are Austria, Belgium, Denmark, Finland, Germany, Luxembourg, The Netherlands, and Sweden. For Austria, see "National Legislation and Standards," Carodog. For others, see *Ibid.*; and Louisa Tasker, on behalf of the World Society for the Protection of Animals (WSPA) and the Royal Society for the Prevention of Cruelty to Animals (RSPCA), "Report-Stray Animal Control Practices (Europe): An Investigation of Stray Dog and Cat Practices Across Europe," (March 2007). http://www.stray-afp.org/nl/wp-content/uploads/2012/09/WSPA-RSPCA-International-stray-control-practices-in-Europe-2006-2007.pdf, accessed May 29, 2018. While dogs are abandoned in Luxembourg, they are quickly adopted in this country of "great animal lovers." See Docs-4Dogs, European Network, "The Situation in Luxembourg." http://www.aerztefuertiere.de/index.php?option=com_content&view=category&id=80&Itemid=522&lang=en&limitstart=12, accessed November 21, 2014.
33. Tasker, on behalf of WSPA and RSPCA, "Report," 28.
34. *Ibid.*, 29.
35. "Top 10 Dog-Friendly Countries," *Puppyset*, August 29, 2013. http://www.puppyset.com/top-10-dog-friendly-countries/, accessed November 19, 2014.

36. Staff, AFP, "'Doggy Deli' too Decadent for some Germans' taste," *San Jose Mercury News*, January 2, 2014. http://www.mercurynews.com/ci_24836097/doggy-deli-too-decadent-some-germans-taste, July 15, 2015.
37. Maddy Savage, "Sweden gets First Food Truck for Posh Dogs," *The Local*, June 16, 2015. http://www.thelocal.se/20150616/stockholm-gets-gourmet-food-truck-for-dogs, July 13, 2015.
38. "Executive Summary—Petcare in France," *Euromonitor International*, July 2015. http://www.euromonitor.com/pet-care-in-france/report, accessed July 22, 2015; "Executive Summary—Petcare in Sweden," *Euromonitor International*, July 2015. http://www.euromonitor.com/pet-care-in-sweden/report, accessed July 22, 2015; "Executive Summary—Pet Care in Italy," *Euromonitor International*, July 2014. http://www.euromonitor.com/pet-care-in-italy/report, accessed July 22, 2015; "Executive Summary—Pet Care in Spain," *Euromonitor International*, July 2015. http://www.euromonitor.com/pet-care-in-spain/report, accessed July 22, 2015; "Executive Summary—Pet Care in Portugal," *Euromonitor International*, July 2014. http://www.euromonitor.com/pet-care-in-portugal/report, accessed July 22, 2015; and "Executive Summary—Pet Care in Greece," *Euromonitor International*, November 2014. http://www.euromonitor.com/pet-care-in-greece/report, accessed July 22, 2015.
39. Michal Piotr Pregowski and Justyna Wlodarczyk, "Researching the Human-Canine Relationship in Democratic Poland," in Michal Piotr Pregowski and Justyna Wlodarczyk, eds., *Free Market Dogs: The Human-Canine Bond in Post-Communist Poland* (West Lafayette, Indiana: Purdue University Press, 2016), 14.
40. Katherine Albro Houpt, et al., "Proceedings of a Workshop to Identify Dog Welfare Issues in the U.S, Czech Republic, Spain and the United Kingdom," *Applied Animal Behavior Science* 106 (2007): 227. There are similar relationships in urban areas of Poland. See Pregowski and Wlodarczyk, "Researching the Human-Canine Relationship," 5–6.
41. "Executive Summary—Pet Care in Eastern Europe," *Euromonitor International*, August 2013. http://www.euromonitor.com/pet-care-in-eastern-europe/report, accessed July 22, 2015. At this site, there are links to executive summaries for several country reports, including Slovakia, the Czech Republic, Hungary, Poland, Bulgaria and Romania. There are also links to executive summaries of country reports for northwestern Europe and the US.
42. On change in purpose, see Pregowski and Wlodarczyk, "Researching the Human-Canine Relationship," 18. On attitudes about training, see Justyna Wlodarczyk, "Canine Performance Sports in Poland: Another Look at the Dog Training Revolution," in Michal Piotr Pregowski and Justyna Wlodarczyk, eds., *Free Market Dogs*, 62.
43. Tania Coates and Sam Morris, *Camper Vans, Ex-pats & Spanish Hounds: The Strays of Spain from Road Trip to Rescue* (Hubble and Hattie, 2013), 37.
44. Anonymous, "Animal Lovers fight 'cruel' put-down rule for strays," *The Local*, July 4, 2014. http://www.thelocal.es/20140704/animal-lovers-challenge-spains-10-day-put-down-policy-for-strays, accessed July 15, 2015.
45. For quote, Coates and Morris, *Camper Vans, Ex-pats & Spanish Hounds*, 39. For methods of killing, see *Ibid.*, 37.
46. Giles Tremlett, "The Dogs left to Die after they 'humiliated' their masters," *The Guardian*, December 31, 2005. http://www.theguardian.com/world/2006/jan/01/spain.animalwelfare, accessed November 20, 2014.

47. For more on this, see Coates and Morris, *Camper Vans*; Beryl Brennan, "The Starving Dogs that Give Spain A Bad Name," *The Telegraph*, March 22, 2011. http://www.telegraph.co.uk/expat/expatlife/8382998/the-starving-dogs-that-give-Spain-a-bad-name.html, accessed September 17, 2014; European Society for Dogs and Animal Welfare (ESDAW), "Hunting Dogs—Spain." http://www.esdaw.eu/hunting-dogs---spain.html, accessed November 19, 2014; and Jackie Todd, *Dog Days in Andalucia: Tails from Spain* (Edinburgh: Mainstream Publishing Company, 2010).
48. Wendy Williams, "Could Spain Be a New Nation of Animal Lovers?" *The Olive Press* February 3, 2011. http://www.theolivepress.es/spain-news/2011/03/02/could-spain-be-a-new-nation-of-animal-lovers/, accessed June 3, 2014.
49. "Hunter Convicted for hanging Greyhounds," *Spanish News Today*, October 31, 2013. http://spanishnewstoday.com/hunter-convicted-for-hanging-greyhounds_18980-a.html#.VG36PsmDHY8, accessed November 20, 2014.
50. Eva Voslářová and Annamaria Passantino, "Stray Dog and Cat Laws and Enforcement in Czech Republic and Italy," *Ann 1st Super Sanitá* 48:1 (2012): 101.
51. Cyprus Dogs Rehoming Association, "Cyprus Dog Law." http://www.cyprusdogsrehomingassociation.com/knowledge-base/cyprus-dog-law/, accessed November 19, 2014. Website no longer available. See https://www.facebook.com/CYDRA-Cyprus-Dogs-Rehoming-Association-719757261392282/?hc_ref=ARQZkjjT1-R8PhCq70c_ciZ1AqHERaM9-V5xlGzEoNT2hZUEvB0DFGP4iUYD6K21OgI for the home of this Association.
52. Eleanor Beardsley, "In France, The (Abandoned) Dog Days of Summer," *National Public Radio*, July 11, 2012. http://www.npr.org/2012/07/11/156609037/in-france-the-abandoned-dog-days-of-summer, accessed June 22, 2015.
53. Petru Clej, "Bucharest Dog Cull Plan divides Romanians," *BBC News Europe*, October 13, 2013. http://www.bbc.com/news/world-europe-24480505, accessed July 5, 2014.
54. Carmen Arsene, *Stray Dog Situation in Romania* (National Federation for Animal Protection, August 2011). http://www.fnpa.ro/imagini/2011/09/Stray-dog-situation-in-Romania.-Animal-cruelty.pdf, accessed June 3, 2015. The original report was updated in July 2014 and the situation continues to be very poor for dogs in shelters. For the update, see https://serbiananimalsvoice.files.wordpress.com/2014/07/stray-dog-situation-in-romania-c-arsene-july-2014-english-version-1.pdf, accessed June 3, 2015.
55. Tasker, on behalf of WSPA and RSPCA, "Report," 8.
56. Arsene, "Stray Dog Situation."
57. On event, see Michal Piotr Pregowski and Justyna Wlodarczyk, "Four Paws of the Third Republic of Poland: A Timeline," in Michal Piotr Pregowski and Justyna Wlodarczyk, eds., *Free Market Dogs*, xxii. On rural practices, see Pregowski and Wlodarczyk, "Researching the Human-Canine Relationship," 26.
58. P. Elizabeth Anderson, *The Powerful Bond Between People and Pets: Our Boundless Connections to Companion Animals* (Westport, Connecticut: Praeger, 2008), 82. For 2012 spending on pet industry, see American Pet Products Association, "Pet Industry Market Size and Ownership Statistics." http://www.americanpetproducts.org/press_industrytrends.asp, accessed November 19, 2014.
59. Michael Schaffer, *One Nation Under Dog: Adventures in the New World of Prozac-Popping Puppies, Dog-Park Politics, and Organic Pet Food* (New York: Henry Holt, 2009), 89.

60. See Grimm, *Citizen Canine*, 12. The percentage of people who consider dogs to be family members varies in survey results from as low as 54 percent to as high as 99 percent. See Clinton R. Sanders, *Understanding Dogs: Living and Working with Canine Companions* (Philadelphia: Temple University Press, 1999), 22; and American Veterinary Medical Association, *U.S. Pet Ownership and Demographic Sourcebook*, 2007 ed. (Schaumburg, Illinois: American Veterinary Medical Association, 2007), 105.
61. See Grimm, *Citizen Canine*, 12 for the lower number and Schaffer, *One Nation Under Dog*, 86, for the latter one.
62. Hunter and Brisbin, Jr., *Pet Politics*, 94.
63. For more on the benefits to humans from these relationships, including social interaction, see Lynette A. Hart, "Dogs as Human Companions: A Review of the Relationship," in James Serpell, ed., *The Domestic Dog: Its Evolution, Behavior and Interactions with People* (New York: Cambridge University Press, 1995), 161–178; and Alan Beck and Aaron Katcher, *Between People and Pets: The Importance of Animal Companionship*, Rev. Ed. (West Lafayette, Indiana: Purdue University Press, 1996). For the tendency to form human attachments from dog-walking, see Julie Walsh, *Unleashed Fury: The Political Struggle for Dog-friendly Parks* (West Lafayette, Indiana: Purdue University Press, 2011), 9–10.
64. ASPCA, "Pet Statistics."
65. M. D. Salman, John G. New, Jr., Janet M. Scarlett, Philip H. Kris, Rebecca Ruch-Gallie and Suzanne Hetts, "Human and Animal Factors Related to the Relinquishment of Dogs and Cats in 12 Selected Animal Shelters in the United States," *Journal of Applied Animal Welfare Science* J:3 (1998): 213–214. Also see National Council on Pet Population Study and Policy, "Exploring the Surplus Cat and Dog Problem: Highlights of Five Research Publications Regarding Relinquishment of Pets," 2001. http://www.petpopulation.org/exploring.pdf, accessed November 20, 2014.
66. For quotation, see Megan Caulfield and Krista Gazzola, "All Roads Lead to Home," *Animal Sheltering: The Magazine for Animal Care Professionals and Volunteers* (July/August 2010): 30–35. http://www.animalsheltering.org/resources/magazine/Jul_Aug_2010/all_roads_lead_to_home.pdf, accessed September 16, 2014. For more on southern population crisis, see Anne Kadet, "Rescue Dogs from the South," *Wall Street Journal*, July 26, 2013; Johanna Luv, "Transporting Dogs from Overpopulated States: Shelters Fill Empty Kennels with Southern Pups," *The Bark* (October 4, 2011). http://thebark.com/content/transporting-dogs-overpopulated-states, accessed September 16, 2014; and Jenifer Champ Wallis, "Why Some Southern Dogs are heading North: The Practical Effects of Animal Population Control Legislation," *American Bar Association Animal Law Committee Newsletter* (Fall 2008). http://www.wallis.law.com/pdfs/ABA_Animal_Law_Article.pdf, accessed September 16, 2014.
67. Patti Strand, "The Global Dog Population Crisis," *National Animal Interest Alliance*, November 17, 2011. http://www.naiaonline.org/articles/article/the-global-stray-dog-population-crisis-and-humane-relocation, accessed November 20, 2014.
68. J. Courtney Sullivan, "Adopt a Dog with a Southern Drawl," *New York Times*, May 25, 2014. http://www.nytimes.com/2014/05/26/opinion/adopt-a-dog-with-a-southern-drawl.html?_r=0, accessed September 16, 2014.

69. Association for Pet Obesity Prevention, "Pet Obesity Rates Rise, Cats Heavier than Ever," 2012 National Pet Obesity Survey Results, March 12, 2013. http://www.petobesityprevention.org/2012-national-pet-obesity-survey-results/, accessed November 19, 2014.
70. Elizabeth A. Clancy and Andrew N. Rowan, "Companion Animal Demographics in the United States: A Historical Perspective," in Deborah J. Salem and Andrew N. Rowan, *The State of the Animals II* (Washington, DC: Humane Society Press, 2003), 22.
71. Rebecca J. Huss, "No Pets Allowed: Housing Issues and Companion Animals," *Animal Law* 11 (2005): 93.
72. Bradley, "The Dog Index."
73. Grimm, *Citizen Canine*, 100.
74. HSUS, "Humane State Rankings 2017."
75. For number of states, see *Ibid*. Also see Aamer Madhani, "U.S. Communities Increasingly Ditching Pit Bull Bans," *USA Today*, November 18, 2014. http://www.usatoday.com/story/news/nation/2014/11/17/pit-bulls-breed-specific-legislation-bans/19048719/, accessed July 8, 2015.
76. Donna J. Miller, "Pit-Bulls No Longer Deemed Vicious by Ohio Law that Takes Effect Tuesday," *Cleveland Plain Dealer*, May 21, 2012. http://www.cleveland.com/metro/index.ssf/2012/05/pit_bulls_no_longer_deemed_vic.html, accessed July 8, 2015.
77. "Pets in U.S. National Parks, Forests, Recreation Areas, Seashores, Lakeshores, Monuments, Historical Parks and Historic Sites—Pet Policies," Pet-Friendly Travel.com. http://www.petfriendlytravel.com/national_parks, accessed October 28, 2014. Also see U.S. Forest Service, "Should I bring my Dog hiking and/or camping?" http://www.fs.usda.gov/Internet/FSE_DOCUMENTS/stelprdb5351574.pdf, accessed June 2, 2016.
78. For more on the San Francisco case, see Walsh, *Unleashed Fury*, Chapters V–VI.
79. For more on state leash laws, see Rebecca F. Wisch, "Table of State Dog Leash Laws," Animal Legal and Historical Center (Michigan State University College of Law, 2012). http://www.animallaw.info/topics/table-state-dog-leash-laws, accessed October 28, 2014.
80. See "Dog Parks in the United States Continue to Be Built," DogPark.com. http://www.dogpark.com/dog-parks-continue-to-be-built/, accessed October 28, 2014.
81. Dog walkers have voiced complaints in several parts of the country. For an example of one case study, see Walsh, *Unleashed Fury*, Chapter IV.
82. On the acceptance of canines, see "Top 10 Dog-Friendly Countries;" Peter Zudeick, "Germans and their Love of Dogs," *Deutsche Welle*, November 29, 2012, http://www.dw.de/germans-and-their-love-for-dogs/a-16410393, accessed November 20, 2014; Staff, "Doggy Deli;" Joanna Robertson, "The Pampered Pooches of Paris," *BBC News*, December 25, 2011. http://www.bbc.com/news/magazine-16268890, accessed June 11, 2015; and Susan Sterling, "Who Let the Dogs Out? Europeans!" *New York Times*, November 26, 2000.
83. Martin Lodge, "Barking Mad? Risk Regulation and the Control of Dangerous Dogs in Germany," *German Politics* 10: 30 (December 2001): 65–82; and Claudia E. Haupt, "Who Let the Dangerous Dogs Out? The German States' Hasty Legislative Action, the Federal Law on Dangerous Dogs and the 'Kampfhunde' Decision of the Federal Constitutional Court," *Journal of Animal Law* 2 (2006): 27–48.

84. The countries are Croatia, Cyprus, Denmark, France, Germany, Hungary, Ireland, Lithuania, Luxembourg, Malta, Poland, Portugal, Slovakia, Spain, Sweden and the United Kingdom. Belgium and Austria allow sub-national restrictions. See European Enforcement Network of Animal Welfare Lawyers and Commissioners, National Animal Welfare Legislation. http://www.lawyersforanimalprotection.eu/national-animal-welfare-legislation, accessed November 19, 2014; and "National Legislation and Standards," Carodog.
85. See Soeren Kern, "'Muslims Declare Jihad on Dogs in Europe," Gatestone Institute International Policy Council, January 31, 2012. http://www.gatestoneinstitute.org/2796/muslims-ban-dogs-europe, accessed 20 November 2014; and Andy Dolan, "Muslim Bus Drivers Refuse to let Guide Dogs on Board," *The Daily Mail*, 18 July 2010. http://www.dailymail.co.uk/news/article-1295749/Muslim-bus-drivers-refuse-let-guide-dogs-board.html, accessed November 20, 2014.
86. "National Legislation and Standards, France," Carodog.
87. "National Legislation and Standards, Germany," Carodog.
88. Article 8—"Keeping companion animals at home," Animal Welfare Act, Greece, available at European Enforcement Network of Animal Welfare Lawyers and Commissioners, "National Animal Welfare Legislation."
89. Robertson, "The Pampered Pooches of Paris."
90. Sterling, "Who Let the Dogs Out?"
91. Jane Common, *Phileas Dogg's Guide to Dog-Friendly Holidays in Britain* (London: Constable & Robinson, LTD, 2014), 20.
92. *Ibid.*, 133.
93. Conor McMahon, "'A victory for common sense': New Rules clear the way for dogs in cafes and pubs," *The Journal.ie*, December 2, 2017. http://www.thejournal.ie/dog-friendly-rules-ireland-3-3739907-Dec2017/, accessed June 3, 2018.
94. Tasker, on behalf of WSPA and RSPCA, "Report," 32.
95. Doc4Dogs, "The Situation in Luxembourg."

Bibliography

Anderson, P. Elizabeth. *The Powerful Bond Between People and Pets: Our Boundless Connections to Companion Animals*. Westport, Connecticut: Praeger, 2008.

Beck, Alan and Aaron Katcher. *Between People and Pets: The Importance of Animal Companionship*. Rev. ed. West Lafayette, Indiana: Purdue University Press, 1996.

Coates, Tania and Sam Morris. *Camper Vans, Ex-pats & Spanish Hounds: The Strays of Spain from Road Trip to Rescue*. Hubble and Hattie, 2013.

EU Dog and Cat Alliance. "The welfare of dogs and cats involved in commercial practices: a review of the legislation across EU countries." https://s3-eu-west-1.amazonaws.com/assets.dogandcatwelfare.eu/live/media/filer_public/f3/c4/f3c44506-728a-4b38-a05e-bc4909214db6/all.pdf, accessed June 3, 2018.

Evans, Erin. "Constitutional Inclusion of Animal Rights in Germany and Switzerland: How Did Animal Protection Become an Issue of National Importance?" *Society and Animals* 18 (2010): 238–239.

Grimm, David. *Citizen Canine: Our Evolving Relationship with Cats and Dogs*. New York: Public Affairs, 2014.

Hankin, Susan J. "What Is the Scope of the Duty to Provide Veterinary Care?" *Maryland Bar Journal* 43:2 (March 5, 2010): 18.

Haupt, Claudia E. "Who Let the Dangerous Dogs Out? The German States' Hasty Legislative Action, the Federal Law on Dangerous Dogs and the 'Kampfhunde' Decision of the Federal Constitutional Court." *Journal of Animal Law* 2 (2006): 27–48.

Houpt, Katherine Albro, et al. "Proceedings of a Workshop to Identify Dog Welfare Issues in the U.S., Czech Republic, Spain and the United Kingdom." *Applied Animal Behavior Science* 106 (2007): 221–233.

Hunter, Susan and Richard A. Brisbin, Jr. *Pet Politics: The Political and Legal Lives of Cats, Dogs, and Horses in Canada and the United States*. West Lafayette, Indiana: Purdue University Press, 2016.

Huss, Rebecca J. "No Pets Allowed: Housing Issues and Companion Animals." *Animal Law* 11 (2005): 69–128.

Lodge, Martin. "Barking Mad? Risk Regulation and the Control of Dangerous Dogs in Germany." *German Politics* 10:30 (December 2001): 65–82.

Müllerová, Hana. "Animals Finally Above Objects and Stricter Criminalization of Cruelty: Some Insights in Czech Animal Legislation." *da Derecho Animal* (March 2012).

Overcash, Elizabeth Ann. "Unwarranted Discrepancies in the Advancement of Animal Law: The Growing Disparity in Protection between Companion Animals and Agricultural Animals." *North Carolina Law Review* 90 (March 2012): 837–883.

Pregowski, Michal Piotr and Justyna Wlodarczyk, eds. *Free Market Dogs: The Human-Canine Bond in Post-Communist Poland*. West Lafayette, Indiana: Purdue University Press, 2016.

Salem, Deborah J. and Andrew N. Rowan, eds. *The State of the Animals II*. Washington, DC: Humane Society Press, 2003.

Salmon, M. D., et al. "Human and Animal Factors Related to the Relinquishment of Dogs and Cats in 12 Selected Animal Shelters in the United States." *Journal of Applied Animal Welfare Science* J:3 (1998): 207–226.

Sanders, Clinton R. *Understanding Dogs: Living and Working with Canine Companions*. Philadelphia: Temple University Press, 1999.

Schaffer, Michael. *One Nation Under Dog: Adventures in the New World of Prozac-Popping Puppies, Dog-Park Politics, and Organic Pet Food*. New York: Henry Holt, 2009.

Serpell, James, ed. *The Domestic Dog: Its Evolution, Behavior and Interactions with People*. New York: Cambridge University Press, 1995.

Tasker, Louisa, on behalf of the World Society for the Protection of Animals (WSPA) and the Royal Society for the Prevention of Cruelty to Animals (RSPCA). "Report-Stray Animal Control Practices (Europe): An Investigation of Stray Dog and Cat Practices Across Europe." (March 2007). http://www.stray-afp.org/nl/wp-content/uploads/2012/09/WSPA-RSPCA-International-stray-control-practices-in-Europe-2006-2007.pdf, accessed May 29, 2018.

Todd, Jackie. *Dog Days in Andalucia: Tails from Spain*. Edinburgh: Mainstream Publishing Company, 2010.

Voslářová, Eva and Annamaria Passantino. "Stray Dog and Cat Laws and Enforcement in Czech Republic and Italy." *Ann 1st Super Sanitá* 48:1 (2012): 97–104.

Wagman, Bruce A. and Matthew Liebman. *A Worldview of Animal Law*. Durham, North Carolina: Carolina Academic Press, 2011.

Walsh, Julie. *Unleashed Fury: The Political Struggle for Dog-friendly Parks*. West Lafayette, Indiana: Purdue University Press, 2011.

Wisch, Rebecca F. "Table of State Dog Leash Laws." Animal Legal and Historical Center, Michigan State University College of Law, 2012. http://www.animallaw.info/topics/table-state-dog-leash-laws, accessed October 28, 2014.

· 3 ·

IN OR OUT OF THE FAMILY?

High Stakes for Canine Status

For the millions of people who consider their dogs full-fledged family members, there is often a palpable unease about how they attained that status. Consider the distaste associated with the word "owner" for those who deem their dog a member of the family. Yet in most cases, the dogs were purchased from a breeder or supplier of some kind or alternatively, were adopted from a shelter or rescue group with some fee charged. In other words, many joined the family as a result of an economic transaction. It is, in fact, very easy to acquire a puppy or dog in most places in the US and EU. Few sellers are likely to discourage buyers! Ideally, responsible breeders and rescue groups would educate buyers about the needs of the dog in question and discourage those buyers who would not be a good match. Reality, of course, veers from this ideal more often than not. Perhaps predictably then, the relinquishment of young dogs, typically one to three years old, is a major problem. Significant rates of relinquishment can result in overcrowded shelters, a population of stray or free-roaming dogs, and the euthanasia of healthy dogs. All of these outcomes are negative ones for canines. Once out of a human family, a dog's life is significantly devalued in many places.

What public policies can not only help to keep canines in human families but also to protect them before and possibly after family life? Of course, regulations to ensure the welfare of dogs and puppies throughout the breeding and sale process are essential. Public campaigns to educate people about the responsibilities of caring for a canine might potentially reduce casual acquisitions as well. Mandatory and permanent identification, such as microchips, can at least induce people to bring their dogs to a shelter, instead of simply abandoning them to the streets, and to face the reality of the dogs' plight. For those dogs taken to shelters, either by previous caretakers or dogcatchers, the best outcome is rehoming. The likelihood of placement is much greater when there is a non-existent or very small stray population. If, alternatively, there is a large stray population, it is much less likely that abandoned dogs will be adopted. Protective policies would certainly prevent the euthanasia of healthy dogs when there is some possibility of rehoming. Even without that chance, there are other options instead of mass euthanasia, such as spay-neuter-release programs.

With its laissez-faire reputation and reluctance to regulate business, it is expected that the US will have lax regulations on breeders. In contrast, the EU and its member states are anticipated to regulate commercial breeding strictly. In reality, both the US and EU have problems with their respective regulatory systems in this area. By and large, though, these expectations will be confirmed, but with a substantial minority in both the US and EU bucking the trend. The EU and its member states are presumed to be more likely to mandate the permanent identification and registration of dogs, while the US and its states are unlikely to require such permanent markers. In this area as well, the data will mostly confirm expectations, yet with exceptions in policy in the EU and practice in the US. Finally, with its individualist strain, the US and its states are assumed to leave the prerogative of euthanizing healthy dogs to owners and shelters, while the EU and its states, with their commitment to the value of animals' lives, are thought to be likely to prohibit this practice. Although policies of the US and its states confirm these expectations, in practice, there are a growing number of no-kill shelters. In the EU, the data do not validate this expectation since a majority of member states do not prohibit the euthanasia of healthy dogs. There is a substantial minority that do, however, and increasingly, EU member states are relying upon catch-sterilize-release programs, rather than mass euthanasia, to prevent an even larger number of free-roaming dogs.

Because the presence of a free-roaming population is not caused solely by the abandonment of animals, the mandatory identification of dogs is only one factor in the effort to minimize the number of dogs without homes. When high rates of abandonment are coupled with low spay/neuter rates, there is likely to be an even greater number of "unwanted" dogs. Compared to the US, there are lower rates of canine sterilization throughout the EU. In some EU member states, there are nonetheless no problems with free-roaming dogs or large shelter populations given highly responsible ethics of care. In other EU member states, the combination of norms of abandonment and low sterilization rates has yielded large populations of roaming dogs. Mainly as a result of abandonment and relinquishment, the US has large shelter populations in parts of the country and localized free-roaming populations. When such populations exist, canine welfare suffers even if euthanasia is not routinely invoked to reduce the numbers. As a result, it is critical to have some information about free-roaming and shelter populations and practices to manage those populations in the US and EU, even though the numbers are by nature estimates only. Such an overview will help to complement the detailed data about regulations for commercial breeding, mandatory identification, and euthanasia and thereby provide a more comprehensive portrait of the treatment of those dogs without human families.

Before Joining the Family: Regulations on Commercial Breeders

Millions of people looking to bring a dog into their home turn to breeders, pet stores, and shelters. Focused on their new pup or dog, most are unlikely to research the conditions under which the puppy was born and weaned, let alone inquire into the conditions for the parents. Given the high demand for puppies especially, people are willing to pay handsomely for their puppy or make a substantial contribution to a shelter. Such a high demand provides strong incentive for breeders to supply puppies to the market. It is the fulfillment of a simple law of supply and demand. Like all industries, absent regulation, there will be some unscrupulous dealers who seek to maximize profit despite a negative impact on the health of puppies and the breeding dogs. When commercial breeding establishments elevate profits over the well-being of dogs, they are dubbed "puppy mills" in the US and "puppy farms" in the EU. Such establishments can operate on a large or small scale. The prioritization of profits, more than the size of the breeder, is what defines the term.[1] Conditions at puppy mills can reach levels of utter depravity, with the dogs and puppies subjected to pain, injury, and disease as well as severe discomfort, fear, and distress. Their presence, in other words, infringes upon several of the canine freedoms. Some of the possible conditions at puppy mills include unsanitary and cramped housing for dogs in some cases with stacked cages and wire flooring in crates; overbreeding of females with inadequate or non-existent medical attention; and inadequate medical care for puppies who are exposed to disease and sold to dealers at too young of an age. The breeding dogs are denied wholesome exercise, companionship, and anything approaching a normal life. There are multiple examples of these problems and other ones of cruelty and neglect at some commercial breeders.[2]

In its report on the puppy trade in Europe, Four Paws International recounts several stories of caretakers who purchased pups who soon died of diseases contracted at the puppy farms or in transport. In Italy, 52 percent of the imported puppies were sick with several serious diseases and infections, such as parvovirus, distemper, and endoparasites.[3] When a Slovakian truck crashed in Germany, officials found more than 100 "puppies…stacked in boxes in a closed-truck bed reeking of urine and feces…."[4] Life is no better for the breeding dogs at these places. The Humane Society of the United States (HSUS) publishes an annual list of the Worst 101 "puppy mills" in the US. In one case, a breeder had left 131 dogs out in the cold without adequate protection. The same breeder housed two females together in an enclosure where three dead puppies were found in "various stages of dismemberment." Another breeder housed 53 adults and 147 puppies in 64 cages in a 24 × 60 trailer![5] Inspectors have observed dogs in dire need of veterinary care, with open sores, eye disorders and swellings, as well as dogs living in filthy conditions, with insects and feces in food, "water bowls with 'green slime' in them, a strong ammonia (urine) odor, and 'at least a four-week buildup of feces in some of the outdoor runs.'"[6] The depravities are endless. The dogs are reduced from sentient beings to commodities, completely objectified. In some cases, the scale is so large that breeders do not care if some of the pups die or the lives of breeding dogs are cut short. Their lives are cheap.

Regulations for Commercial Breeders: Strong or Lax?

To assess whether strong regulations are in place for commercial breeders, six factors are considered. First, are commercial breeders required to obtain a license and be subjected to inspections? Ideally, such breeders would have to apply for a license and document the adequacy of their facilities and staff for animal care. Governmental inspectors would visit these facilities on a routine or regular basis to ensure compliance with animal welfare standards. The US government, and American and EU states were classified as having "licensing with mandatory inspections" if at least one inspection was mandatory. If governmental inspectors could demand entry but were not guaranteed to do so, then such states were labeled as having "licensing with possible inspections." If licensing procedures were in place, but with no inspections, the states were noted as having "licensing only." Protections in those states would be lax and in states with no licensing requirements at all, non-existent.

Even if states have licensing and mandatory or possible inspections, there can be significant loopholes if such regulations attach only to large-scale breeders. As the reader will recall, small operations can be abusive as well. Categories were established for states that apply licensing standards to all commercial breeders, those with either 2–5 breeding dogs and/or litters per year, those with 6–10, 11–15, or over 16. Some states apply standards based on the number of litters and others based on the number of intact females and/or male dogs used for reproduction. If a state made a determination based on the number of dogs sold in a year, it was assumed that ten puppies were in a litter for classification purposes. States applying regulations to those with ten or fewer breeding dogs and/or litters are deemed to have strong regulations. Anything over that is classified as lax.

It is optimal for states to stipulate explicit conditions of care for commercial breeders. These typically include regulations about the structure of buildings, sanitation, ventilation, temperature, lighting, adequacy and safety of enclosures, mandatory segregation of ill dogs/puppies, contracted services with a veterinarian, and enrichment and socialization requirements. When states have such regulations in place, they are deemed to have strong regulations and are labeled as having "breeder standards." Other states have strong and affirmative obligations for all keepers of animals. These too can be considered as providing strong obligations, as they apply to all breeders. However, it is more desirable to have codes for breeders since they explicitly cover areas, such as enrichment, socialization, and facilities, that codes for all keepers address only generally, if at all. Those states that have no explicit standards of care other than animal cruelty prohibitions are classified as lax in their regulations.

It is additionally helpful to require that those working in the commercial breeding industry have sufficient knowledge and expertise, and optimally, undergo training. Those states that require proof of such training and/or credentials are labeled as having strong regulations, while those states omitting any mandate for credentials and/or training are considered lax. A fifth factor concerns limitations on the breeding of female dogs. Legislation protective of animals would limit the number of times that a female could be bred in a given period and throughout her life. It would also stipulate a minimum and maximum age for the female to be bred. The more explicit the requirements are in this area, the better for the dogs. Those states with specific limitations are classified as having strong regulations and those without them are considered to be lax. Finally, states that prohibit the breeding of defects, such as inherited diseases or painful conditions, are deemed to have strong regulations and those that have no such prohibitions are labeled as lax. In many dog breeds, as publicly highlighted in the BBC documentary *Pedigree Dogs Exposed*, people have purposefully bred conditions for the sake of appearance that are painful and potentially deadly for dogs. Examples include heads too small for brain size, noses that result in breathing problems, and musculoskeletal disorders. The reduced gene pool in many breeds can also increase risks for genetic diseases, such as forms of cancer. Obviously, some states will have strong regulations in some of these areas and lax ones in others. Collectively, however, these criteria should provide enough data to conclude as to the overall strength of regulations on commercial breeders.

Missing: Effective Regulations at a Central Level

In order to prevent systematic abuse and cruelty, central governments must regulate effectively. Otherwise, if only one state has weak regulations, mills can flock there and sell puppies all over. To date, neither the US nor the EU has such strict and effective regulations. Because puppies are sold across state lines, there is an opportunity for national regulations to apply to these mills in the US. Indeed, the national government could play a critical role in eradicating offending kennels if it had the political will to do so. Instead, it regulates the commercial breeding of dogs, but with lax enforcement. In the early 2000s, US Representative Whitfield introduced legislation that would have placed limitations on the frequency and age at which dogs could be bred. Additionally, the bill would have empowered the US Department of Agriculture (USDA) to revoke the licenses of breeders with three regulatory violations over an eight-year period. The American Kennel Club, animal researchers, and commercial breeders lobbied successfully against the bill.

As a result, the operative law for the regulation of commercial breeding remains the AWA. This law requires both "people who breed dogs and cats for use as pets or for other purposes and sell them sight unseen at the retail level," or Class A dealers, to obtain licenses from the USDA.[7] Before a license is granted, a preliminary inspection is conducted. Following that, unannounced and routine inspections are typically done once per year, but with the frequency dependent upon risk analysis. Commercial breeders, with five or more breeding females, that sell dogs wholesale, such as for distribution to pet stores, those who sell 25 or more dogs to research facilities, and those, with more than four breeding females, that sell animals sight unseen, such as over the Internet, at the retail level are subject to licensing requirements. The law does not cover breeders selling retail if done face-to-face. The USDA has breeder standards of care, which include requirements for adequate housing, veterinary care, and husbandry, such as sanitation and feeding. However, the standards are wanting in at least two respects. The exercise requirements have a loophole that allows breeders housing dogs in groups exemption provided the enclosures meet minimal space requirements. Additionally, potable water need not be readily available at all times, but only for at least one hour two times a day. The law additionally requires that workers at breeding operations have training to perform tasks in veterinary plans. However, there are no limits on the number of times a female can be bred, no age restrictions for breeding dogs, and no prohibition on breeding defects.[8]

While on paper, the US government appears to have strong regulations for licensing, inspections, and standards of care, there are woefully deficient resources committed to the enforcement of these laws and "no significant federal effort to locate and penalize operators of unlicensed breeding kennels."[9] In 2010, the Office of the Inspector General issued a negative audit report about the regulatory system for commercial dog breeders. Referring to a past audit that found the USDA's Animal and Plant Health Inspection Service (APHIS) "not aggressively pursuing enforcement actions against violators of the AWA," this report again identified "major deficiencies." Preferring to achieve compliance via education, inspectors inflicted only minimal penalties on violators and some misused guidelines to do so. As a result, 2,416 of 4,250 establishments had repeat violations, "some that ignored minimum care standards."[10] Animal welfare groups complain about the standards themselves, with the American Society for the Prevention of Cruelty to Animals (ASPCA) describing them as far from what most people would consider to be "humane," and the leniency of inspectors.[11] In 2018, there is a proposal for third parties to be empowered to conduct inspections, which would no longer be done on a surprise basis. Those third parties would most likely be industry-friendly groups, such as the AKC, and their favorable reports would prevent APHIS inspections. In the case of the

US national government, the hypothesis that it "will have lax regulations on commercial breeders for the benefit of consumers only" is confirmed only if enforcement is considered in the evaluation. On paper, four of the six regulations are in place, but the breeder standards are wanting.

The EU, which possesses nothing close to the governmental powers of the US national government over states, has instructed the Commission to study the welfare of dogs and cats involved in commercial practices. In the coming years, it is possible that the Commission will regulate in this area.[12] If it does so, there is a better chance that the regulations and enforcement will not be as lax as in the US. For now, however, EU member states are entirely responsible for the regulation of commercial breeding. Accordingly, the hypothesis that "the EU…will strictly regulate the commercial breeding of dogs and sale of puppies for purposes of protecting *both* the animals and prospective caretakers" is not validated to date.

US States: A Slow Move Away from the American Model?

Given the weakness of national standards in the US, some states have stepped up to fill the regulatory gap to some degree. Indeed, 14 states require licensing and mandatory inspections of commercial breeders, while 14 more license with the threat of possible inspections. Slightly more than half, then, have regulations in place, while 22 or 44 percent have lax or non-existent regulations in this area. For those states that license commercial breeders, 16 have fairly comprehensive coverage with licensing required if five or fewer breeding dogs or litters per year. Eight more states mandate licensing if there are ten or fewer breeding dogs or litters per year. As a result, 24 states, almost half, have strong or adequate coverage in this area. On the flip side, that leaves eight states with licensing standards that omit small- or even medium-sized operations from coverage. Four, in fact, do not license unless there are over 15 breeding dogs or litters per year. Added to those that do not license at all, there are 26 states with weak regulation in this area.

Somewhat similarly, 26 states have standards of care for breeders and two more have affirmative duties for all keepers of animals. In contrast, 22 or 44 percent rely only on anti-cruelty statutes to police commercial breeders. Slightly more than half have strong regulations in this area, then, with a substantial minority lax in its regulation. In the remaining three areas, US states are overwhelmingly lax in their regulation. Only five states or ten percent demand knowledge, expertise, or training for those breeding dogs. Only one state, Nevada, limits the number of litters for female dogs to one per year. Two others, Missouri and Texas, call for adequate rest between breeding cycles, but that is a vague guideline. Just three states, Nevada, Oklahoma, and Virginia, posit a minimum age before females can be bred and only one, Virginia, sets a maximum age for breeding. The overwhelming majority of states in these two areas therefore have lax regulations. Finally, no US state effectively legislates against the breeding of genetic defects in dogs (see Table 3.1).

Table 3.1: US National and State Regulations for Breeders.

	Licensing & Inspections	**Licensing Applies *If***	**Conditions of Care**	**Training for Workers**	**Limits on Breeding**
US government	licensing, mandatory inspections (initial & routine)	wholesale distributor with 5 or more breeding females; sells 25 or more dogs to research facility/year; or more than 4 breeding females & sells retail sight unseen (i.e., Internet)	breeder standards	yes	no
Alabama	none	n/a	anti-cruelty standards	no	no
Alaska	none	n/a	standards for keepers	no	no
Arkansas	none	n/a	anti-cruelty standards	no	no
Arizona	licensing, mandatory (over 20 dogs) and possible (5–20 dogs) inspections	over 5 dogs	anti-cruelty standards	no	no
California	none	n/a, but defined as 3 or more litters or 20 or more dogs bred on premises sold/transferred in 12 months	breeder standards	no	no
Colorado	licensing, possible inspections	breeds or raises dogs for sale/transfer	breeder standards	no	no
Connecticut	Licensing, possible inspections	breeds more than 2 litters annually	breeder standards	no	no

	Licensing & Inspections	Licensing Applies *If*	Conditions of Care	Training for Workers	Limits on Breeding
Delaware	licensing, possible inspections	keeps more than 4 dogs for breeding	Breeder standards	no	no
Florida	none	n/a	anti-cruelty standards	no	no
Georgia	licensing, mandatory inspections (initial and routine)	more than 1 litter in 12 month period or over 30 adult dogs	breeder standards	no	no
Hawaii	none	n/a	anti-cruelty standards	no	no
Idaho	none	n/a	anti-cruelty standards	no	no
Illinois	licensing, possible inspections	5 or more intact females and sells, exchanges, gives dogs or cats	breeder standards	no	no
Indiana	licensing, no inspections	more than 20 intact females for at least 12 months	breeder standards, but akin to anti-cruelty	no	no
Iowa	licensing, possible inspections	4 or more breeding dogs or cats, & sells or exchanges dogs/cats	breeder standards	no	no
Kansas	licensing, initial inspection and possible inspections thereafter	all or part of 6 or more litters (dogs/cats) or 30 or more dogs, cats or both sold or offered to another primarily at wholesale	breeder standards	yes, supervision by one with knowledge, experience in care of dogs	no
Kentucky	none	n/a	anti-cruelty standards	no	no
Louisiana	licensing, no inspections	5 or more dogs bred/ sold; maximum of 75 dogs over age of one for breeding purposes	anti-cruelty standards	no	no

	Licensing & Inspections	Licensing Applies *If*	Conditions of Care	Training for Workers	Limits on Breeding
Maine	licensing, inspections possible	5 or more intact females and some/all offspring sold *or* more than 16 dogs/cats raised on premises sold to public in 12 month period	breeder standards	no	no
Maryland	licensing, inspections possible	15 or more intact females over 6 months *and* sells dogs from 6 or more litters/year	anti-cruelty standards	no	no
Massachusetts	licensing, inspections possible	more than 3 dogs 3 months or older for whatever purpose	anti-cruelty standards	no	no
Michigan	licensing, inspections possible	more than 15 intact female dogs that have been bred	breeder standards	no	no
Minnesota	licensing, mandatory inspections (initial and routine)	10 or more adult intact animals *and* production of more than 5 litters/year (dogs/cats)	breeder standards	no	no
Mississippi	none	n/a	anti-cruelty standards	no	no
Missouri	licensing, mandatory inspections (initial and routine)	more than 3 intact females for purpose of breeding animals for sale	breeder standards	no	"adequate rest between breeding cycles"
Montana	none	n/a	anti-cruelty standards	no	no
Nebraska	licensing, mandatory inspections	sells 31 or more dogs/cats in 12 month period; *or* harbors 4 or more dogs/cats intended for breeding in 12 month period; **or** dogs/cats produce 4 or more litters in 12 month period; **or** knowingly sells for later retail	breeder standards	no	no

	Licensing & Inspections	Licensing Applies *If*	Conditions of Care	Training for Workers	Limits on Breeding
Nevada	licensing, inspections possible	engaged in breeding dogs/cats for sale or trade; not application for hobby breeder	breeder standards	no	must be 15 months; only 1 litter/year
New Hampshire	licensing, inspections possible	transfers 10 or more litters or 50 or more puppies in 12 month period	breeder standards	no	no
New Jersey	licensing, local annual inspections by health department	in business of selling or breeding dogs: regular and purposeful breeding, routine sales, separate kennel housing as markers	anti-cruelty standards	no	no
New Mexico	none	n/a	anti-cruelty standards	no	no
New York	licensing, mandatory inspections (initial and routine)	sells more than 9 dogs/year *or* 25 or more born and raised on premises/year	breeder standards	yes	no
North Carolina	none	n/a	anti-cruelty standards	no	no
North Dakota	none	n/a	anti-cruelty standards	no	no
Ohio	licensing, possible initial inspection and mandatory routine inspections	at least 9 litters/year in return for fee, *and* sells 60 or more dogs/year	breeder standards	no	no
Oklahoma	licensing, mandatory inspections (initial and routine)	possesses 11 or more intact females for use in breeding animals for sale	breeder standards	no	must be at least second cycle and healthy
Oregon	not stated	10 or more intact dogs 8 months or older; maximum of 50 intact dogs 2 years or older for purposes of reproduction	breeder standards	no	no

	Licensing & Inspections	Licensing Applies *If*	Conditions of Care	Training for Workers	Limits on Breeding
Pennsylvania	licensing, mandatory inspections	sells or transfers any dog to dealer/pet shop; *or* sells/transfers more than 60 dogs/year	breeder standards	no	no
Rhode Island	licensing only	engage in propagation of purebred or crossbred dogs	anti-cruelty standards	no	no
South Carolina	none	n/a	anti-cruelty standards	no	no
South Dakota	none	n/a	anti-cruelty standards	no	no
Tennessee	licensing, inspections possible	20 or more unsterilized adult females (dogs/cats) for purposes of selling offspring	breeder standards	knowledge, education, or experience required for supervisor	no
Texas	licensing, mandatory inspections (initial & routine)	possesses 11 or more adult females intact (dogs/cats) and engaged in business of breeding; *or* offers to sell not fewer than 20 animals in calendar year	breeder standards	yes	"adequate period between breeding cycles consistent with breed standards"
Utah	none	n/a	anti-cruelty standards	no	no
Vermont	licensing, inspections possible	sale of more than 1 litter/year; *or* 2 or more animals over 6 months for money	breeder standards	trained, experienced supervisor	no
Virginia	licensing, inspections possible	30 or more adult female dogs maintained during 12 month period for purpose of sale of their offspring	standards for keepers	no	must be 18 months and no older than 8 years; vet must certify health annually
Washington	not stated	10 or more intact dogs over 6 months kept in enclosures for majority of day	breeder standards	no	no

	Licensing & Inspections	Licensing Applies *If*	Conditions of Care	Training for Workers	Limits on Breeding
West Virginia	licensing, mandatory inspections	11 or more intact dogs over 1 year for purpose of breeding	breeder standards	no	vet must certify in suitable health
Wisconsin	licensing, mandatory inspections (initial & routine)	4 litters or more; *and* selling 25 or more/ year that person has bred/raised	breeder standards	no	no
Wyoming	none	n/a	anti-cruelty standards	no	no

Sources: Laws accessed and information gathered from: Rebecca F. Wisch, "Table of State Commercial Pet Breeder Laws," (Animal Legal and Historical Center, Michigan State University College of Law, 2017). https://www.animallaw.info/topic/table-state-commercial-pet-breeders-laws, accessed June 15, 2018; U.S. Department of Agriculture, APHIS, "Regulatory Compliance for Commercial Dog Breeders: Introductory Course," April 25, 2016. https://www.aphis.usda.gov/aphis/ourfocus/animalwelfare/caw/education+and+training/ct_commercial_dog_breeders, accessed June 14, 2018; and "State Statutes Regulating Pet Breeding," (The Animal Council, April 2018). http://www.theanimalcouncil.com/BreedingRegState.html, accessed June 15, 2018.

In the US, for just over half of the states, there is evidence in the areas of licensing/inspection and coverage that confirms hypothesis #3 that *the US government and American states will have lax regulations on commercial breeders for the benefit of consumers only*. Yet a majority would refute that hypothesis in the area of standards of care and two more states adding licensing, inspection, and coverage would flip the majority and refute the hypotheses in those areas. In fact legislation is currently proposed in several states that do not oversee breeders. For example, North Dakota legislators proposed a regulatory bill in 2017 following several seizures of animals from cruel conditions, but it has not passed. The issue has been placed in the public spotlight in Montana and South Carolina as well. Again, horrific cases with animals in unsanitary conditions and poor health have galvanized public opinion and motivated legislators to consider regulation.[13] Yet in the other three areas, training of caregivers, protection of breeding females, and the prohibition of breeding defects, the evidence clearly confirms hypothesis #3 that US states will have lax regulations. Even in those states with strong regulatory frameworks, such as

Missouri, there are still problems with enforcement. In that state, there is still the largest number of problematic facilities with 22 making the HSUS annual list of the worst 101 puppy mills.[14] It should be noted, however, that Missouri, with 558, has by far the largest number of Class A dealers or large commercial breeders in the country. Iowa, which has the second greatest number of dealers, is way behind, with 208. There are only eight other states with over 50 breeders, namely, Arkansas, Indiana, Kansas, Nebraska, Ohio, Oklahoma, Pennsylvania, and Texas.[15] Two of these states, Arkansas and Indiana, have lax regulations and Oklahoma excludes from coverage those without at least 11 intact females. In short, practices have not yet caught up to laws even in states with decent regulations.

EU Member States: Stricter Regulations but Still Loopholes?

True to expectations, 18/28 or 64 percent of EU member states require licensing and mandatory inspections of commercial breeders. Three more mandate licensing with the possibility of inspections. Only 7/28 or 25 percent have lax regulations in this area. Latvia, the Czech Republic, and Malta inspect only if complaints are filed. The other four states, Estonia, Hungary, Poland, and Slovakia, do not have a program for inspections. For those 21 member states conducting either mandatory or possible inspections, 13 have comprehensive coverage or demand licensing for all commercial breeders or those with five or fewer breeding dogs or litters per year. Four require licensing for establishments with ten or fewer breeding dogs or litters and only one, Luxembourg, sets the limit over ten. Three member states do not specifically state the criteria for licensing at the national level. In sum, it is reasonable to conclude that 17 member states, over half, have strong or adequate regulations in this area. However, 11/28 or almost 40 percent have a weaker legislative framework and therefore do not conform with the hypothesis. The difference with US states is not tremendous in this area, as slightly more than half of US states had lax regulations, but it is the direction expected.

In contrast, 13 or almost half of EU member states have breeder standards and 12 others have affirmative obligation for keepers that would be applicable to breeders. Just 3/28 or about 11 percent have lax standards on this criterion. Additionally, 21/28 states or 75 percent require training and/or knowledge and experience for breeders. In fact, all of the member states that have ratified the ECPPA are expected to do so. Almost half or 12/28 have specific prohibitions against the breeding of defects. Two others have general or vague language and therefore are not counted as having such regulations in place. Finally, 11/28 or close to 40 percent limit the number of litters or periods between litters for female breeding dogs and 6/28 and 3/28 prescribe a minimum and maximum age for breeding, respectively.

In the areas of standards of care and training for breeders, hypothesis #10 that *the EU and its member states will strictly regulate the commercial breeding of dogs and sale of puppies for purposes of protecting both the animals and prospective human caretakers* is validated. There is also decidedly more EU member states than US states placing limitations on the breeding of females and prohibiting the breeding of defects, facts that help to sustain the hypothesis as well. However, in the area of licensing and inspections, the differences between EU and US states are not as stark, though a slightly greater percentage of EU member states are likely to have strict regulations there too. Importantly, a substantial minority of states in both the US and EU defy expectations (see Table 3.2).

Table 3.2: EU Regulations for Breeders.

	Licensing and Inspections	**Licensing Applies *If***	**Conditions of Care**	**Training for Workers**	**Limits on Breeding**	**Prohibits Breeding Defects**
Austria*	licensing, mandatory inspections (initial and routine)	keeping animals for breeding/sale	breeder standards	yes, proof required	not stated	yes
Belgium*	licensing, mandatory inspections (initial and routine)	3 or more litters/year	breeder standards	yes, proof required	not more than 2 litters/year	yes
Bulgaria*	licensing, mandatory inspections (initial and routine)	dog owner who raises a dog with purpose of breeding	keeper and breeder standards	yes, proof required	not stated	no
Croatia	licensing, initial mandatory and then based on risk, random selection and complaints	3 or more breeding females	breeder standards	yes, proof required	must be at least 15 months and no older than 8 years; only one litter/year	no

	Licensing and Inspections	Licensing Applies *If*	Conditions of Care	Training for Workers	Limits on Breeding	Prohibits Breeding Defects
Cyprus*	licensing, inspections possible	premises where dogs kept, reared, bred; female dogs acquired for breeding must be declared	standards for keepers	yes, proof required	not stated	no
Czech Rep.*	registration only, inspections only if complaints	all commercial must register	standards for keepers	per PPA, professional training or sufficient experience	for small and large breeds, must be 14 and 17 months and no older than 8 years; max. of 3 litters/2 years	yes
Denmark*	licensing, mandatory inspections (initial and routine)	minimum of 3 females which have 3 or more litters/year	breeder standards	yes	no	not stated
Estonia	none	n/a	very general, applies to all keepers	no	"must not give birth too often"	yes
Finland*	licensing, inspections based on sampling and complaints	6 breeding females which have given birth	standards for all keepers	yes, proof required	not stated	yes
France*	registration, mandatory inspections	registration for owning female that has birthed a litter; for inspections, more than 9 dogs older than 4 months	breeder standards	yes, proof required	no more than 3 litters/2 years	yes
Germany*	licensing, initial mandatory inspection	3 or more intact females *or* more than 3 litters/year	breeder standards	yes, proof required	not stated	yes

	Licensing and Inspections	Licensing Applies *If*	Conditions of Care	Training for Workers	Limits on Breeding	Prohibits Breeding Defects
Greece*	licensing, mandatory inspections (initial and routine)	more than 2 females bred *or* more than 2 litters/year	standards for all keepers	per PPA, professional training or sufficient experience; authorities to organize trainings	must be at least second cycle and no older than 9; minimum of 9 months between birth and next pregnancy	yes
Hungary	not explicit	n/a	standards for all keepers	no	not stated	yes
Ireland	licensing, mandatory inspections	6 or more intact females	breeder standards	experience, with regular training recommended	no more than 6 litters in life; no more than 3/3 years	no
Italy*	licensing, initial inspection and then possible	not stated	standards for all keepers	competence, but training not required	not stated	no
Latvia*	licensing, inspections only if complaint or suspicion of violation	not stated	standards for all keepers	yes, proof required	no more than 1 litter/year	yes
Lithuania*	licensing, mandatory inspections (initial and routine)	any commercial breeding	breeder standards	"competent staff"	"sufficient time" between litters	yes
Luxembourg*	licensing, inspections possible	breeding establishment with more than 10 animals	standards for all keepers	yes, proof required	not stated	yes
Malta	register, inspections only if complaints	more than 4 litters/year	general only, not explicit standards	no	must be 12 months; no more than 1 litter/year, 6 litters in life	no

	Licensing and Inspections	Licensing Applies *If*	Conditions of Care	Training for Workers	Limits on Breeding	Prohibits Breeding Defects
Netherlands	register, inspections possible for all but targeted at those who have sold or are keeping more than 20 dogs in 12 month period	if selling any, must register	standards for all keepers	yes, proof required	not more than one litter within 12 months	yes
Poland	none	n/a	general only, not explicit standards	no	not stated	no
Portugal*	licensing, mandatory inspections	all breeders	breeder standards	per PPA, professional training or sufficient experience	not stated	no
Romania*	licensing, mandatory inspections mainly for hygiene	not stated	standards for all keepers	per PPA, professional training or sufficient experience	not stated	no
Slovakia	notification, but no inspections	not stated	breeder standards	no	not stated	"should not show serious genetic diseases"
Slovenia	licensing, mandatory inspections (initial and routine)	commercial and those with more than 5 dogs	up to 10 dogs, standards for keepers; breeder standards for above 10	yes if 10 or more dogs	must be 14 months; cannot mate before 290 days after giving birth	yes
Spain	licensing, mandatory initial inspection	not stated	standards for keepers	no (only one region)	no national guidelines	no (only one region)

	Licensing and Inspections	Licensing Applies *If*	Conditions of Care	Training for Workers	Limits on Breeding	Prohibits Breeding Defects
Sweden*	licensing, mandatory initial inspection	10 or more dogs over 12 months *or* 3 or more litters/year	breeder standards	per PPA, professional training or sufficient experience	second cycle and must be 18 months; if 2 litters within 12 months, must have 12 months of rest	yes
UK	licensing, mandatory inspections (initial and routine)	England and Scotland: 5 litters or more in 12 month period. Wales and N. Ireland: 3 or more females *and* breed 3 or more litters in 12 month period.	standards for keepers	no	England and Scotland: must be 1 year; only 1 litter in 12 month period; no more than 6 litters. N. Ireland: no older than 8; no more than 3 litters in 3 year period; no more than 6 litters	no

*Signed and ratified ECPPA

Sources: Laws accessed and information gathered from EU Dog & Cat Alliance, "The welfare of dogs and cats involved in commercial practices: a review of the legislation across EU countries," (London, 2017). https://s3-eu-west-1.amazonaws.com/assets.dogandcatwelfare.eu/live/media/publicationtemp/all.pdf, accessed June 15, 2018; European Enforcement Network of Animal Welfare Lawyers and Commissioners, "Country Profile," (Vier Pfoten, European Policy Office). http://www.lawyersforanimalprotection.eu/country-profile/, accessed June 15, 2018; and Carodog: Companion Animal Responsible Ownership, "National Legislation." http://www.carodog.eu/national-legislation/, accessed June 15, 2018.

Because regulations on commercial breeding are not consistent across the EU, in practice, puppy mills or farms can operate in areas with either a poor legislative framework or lax enforcement. Both the Czech Republic, which has detailed rules for breeders, and Poland, which outlaws cruel means of breeding, are described as "key puppy production countries" in the Four Paws Report about mills.[16] In the EU, most of the mill puppies are from the East and sold to countries in the West. For example, between 2011 and 2013, "the number of dogs entering the United Kingdom from Poland, Romania, Hungary, and Lithuania rose from two thousand to twelve thousand."[17] Networks of unscrupulous small-scale breeders, which are exempted from regulations, can make enforcement of standards extremely difficult. In Eastern Europe, dealers and transporters can collect puppies from as many as 3,000 breeders.[18]

Unfortunately in the EU, there is big money in the illicit trade of puppies. According to one estimate, the illegal industry is worth more than 100 million pounds for dogs smuggled into the UK. At the high end, smugglers can earn 35,000 pounds a week and face minimal criminal penalties. Unlike jail terms for smuggling drugs, those for animal cruelty are lax or limited to six months. As a result, member states, such as the UK, with strict laws to ensure that only healthy puppies are imported, nonetheless have abused and sickly pups marketed to an unsuspecting public. The trade is on display in such places as Pecs, Hungary, where a puppy market takes place with "puppies stuffed in the back of car boots in cages and baskets" and with "many of the animals desperately sick." With the help of unethical veterinarians and dealers who falsify records, those pups are destined for homes in western and southern Europe, such as Italy and the UK.[19]

Central Help Needed!

Absent financial help and regulation from a central and wealthier layer of government, some states are going to either have lax regulations and/or fail to enforce any regulations on the books. Unscrupulous operators take advantage of this situation to breed dogs in poor conditions and market sickly pups. Only central governments, supranational in the EU and national in the US, can tackle the trafficking of such puppies across state borders and improve the lives of dogs at the breeding facilities. When that truckload of puppies stacked in cramped and dirty cages crashed in Germany, the authorities could not file criminal charges given the production of valid vaccination certificates. As Overdorf notes, "The impotence of the authorities in Germany—where regulations governing the treatment of animals are among the toughest in the world—highlights the difficulty of stopping the cruel trade."[20] Depending on the Commission's recommendations in this area, it is conceivable that the EU will legislate and work to close these gaps. It is less likely that the

US government will strengthen its regulations, but there have been notable successes at the state level. Indeed, the monolithic American and European policy models fail to capture the reality in this policy area despite the validation of hypotheses.

Giving Up on Friends

Many people consider their dogs family members and therefore priceless, but others indisputably cannot shed the notion of a dog as a commodity. That latter conception is implied in the transaction through which millions of dogs are acquired and also in the language of "ownership." Testifying to the lingering conception of dogs as commodities are the large numbers of dogs given up, surrendered to shelters or simply abandoned, in the US and EU. To be sure, there are myriad reasons why people relinquish dogs. Although the explanations are ranked differently, several studies about the US identify aggressive companion animal behavior, moving, rental or housing issues, and caretaker personal issues, such as a lack of time, resources, illness, or allergies.[21] According to one US study, the majority of relinquished dogs were between five months and three years old and "owned" from seven months to one year.[22] Relinquishment rates are high in other countries as well. In the UK, shelters were at a "breaking point" in 2015 because thousands had surrendered pet dogs.[23] Likewise, in France, thousands give up their dogs to shelters each year to go on summer vacations, a troublesome practice found also in Spain and Italy.[24] As the reader may recall, in places with a low value on canine life, such as select parts of rural Spain, dogs are simply discarded at the end of hunting season. For some people, the surrender of a dog is a wrenching decision triggered by aggression in the dog, illness, or economic imperative and for others, it is a cavalier choice with little or no thought for the dog. Perhaps there is a continuum but it seems safe to reason that a large number of relinquishments is likely to indicate the prevalence of a more cavalier attitude toward dogs and/or poor contemplation of caretakers' responsibilities before purchase.

There is no accurate census for the number of unwanted dogs in the US and Europe. Such dogs are not only found in shelters, but are free-ranging or living on their own. While it is unfortunate when a person relinquishes a dog to a shelter, it is most often worse for the dog when abandoned to the streets. There are exceptions, of course, for those places with horrific conditions in their shelters. However, it is a delusion to think that the abandoned dog is in a satisfactory environment. When there are significant numbers of free-roaming dogs, they are usually of different backgrounds. In some cases, these dogs are "strays" who "maintain social bonds with humans." Because they have been abandoned or are lost, they are seeking another relationship with a human being. In other cases, these dogs are feral, "living successfully without any contact with humans" and any social bonds are with other dogs. Such dogs are skittish around humans and tend to avoid any contact with them. According to scholars, these two categories as well as that of "owned" or adopted are fluid since "a dog may change its status during its lifetime."[25] For example, a beloved companion, if lost, could become a stray and ultimately feral under certain conditions, though feral dogs are most often the offspring of strays and not the strays themselves. In other words, companion animals are not at all immune from the consequences of societal treatment of stray and feral dogs.

In countries with very small or non-existent stray populations, chances are much better that any such dogs will be taken to shelters and re-homed, if not reunited with their original caretakers. Unfortunately, however, there are substantial stray/feral populations found in both the US and EU. As the reader may recall, there are especially large stray/feral populations in eastern and southern Europe, with the only exception of Slovenia.[26] The problem is also found, though not nearly to the same extent as in those areas, in the American South, American plains, several large cities in both the US and EU, and a few western/northern EU member states, such as France and the United Kingdom. There are at least eight EU member states with virtually no stray populations, but the European Society for Dog and Animal Welfare (ESDAW) nonetheless estimates that there are approximately 100 million strays in the EU.[27] While some EU member states, such as Bulgaria, are taking steps to address the problem and have a slightly improving situation, there are still large populations in many places, including Italy, Spain, Cyprus, Greece, Romania, and Slovakia. It is estimated that there are 50,000–100,000 stray dogs on the streets of Bucharest alone. In the south of Europe, Italy, for example, has a stray population of approximately 600,000. Even in the UK, there are estimated to be about 81,000 stray dogs.[28]

In the US, there is a problem with strays in big cities, particularly in low-income areas, and in some rural sections of the country. Beginning a few years ago, Detroit, Michigan has become exemplary of this potential crisis. Pushed into economic disaster by the withdrawal of manufacturing jobs in the automobile industry, Detroit has thousands of stray/feral dogs in its neighborhoods. While some estimates are as high as 50,000, the Stray Project claims that there are no more than three thousand such dogs on any given day.[29] Although Detroit has garnered the most publicity for its stray problem, other major cities, such as St. Louis, Los Angeles, and Cleveland, also report feral/stray populations. Since the 1980s, the problem intensified in big cities given an increase in dogfighting. Unneutered dogs, bred and trained for aggressiveness, were often dumped in abandoned areas to fend for themselves.[30] It is impossible to determine the exact number of strays in the US, but there are clearly pockets in the country with a "stray problem."[31] One journalist labeled it "an underground epidemic in most cities."[32] Predictably, it is a private, not public, initiative, the Stray Project, that is working to assess the scope of the problem.

Life for these dogs is, to use the words of Thomas Hobbes, "nasty, brutish and short."[33] As noted in the Royal Society for the Prevention of Cruelty to Animals (RSPCA) and World Society for the Protection of Animals (WSPA) Report, free-ranging dogs are prone to injuries from car accidents and encounters with other animals during competition for limited resources, malnutrition, disease, inhumane collection and culling methods, and deliberate abuse.[34] In his seminal study of free-roaming dogs in Baltimore in the early 1970s, Beck provides substantiation for these concerns. He writes, "Death comes to free-ranging urban dogs primarily from disease, collision with automobiles, being collected by the Animal Shelter and subsequently disposed of, or being killed intentionally by human beings without public sanction."[35] Per the results of his study, malnutrition was mainly a problem for animals suffering from disease, as others were able to procure edible food primarily from trash. In places with larger stray populations, such as East European cities, the availability of food for each dog might be more limited than in this case. Animal advocates, such as ESDAW, chronicle in gruesome detail the horror stories of individual dogs who experience the hardships and deaths described in these studies and reports. For example, such dogs, if injured severely in a traffic accident and unable to move, can die a slow and agonizing death of starvation by the side of the road. Some people view them as "vermin" and abuse them with impunity.[36] In St. Louis, according to Grim, 70 percent of the 500–600 dogs in the shelter system have gunshot wounds.[37] Not surprisingly, these dogs have short life spans, with some estimates as low as one to two years.[38]

In a tragic reversal of societal tendencies to protect endangered species, there seems to be a tendency to brutalize stray dogs. When present in significant numbers, their lives, and with them those of all dogs, are cheapened or devalued. It is as though the laws of supply and demand apply to the value of the lives of sentient beings. With such assumptions in place, there are at times attempts to wipe out these populations via cruel means. In Romania, for example, there was a massive campaign to round up and kill stray dogs in the aftermath of a deadly attack on a young boy in 2013 about which there is now question if stray dogs were involved. Although the law was changed somewhat in response to international pressure, the killings and abuse of strays continue in that country. On the American side of the Atlantic, an internal police memo in Harrisburg, Pennsylvania instructed officers to stop bringing stray dogs to the shelter, which was getting overcrowded. Instead, it advised them to release the dogs in another area, adopt them, or "just put a bullet in them."[39] Clearly, the life of a feral or stray dog is a perilous one. At best, they are vulnerable to all manner of hazards, and at worse, they are subjected to torture and inhumane deaths.

An Ounce of Prevention Is Worth a Pound of Cure

Education and Screening

The acquisition of a dog requires a long-term commitment of time, emotion, and financial resources. As Fournier and Geller note, "Studies consistently find that caretakers who relinquish their animals," versus those who do not, "have much less knowledge about animal behavior, health care, the expenses of animal caretaking, and female canine cycles."[40] Their expectations are unreasonable. Clearly, better education of potential caretakers might help to alleviate the problem of relinquishment. What is more, there is need for breeders and sellers to do a better job screening potential caretakers. Some of the personal reasons which are commonly cited upon surrendering dogs, such as allergies or insufficient time or space, are foreseeable in advance of any adoption. More could be done to match people with breeds and individual dogs compatible with their lifestyles.[41]

There are many breeders who attempt to do just that. However, others are simply trying to maximize sales. As part of the requirements placed upon the sale of dogs, governments could easily require that those purchasing dogs be provided with information about exercise, behavioral, and health care needs. For non-profit shelters and rescue organizations, there should be similar protocols in place to educate those adopting dogs. In one study of an Italian animal shelter, the researchers found that almost all of the dogs were returned because of behavioral problems. Some dogs were returned more than once, with 20 percent reporting the same behavioral issue for that dog.[42] Such findings indicate a need for staff to engage in training dogs with such issues or at a minimum, to inform potential adopters of the problem. The more that breeders and shelters can do to educate prospective canine caretakers about their responsibilities, the better.

Ideally, those who are not willing to commit to a dog's care would refrain from adopting without thought. There seems to be a relationship between higher percentages of households with dogs and relinquishment. In the EU, for example, member states with higher percentages of households with dogs tend to have serious problems with large shelter populations and/or free-roaming dogs. Per the 2014 numbers of the European Pet Food Industry, Romania, which is notorious for its free-roaming and shelter dogs, has the highest percentage of households with at least one dog or 45 percent. The Czech Republic (41 percent), Hungary (33 percent), Lithuania (37 percent), Poland (37 percent), and Portugal (32 percent), all states with problems with relinquishment, have comparably higher rates of households with at least one dog as well. In contrast, those states in north-central Europe with virtually no free-roaming dogs and minimal shelter populations have comparably lower rates of households with at least one dog, under 25 percent, with Austria and Sweden as low as 12 and 13 percent, respectively. This relationship is by no means perfect or without exception. For example, Greece, which has a large free-roaming population due to abandonment and other factors, reports only 14 percent of households with one dog and in Slovenia, which has a minimal problem, 30 percent of households have at least one dog. However, it is not unreasonable to conclude that high rates of households with at least one dog might indicate a lower threshold of contemplation before acquisition.[43]

In the US, the number of households with at least one dog tends to be lower in the Northeast and Upper Midwest, sections of the US where there are small shelter populations, and higher in the South, where there are large shelter populations. Nine southern states have 40 percent or more of households having at least one dog. With the exception of Louisiana, every southern state reports rates of 35 percent or more of households with at least one dog. In the Northeast, every state but Vermont has rates below 35 percent. No state in either the upper Midwest or Northeast has a rate over 40 percent.[44] Again, such high rates tend to be associated with bigger shelter populations and higher relinquishment rates.

Mandatory Identification

Recognizing that there will be those who relinquish dogs, it is better to encourage surrender to reputable shelters. The mandatory registration and identification of dogs with microchips or other permanent markers help not only to deter abandonment to the streets but also to reunite lost dogs with their caretakers. Inserted under the skin between an animal's shoulder blades, a microchip, which is the size of a grain of rice, bears "a unique code number that is entered" onto a database with the caretaker's information.[45] Consistent with expectations, there are clear differences in the use of such permanent forms of identification in the US and EU. Both hypothesis #2, which states *neither the US government nor the states will require permanent markers, such as microchips, on dogs*, and hypothesis #9, which states *the EU and its member states will mandate both the permanent identification and registration of dogs*, are clearly sustained. The *supra*-national government has taken the lead in promoting permanent identification in the EU. According to EU law, dogs traveling with their human companions across national borders must have a "pet passport," which requires, among other things, microchipping. That *supra*-national regulation has not only ensured that travelers chip their dogs but it has undoubtedly raised awareness about the benefits of the practice.

Following the EU, the trend among member states is toward compulsory registration with permanent identification, such as a microchip or tattoo. The benefits of permanent markings are clear. In Sweden, for example, where microchipping has been compulsory for over a decade, more than 90 percent of lost dogs are reunited with their caretakers within 24 hours.[46] As of 2018, 21/28 member states required that dogs be permanently identified (see Table 3.3). With very few exceptions, all of these member states maintain a national database on which the dogs' and caretakers' information is recorded. Only eight member states, however, connect their databases to a European-wide one. In some cases, it is up to regional or local governments to carry out the program. In Italy, that delegation has resulted in "regional variations in enforcement and effect of the microchipping scheme."[47] There have also been concerns with the keeping of multiple databases, such as in the UK, as dogs can wander considerable distances. In those member states that do not have national requirements for microchipping, there are nonetheless in some cases regional laws in place to compel it. For example, all "dangerous" dogs must be chipped in Germany, but only two states or Lander require chipping for all dogs.[48] Likewise, the Czech government delegates the microchipping decision and enforcement to local governments. That policy in the Czech Republic has not yet resulted in widespread microchipping.[49] Despite these exceptions, the trend in the EU is clearly toward compulsory microchipping of dogs. Arguably, the EU's leadership on this issue has helped to spread the practice. However, the public's acceptance of this requirement bespeaks of a tolerance for regulations for animal care that is not as prevalent in the US.

Table 3.3: EU Regulations: Microchipping and Euthanasia.

	Requires permanent markings?	**National database for registrations?**	**Linked to European Database?**	**Prohibits euthanasia of healthy dogs?**
Austria	yes	yes	not yet	Yes
Belgium	yes	yes	yes	no
Bulgaria	yes	yes	no	yes
Croatia	yes	yes	no	no
Cyprus	yes	yes	no	no
Czech Republic	no	n/a	n/a	yes
Denmark	yes	yes	yes	no
Estonia	no	n/a	n/a	no
Finland	no	n/a	n/a	no
France	yes	yes	yes	no
Germany	no	n/a	n/a	yes
Greece	yes	yes	no	yes
Hungary	yes	yes	yes	no
Ireland	yes	yes*	yes	no
Italy	yes	yes	no	yes
Latvia	yes	yes	yes	no
Lithuania	no	n/a	n/a	yes
Luxembourg	yes	yes	yes	no
Malta	yes	yes	no	no
Netherlands	yes	yes**	no	yes
Poland	no	n/a	n/a	no
Portugal	yes	yes	no	no
Romania	yes	yes	no	no
Slovakia	no	n/a	n/a	no

	Requires permanent markings?	National database for registrations?	Linked to European Database?	Prohibits euthanasia of healthy dogs?
Slovenia	yes	yes	no	no
Spain	yes	no***	yes	no
Sweden	yes	yes	no	yes
UK	yes	no	no	no

*There are four databases, but all are members of European central database.
**Central database used for law enforcement only.
***There are separate databases for all of the autonomous communities, but all are linked to European central database.

Sources: EU Dog & Cat Alliance, "The welfare of dogs and cats involved in commercial practices: a review of the legislation across EU countries," (London, 2017). https://s3-eu-west-1.amazonaws.com/assets.dogandcatwelfare.eu/live/media/publicationtemp/all.pdf, accessed June 15, 2018; Carodog: Companion Animal Responsible Ownership, "National Legislation." http://www.carodog.eu/national-legislation/, accessed June 15, 2018; and Vier Pfoten, "Killing of Healthy Dogs in Europe: Legal Research," (Brussels: European Policy Office, 2014). http://www.carodog.eu/wp-content/uploads/2014/06/legal-overview-where-killing-of-dogs-is-allowed2.pdf, accessed June 15, 2018.

There are no national or statewide requirements to microchip or tattoo dogs in the US. States require that dogs wear tags or licenses, which are issued only with proof of vaccination for rabies. Unless a dog is lost, however, there is rarely enforcement of this mandate. Tags can certainly be helpful in returning lost dogs to their people. According to the ASPCA, approximately 542,000 dogs in shelters are returned to their caretakers annually.[50] However, tags can easily be lost or a dog's collar can be removed. In such cases, the return of dogs to their homes is less likely, especially if a dog has wandered or been taken far away. There is no national registration of dogs in the US, as this matter is delegated entirely to the states. Indeed, as Clancy and Rowan explain, "The US has never had a national system in place to collect, store and analyze data relating to pet care giving."[51] Such a centralized system with routine microchipping would substantially reduce the risk of permanently lost dogs, with all the fear and distress that entails. One of the few studies on this issue in the US found that dogs were 2.5 times more likely to be returned to their caretakers if microchipped.[52]

According to Found Animals, a non-profit group, there are many cities and counties in California, Texas, and Illinois that mandate microchipping.[53] Without statewide requirements, though, there are likely to be substantial gaps in the coverage of dogs. State legislators might be reluctant to pass such requirements for budgetary reasons or for fear of triggering a populist backlash in view of American mistrust of government. Without legislative compulsion, approximately 26 percent of dogs in the US were microchipped as of 2010. That percentage has undoubtedly climbed since then in light of highly publicized stories of pets united with caretakers.[54] In Nevada, commercial breeders are now required to microchip puppies. Yet overall, American states have kept the decision to microchip a prerogative of "owners," not a social or legal duty out of concern for the welfare of the animal. The hypotheses in this area are therefore confirmed. Requirements for permanent markers are much more likely in the EU, though 25 percent of EU member states do not have national requirements for microchips.

Sterilization and the Controversy

Since the 1970s, many governments and animal welfare organizations have advocated for the sterilization of companion animals as a primary means to manage canine population levels. In the US, animal welfare groups, such as HSUS and ASPCA, would attribute the decline in the numbers of canines euthanized since that time to the widespread application of sterilization. Nationally, approximately 70 percent of dogs are sterilized.[55] However, scholars and scientists have questioned the effect of sterilization on shelter populations. Scientists, in particular, highlight the obvious fact that dogs cannot reproduce unless humans allow them access to one another. Societies with highly responsible ethics of care, such as those in north-central Europe, can and do have very low sterilization rates and virtually no unwanted dogs. What is more, critics note that the relinquishment of dogs is the main cause of shelter populations at least in the US. There is high demand for puppies. As a result, some claim that sterilization is an ineffective tool for managing canine population levels.

Increasingly as well, there is controversy over the effects of sterilization on individual dogs. In several European cultures, spaying and neutering are considered to be unnecessary surgeries that cause discomfort and distress to dogs. This attitude is currently winning some advocates in the US. Opponents of sterilization claim adverse health effects and cite a few studies in support of their case, particularly for early sterilization. Advocates maintain that there are health benefits to sterilization for dogs and also cite the lifelong distress of dogs unable to satisfy a physical need, limitations placed upon dogs to ensure no unintended breeding, and concerns with aggression in some males.[56] Whatever the resolution of this debate, it is clear that enforced abstinence can work and is used successfully in north-central Europe. This approach is quite consistent with the European model, reliant as it is on social responsibility and attuned to the distress of dogs.

However, this approach's success is dependent upon human behavior. As Fournier and Geller observe, "it is the behavior of people that has resulted in an overabundance of animals, and to solve the problem, people must change their behavior."[57] Laws and their associated inducements impact human behavior and must comport with the mores and practices of particular places. In societies where virtually no one abandons dogs and all exercise highly responsible ethics of care, there is no need for incentives to sterilize dogs. What about in societies where such norms are not in place? If people abandon dogs or occasionally allow them to roam, do sterilization rates and incentives have any impact on the population of "unwanted" dogs? There is not agreement on this answer and the scholarly findings are somewhat mixed.

Several studies could not establish any effect of sterilization procedures on shelter intake. For example, one study assessed the impact of New Hampshire's Animal Population Control Program, which encouraged and subsidized canine sterilization. Comparing shelter intake and euthanasia data before and after its implementation, the researchers found "no decrease in dog intake or euthanasia."[58] Other studies stipulate the uncertainty of any effect, but imply that there is likely to be some benefit. For example, Fournier and Geller argue that "sterilization is a critical behavior that should be targeted in efforts to reduce overpopulation," but acknowledge that there are "no public evaluations" to determine "if it has any impact on the problem."[59] It has also been observed that cost is not the deterrent in many people's decisions not to sterilize their dogs, a fact which casts doubt on the efficacy of public subsidies for sterilization.

However, others emphasize the importance of sterilization in the management of canine populations. The same study that found no impact for New Hampshire's sterilization initiative had different results for a program in Austin, Texas. Comparing shelter intake and euthanasia data from the targeted program areas versus non-targeted areas, researchers discovered a "significantly lower rate of increase for dog…intake and euthanasia in the program areas."[60] Frank maintains that sterilization policies must be evaluated over a long period of time "since full impact may not be achieved for thirty years or more. Spay/neuter efforts can have a large impact even if they effect a small portion of the human population."[61] Similarly, an Italian study estimated a substantial effect on the canine population in response both to the female sterilization rate and the age at which females are spayed.[62] Based on these studies, there are clearly instances in which sterilization is beneficial. With that said, it is difficult to disentangle the causes of large abandoned and/or shelter populations.

Those who promote sterilization readily note that relinquishment and abandonment contribute as well to an "unwanted" population. Logically, in areas where the abandonment of dogs to the streets is either common or sporadic, sterilization rates would be likely to exert impact even if only to slow the rate of increase in the population. One would anticipate some effect as well in places with more casual approaches to caretaking and high relinquishment rates. If caretakers are unaware of the precautions to prevent reproduction or unwilling to take them, unplanned litters are more likely to result. In the US, a 2002 PetSmart survey found that 13 percent of dogs "purchased in the previous year had borne litters, with 50 percent of those unplanned."[63] While puppies are not hard to place, there is likely some opportunity cost. In other words, some individuals who might have adopted an adolescent opt for the readily available pup instead. More significantly, such unplanned litters are likely to contribute to casual adoptions. Far from screening potential caretakers, those with unplanned litters are aggressively seeking people to take a pup.

While it is clearly possible to have no unwanted population without sterilization and there are mixed results about its efficacy, it is the opinion of many governments and animal advocacy groups that sterilization programs are beneficial until societies shift toward universal responsibility in caretaking. How supportive are governments in the US and EU of these programs? In the US, as of 2017, 33 states required all animals released from shelters to be spayed or neutered before adoption. However, several states exempt dogs who are being re-claimed by caretakers from this requirement despite the fact that they were roaming free or otherwise would not have landed in the shelter. Additionally, there are exceptions in some cases for small counties and for lack of veterinary facilities in the area.[64] Some states, such as New Hampshire, have instituted comprehensive programs to control the population of companion animals. In that state, sterilization procedures are subsidized and it is unlawful for dogs to run at large or not under the control of caretakers. The state funds the plan with licensing fees and a special spay/neuter license plate for automobiles, which also contributes to public awareness.[65] By 2017, at least 27 states offered these pet-friendly license plates and used the proceeds to subsidize spay/neuter programs. In addition, some states and counties implement other means to finance spay/neuter programs, such as a voluntary state tax check-off and voluntary or mandatory surcharges to dog licensing fees.[66] In the South, which has a large population in shelters, all states with the exceptions of Kentucky, Mississippi, and North Carolina, now require that dogs be spayed or neutered before their release from shelters and several offer pet-friendly license plates. Nationally, 38 states subsidize the cost of sterilization and 21 states provide a licensing fee differential.[67]

In sum, several state governments have enacted comprehensive population control programs for canines. They include regulations for shelters to spay/neuter before adoption, subsidies and incentives for caretakers to sterilize companion animals, and public education. Such proactive policies are closer to the European than American model. However, these programs are funded, for the most part, in ways consistent with the American approach. Specialty license plates and tax check-offs are voluntary and thereby unlikely to trigger anti-government sentiments. Private organizations, such as the ASPCA and the HSUS, have contributed to public education and worked in collaboration with state governments to address the issue as well. While a few states have delegated all responsibility to these groups, most others have adopted an active role, albeit one compatible with the American model.

Similarly to the US, birth control is handled at the member state level in the EU. However, in response to a large number of petitions from citizens of the EU, a resolution was passed in 2012 calling upon the European Commission to develop stray animal management strategies.[68] The exercise of central leadership could help to spread best practices across problematic areas. At the member state level, there is currently more diversity in the handling of this issue than in the US. In those eight member states with no stray problem, there are no subsidies for sterilization.[69] Indeed, it is uncommon in most of this subset to spay/neuter dogs at all. According to one study, less than seven percent of females and four percent of males were spayed/neutered in Sweden.[70] Instead of reliance on sterilization, these member states control the canine population via highly responsible ethics of caretaking. Dogs are not allowed to roam and females are kept apart during heat cycles.

The other 20 member states, all of which have at least a minor problem with strays, place some reliance on sterilization as a means of birth control.

However, spaying/neutering rates are still much lower than in the US. For example, Torres de la Riva et al. cite studies noting an intact rate of 57 percent in Hungary and 46 percent in the UK.[71] Nor is it common practice to sterilize dogs in France and most other EU member states. Given that these member states have issues, major ones in some cases, with stray/feral populations, several governmental bodies and animal welfare organizations publicize the benefits of sterilization and at least 12 member states offer some form of subsidies for neutering/spaying. In Slovenia, for example, municipalities "run twice yearly neutering schemes for owned dogs at low cost to their owners."[72] Similarly, in Poland, the City of Warsaw began providing free sterilization of companion animals for its residents in 2015. In addition, there are many campaigns in rural areas of the country to promote sterilization and the associated costs of so doing are lower than they once were.[73] Several others, including Ireland and the UK, subsidize sterilization for those with low incomes. Animal welfare organizations, veterinary associations, and municipalities administer and fund almost all of these programs, with virtually no involvement from central or national governments.[74] What is more, several member states, including Cyprus, Slovakia, and others, struggle to educate people to refrain from allowing unneutered dogs to roam. In Cyprus, as in parts of Spain, it is common practice to dump or release hunting dogs, who are not neutered/spayed, after one season. Slovakia also confronts a large-scale "problem of uncontrolled reproduction not only of stray animals but also of dogs and cats owned by irresponsible" people.[75] In short, sterilization in these member states is used as a means of birth control, but not on the scale of the US. In some cases, responsible caretakers prevent intact dogs from reproducing, but in others, the combination of irresponsible care and intact dogs yields large stray populations.

In those member states with such large populations, there are some, including Bulgaria, and Greece, that now require neutering before an animal is adopted from a shelter. Slovenia and the UK also mandate sterilization before adoption. In France, some shelters sterilize dogs before adoption, but others leave the task up to the adopter. In member states overrun with strays, such as Cyprus, a paucity of resources sometimes prevents animal welfare organizations from spaying/neutering all dogs before adoption. In other words, adopted strays or shelter dogs do not necessarily come neutered or spayed in several EU member states. While animal welfare organizations and governments encourage sterilization in those EU member states with significant stray populations, there is, in some cases, a reluctance to perform unnecessary surgeries on dogs and in other cases, an unwillingness to pay for the procedure, and/or assume responsibility for the care of the animal.

For those strays who are not adopted, there has been a trend in EU member states with large stray/feral populations toward spay-neuter-release programs. In Sofia, Bulgaria, for example, a pilot program was introduced to neuter/spay, vaccinate against rabies, and then return healthy and non-aggressive dogs to the streets. This one and other such programs have proven to be more effective than capture-and-kill strategies in reducing stray populations.[76] Several other EU member states with large stray populations, including Greece, Lithuania, and Latvia, are employing this policy at least in some parts of the country. With this program, EU member states ironically demonstrate a greater reliance than US states on sterilization to control stray/feral populations. If dogs are not adopted in the US, they are typically euthanized. This newer approach of spay-neuter-release is more in keeping with the European model, as it values the lives of the strays and attempts to keep them alive for as long as possible.

When Prevention Fails, What?

Confronted with unwanted dogs in numbers too large to place in homes, authorities have a few options, none of which is ideal. The implementation of no-kill policies without a release program and sufficient facilities results too often in overcrowding and poor conditions for the dogs. Long-term housing in such shelters is not humane and even if conditions at kennels are decent, the environment can still be very distressful for dogs. Nor is the mass killing of healthy animals an acceptable alternative for either the dogs or canine population control. Spay/neuter/release programs spare the animals' lives. Yet, sadly, there are multiple examples for which none of these options is in the dog's interest. As the reader may recall, life on the streets can be brutal. If there are not sufficient food resources and open areas without automobiles, release can be a fate worse than death, especially for dogs relinquished from homes and not used to surviving on their own. Effective management of the canine population is the far, far better alternative.

At present, euthanasia remains the number-one killer of all companion animals, including dogs.[77] In the EU, it remains a common practice to euthanize healthy stray, lost, or abandoned dogs after a specified holding period, usually between seven and fifteen days. A few member states do not even specify a minimum time frame at all, an omission that could result in the immediate euthanasia of lost dogs. Nothing in the ECPPA forbids these killings, though they are supposed to be carried out humanely. Nor is there any EU prohibition on the killing of healthy dogs. Likewise, in the US, there is no such national prohibition. Indeed, as the reader may recall, approximately 1.2 million dogs who enter shelters are euthanized annually in the US.[78]

Among EU member states, there is a wider range of difference on this issue than found among US states. Unlike in the US, there are member states, nine in total, that prohibit the euthanasia of healthy dogs. One region in Spain, Catalunya, also has such a prohibition (see Table 3.3 , p. 98). In Austria, Germany, The Netherlands, and Sweden, all places where the euthanasia of healthy animals is forbidden, shelters can comfortably accommodate any lost or unwanted dogs until they can be placed with a family. However, member states with large stray populations, such as Bulgaria and Lithuania, must rely upon spay-neuter-release programs to prevent overcrowding with this prohibition in place. Italy's shelters, in the first year of the prohibition, were extremely overcrowded, an outcome resulting in the spread of disease. If conditions at shelters are such as to turn healthy dogs into diseased ones, the prohibition is not working as intended or to the benefit of dogs. In this case, the Italian Ministry of Health subsequently financed the development of a highly praised protocol for shelters.[79] In the Czech Republic, which also forbids the euthanasia of healthy dogs, there is "considerable doubt" as to the consistent application of the policy given the number of abandoned animals and the overcrowding at shelters.[80]

In the other 19 member states, the euthanasia of healthy dogs is either expressly permitted or at least, not forbidden, but there are stark differences in the scale of programs or numbers of dogs killed. In Slovakia, for example, there is a "widespread practice of exterminating stray dogs."[81] In fact, local people refer to the overcrowded, dirty kennels in Slovakia where dogs are left hungry prior to their extermination as "concentration camps for canines."[82] The conditions in shelters in Romania are no better. In an investigation, Vier Pfoten found that not one of the 50 public shelters visited conformed to the law, though some were much worse than others. Half of the shelters were overcrowded, 74 percent had food mixed with waste, 40 percent had unclean drinking water, and 53 percent mixed dogs despite health, gender, age, or aggression. In seven percent, investigators found canine corpses inside shelters and in contact with living dogs. Under a 2013 Romanian law, dogs can be killed after 14 days and almost one-third of the shelters euthanize at that point.[83] The mass euthanasia of dogs in Romania is a business with vested interests for those involved, including those who catch the strays in the first place often via brutal means. There have been trials of spay-neuter-release programs in parts of Romania, but catch-and-kill remains the dominant model.[84] In Poland, at least 75,000 dogs were killed in one year alone.[85] According to Pregowski and Wlodarczyk, Poland has more recently committed to caring for homeless dogs. However, with the standard of care not well defined, public shelters are extremely overcrowded with one infamous shelter housing 100 dogs in a single run.[86] In Cyprus, where dozens of stray dogs are found every day, approximately 20,000 healthy and unhealthy dogs will be euthanized annually "because municipal and private shelters are overcrowded and there are not sufficient resources or capacity to keep them."[87] In Spain, the scale of the killing is extraordinary as well. On the other end of the spectrum are those member states with no stray problem, such as Belgium, Denmark, Finland, and Luxembourg. Despite the lack of a prohibition on the practice, there is minimal killing of healthy dogs in such states. In between are member states such as the UK where the practice is declining but still in use. Though difficult to estimate, the RSPCA puts the number of healthy dogs euthanized at approximately 7,000 in a one-year period.[88] All told, the scale of euthanasia remains massive in several eastern and southern member states and present elsewhere as well.

While silent on the legality of euthanasia, the ECPPA requires that "only a veterinarian or another competent person" perform the killing and the individual is to ensure "the minimum of physical and mental suffering." Specifically, the method should either "cause immediate loss of consciousness and death" or "begin with the induction of deep general anesthesia."[89] Even in all of the 18 signatories, these specifications are not always met. There are serious concerns, for example, in Romania and Portugal. The latter member state delegates responsibility for collecting and euthanizing strays to localities where there is variation in treatment. In Romania, "stray animals…continue to be beaten, tortured, poisoned or killed by the tens of thousands by more or less barbaric methods in the…dog pounds…."[90] In Spain, which is not a signatory, authorities do not oversee the killing stations and as a result, there are reports of widespread use of illegal methods, such as burning and drugs that paralyze dogs so that they choke to death.[91] In the EU, there are at least 11 member states that do not require a veterinarian to euthanize an animal.[92] On the use of euthanasia on healthy dogs, then, hypothesis #11 that *the EU and its member states will prohibit the euthanasia of healthy dogs* is not sustained. Even if the nine states where it is prohibited are added to the four member states that permit the practice but have a non-existent or very low stray population, the number falls short of half the EU member states. With that said, roughly one-third of the states have a legal prohibition on the practice and the trend seems to be in that direction.

In the US, all states allow the euthanasia of healthy dogs. However, two states, California and Illinois, have passed laws that mandate pounds to release dogs to animal shelters or adoption organizations instead of euthanizing them. In fact, it is now the policy of California that no animal should be euthanized if adoption to a suitable home is possible. According to Huss, a few other states allow the transfer of animals to humane societies or rescue organizations but do not mandate it.[93] In contrast, most states routinely euthanize dogs if not claimed by an owner within five-to-seven days. Additionally, most state laws fail as well to prevent pet dogs from "convenience euthanasia," or the practice of owners euthanizing dogs because they no longer want them. Delaware's law, which defines cruelty to include "unnecessary" killing, should protect dogs from this practice, but state laws elsewhere either expressly permit such killings or fail to prohibit them effectively. Clearly, hypothesis #4 that *neither the US government nor American states will prohibit the euthanasia of healthy dogs, instead leaving the prerogative to individual owners and shelters* is upheld. What is more, only three US states require a veterinarian to euthanize a dog, though most others, or 35, require the direct or indirect supervision of a veterinarian.[94] In comparison to the EU, the US still has more lax regulation in this area.

While there is consistency with the American model legislatively in the vast majority of states, there are some signs of change. Compared to the 1970s, the number of dogs euthanized has been substantially reduced and over the last decade, there has been a concerted effort among animal advocacy groups to reduce the euthanasia rate of "healthy and treatable companion animals" in the US.[95] The efforts to transport dogs from southern shelters, where euthanasia rates are high, to northern ones, where they will be adopted, are also aimed at minimizing the number of healthy animals killed. According to Grimm, there are "more than 500 cities and towns in the US that are No Kill or approaching" that status.[96] However, all but two state governments have yet to legislate policies in promotion of No Kill.

Conclusion

For those canines who do not have a human companion, it is not so clear that the EU is the better place to be. There is a greater problem with the management of the canine population in the EU, but there are of course persistent concerns with this issue in areas of the US as well. In both, non-profit organizations attempt to place shelter dogs in homes, often re-locating them from one region to another. However, the euthanasia of these unwanted friends remains a common practice in both the US and EU. As a result, the hypothesis that neither the US government nor American states will prohibit the euthanasia of healthy dogs is confirmed, but the hypothesis that the EU and its member states will prohibit it, is not. To be sure, there is more legal progress in the EU toward other alternatives than in the US, as nine EU member states and one region in Spain prohibit the euthanasia of healthy dogs. It should be noted as well that there have been inroads in the US toward no-kill or low-kill shelters, but not as a result of changes in law. Yet the number of stray dogs is not nearly as large in the US as in the EU either.

The experiences of select EU member states, mainly in north-central Europe, demonstrate that practices of highly responsible care can work to prevent a population of unwanted canine friends. In parts of the US as well, such as the Northeast, there is a minimal problem with unwanted dogs. However, in many EU member states and large sections of the US, shelters are at or above capacity. One contributor to an "unwanted" population is abandonment, which can possibly be discouraged by requirements to permanently identify and register dogs. As expected, the EU and its member states are much more likely to mandate those steps than the US, where neither the US government nor states require permanent markers on dogs. In the EU, though, abandonment has been a bigger problem than in the US. Relinquishment of dogs is the most direct source of the problem in the US, a fact indicative of poor screening of potential caretakers and the casual acquisition of puppies. In the EU, where there has been more reluctance to sterilize dogs even in cultures where canine roaming and abandonment are common, shelter populations are additionally fueled by unplanned litters. There has been more focus and accompanying success at increasing sterilization rates for companion animals in the US. Critics of this American approach argue that relinquishment, not the lack of sterilization, is the driver of unwanted canine populations. While EU member states have lower rates of sterilization for companion animals, many are experimenting with spay/neuter-release programs for free-roaming canines as a means to slow population increases. Unfortunately, neither the EU nor the US has found the proper formula to minimize an "unwanted" canine population, but there are sub-units or states that have had success at this goal.

The scale of commercial breeding is larger in the US than EU. Somewhat true to expectations, the US government and American states have lax regulations on commercial breeders. However, close to a majority of states have passed stronger regulations in this area and others are considering changes. The regulations are not as comprehensive as those found in EU member states, as they do not typically restrict the number of breedings for a female dog, prohibit the breeding of defects, or mandate the education and training of personnel in breeding operations. They have established standards of care and systems of licensing and inspections for large-scale breeders at least. Similarly, the expectation that the EU and its member states will strictly regulate the commercial breeding of dogs was validated but with exceptions. A majority of EU member states have such regulations. However, there are member states that have lax regulations. In neither the US nor EU are there central regulations with reliable enforcement so as to prevent abusive practices. Given improving laws at the state level, the situation is not as dire as it once was in the US. Because puppies are sold across national and state lines, uniform regulations are more likely to eliminate rogue operators who take advantage of one place's weak standards. In these areas, the EU has the potential to make protections universal and therefore more effective, while the US is more likely to keep regulation at the state level with minimal national standards. With that said, there are currently just too many exceptions to validate the American and European approaches without qualifications in the area of commercial breeding.

Notes

1. Kim Kavin, *The Dog Merchants: Inside the Big Business of Breeders, Pet Stores, and Rescuers* (New York: Pegasus Books, 2016), 72.
2. HSUS (The Humane Society of the United States), "101 Puppy Mills: A Sampling of Problem Puppy Mills in the United States," May 2014. http://www.humanesociety.org/assets/pdfs/pets/puppy_mills/101-puppy-mills-report-2014.pdf, accessed September 14, 2014.
3. Four Paws International, "Puppy Trade in Europe: Research on the Impact of Illegal businesses on the market, on consumers, on the one-health concept and on animal welfare,"

November 2013. http://www.vier.pfoten-eu/files/EPO/materials_conf/Puppy_Trade-in_Europe/REPORT_EUROPEAN_PUPPY_TRADE.pdf, accessed September 17, 2014.

4. Jason Overdorf, "Europe Has a Puppy Mafia Problem," *Global Post*, August 7, 2014. http://www.globalpost.com/dispatch/news/regions/europe/germany/140806/europe-germany-puppy-mafia-animal-smuggling, accessed June 3, 2015.
5. HSUS, "A Horrible Hundred Problem Puppy Mills in the United States," May 2013, 4. http://www.humanesociety.org/assets/pdfs/pets/puppy_mills/100-puppy-mills-report.pdf#Top, accessed June 2, 2015.
6. *Ibid.*, 9.
7. See Animal and Plant Health Inspection Service (APHIS), "Fact Sheet, Animal Care—Questions and Answers: Regulation of Dog/Cat Breeders and Dealers," February 2014. http://www.aphis.usda.gov/publications/animal_welfare/content/printable_version/faq_animal_dealers.pdf, accessed September 16, 2014. APHIS, part of the U.S. Department of Agriculture, is responsible for the enforcement of these regulations.
8. U.S. Department of Agriculture, APHIS, "Regulatory Compliance for Commercial Dog Breeders: Introductory Course," April 25, 2016. https://www.aphis.usda.gov/aphis/ourfocus/animalwelfare/caw/education+and+training/ct_commercial_dog_breeders, accessed June 14, 2018.
9. Susan Hunter and Richard A. Brisbin, Jr., *Pet Politics: The Political and Legal Lives of Cats, Dogs, and Horses in Canada and the United States* (West Lafayette, Indiana: Purdue University Press, 2016), 209, 208.
10. USDA—Office of Inspector General, "Animal and Plant Health Inspection Service Animal Care Program Inspections of Problematic Dealers," Audit Report 33002–4-SF (Washington, DC: May 2010). https://www.usda.gov/oig/webdocs/33002-4-SF.pdf, accessed June 14, 2018.
11. ASPCA, "Laws that Protect Dogs in Puppy Mills." http://www.aspca.org/fight-cruelty/puppy-mills/laws-protect-dogs-puppy-mills, accessed September 16, 2014.
12. See Alberto Laddomada, European Commission, "EU Legislation on Dogs and Cats." http://ec.europa.eu/dgs/health_consumer/information_sources/docs/28102013-7-aladdomada_en.pdf, accessed September 17, 2014. In his presentation, Laddomada includes the text of the Communication from the Commission to the European Parliament, the Council and the European Economic and Social Committee on the European Union Strategy for the Protection and Welfare of Animals 2012–2015.
13. About North Dakota, see Kalsey Stults, "Commercial dog breeding bill would impact puppy mills in the state, if passed by legislators," *The Dickinson Press*, February 6, 2017. http://www.thedickinsonpress.com/news/4213211-commercial-dog-breeding-bill-would-impact-puppy-mills-state-if-passed-legislators, accessed June 12, 2018. On Montana and South Carolina, respectively, see Ariana Lake, "There are no Montana laws for dog-breeding operations," *WorldNow*, July 28, 2016. http://cordilleramontana.worldnow.com/story/32562967/there-are-no-montana-laws-for-dog-breeding-operations, accessed June 12, 2018; and "Lax Laws make South Carolina a magnet for puppy mills," *WMBF News*, September 22, 2014. http://www.wmbfnews.com/story/26596694/lax-laws-allow-breeders-to-turn-south-carolina-into-a-puppy-mill-magnet, accessed June 12, 2018.
14. HSUS, "101 Puppy Mills."

15. See HSUS, "Estimate of USDA Licensed Breeders 2014: Based on Data published by the United States Department of Agriculture (USDA)," January 2014. http://www.humanesociety.org/assets.pdfs/pets/puppy_mills/map_USDA_licensed_pm.pdf, accessed September 16, 2014.
16. Four Paws International, "Puppy Trade in Europe."
17. Kavin, *The Dog Merchants*, 75.
18. *Ibid.*, 74.
19. Amy Jones, "Puppy Dog Lies," *The Sun*, April 29, 2017. http://www.thesun.co.uk/news/3440525/sick-pet-car-boot-sales-dogs-crammed-cages-filth-smugglers/, accessed June 14, 2017.
20. Overdorf, "Europe Has a Puppy Mafia."
21. Coe, J. B., Young I., Lambert K., Dysart L., Noqueira Borden L., and Rajić A., "A Scoping Review of Published Research on the Relinquishment of Companion Animals," *Journal of Applied Animal Welfare Science* 17:3 (2014): 253–273. This article provides an overview of studies in this area. For examples of individual studies, see Shor, E. R., Petersen, C. L., and Douglas, D. K., "Moving as a Reason for Pet Relinquishment: A Closer Look," *Journal of Applied Animal Welfare Science* 6:1 (2003): 39–52; Kwan, J., and Bain, M., "Owner Attachment and Problem Behaviours Related to Relinquishment and Training Techniques of Dogs," *Journal of Applied Animal Welfare Science* 16:2 (2013): 168–183. For a study about the UK, see Diesel, G., Brodbelt, D., and Pfeiffer, D. U., "Characteristics of Relinquished Dogs and their Owners at 14 Rehoming Centers in the UK," *Journal of Applied Animal Welfare Science* 13:1 (2010): 15–30.
22. American Animal Welfare Society, "Summary of the Projects of the National Council of Pet Population Study and Policy." http://www.americananimalwelfare.com/overpopulation.html, accessed August 26, 2016.
23. Oli Smith, "Healthy Dogs having to be killed by Councils struggling to cope with dumped Pooches," *Express UK*, October 2, 2015. http://www.express.co.uk/news/uk/609459/dogs-dumped-Scottish-streets-Britain-abandoned-pet-crisis-put-down, accessed August 26, 2016.
24. Eleanor Beardsley, "In France, The (Abandoned) Dog Days of Summer," *National Public Radio*, July 11, 2012. http://www.npr.org/2012/07/11/156609037/in-france-the-abandoned-dog-days-of-summer, accessed August 26, 2016.
25. L. Boitani, F. Francisci, P. Ciucci, and G. Andreoli, "Population biology and ecology of feral dogs in central Italy," in James Serpell, ed., *Domestic Dog: Its Evolution, Behavior and Interactions with People* (New York: Cambridge University Press, 1995), 232.
26. See Viktoriya Gueseva, "Dog Ownership through the Eyes of a Stray Dog: Property Rights and the Stray Dog Population," University of Colorado, Boulder, 2013. http://scholar.colorado.edu/egi/viewcontent.cgi?article=1565&context=hone_theses, accessed June 20, 2015; and Louisa Tasker, on behalf of the World Society for the Protection of Animals (WSPA) and the Royal Society for the Prevention of Cruelty to Animals (RSPCA), "Report—Stray Animal Control Practices (Europe): An Investigation of Stray Dog and Cat Practices across Europe" (March 2007): 22. http://www.fao.org/fileadmin/user_upload/animalwelfare/WSPA_RSPCA International Stray Control Practices in Europe 2006_2007.pdf, accessed September 17, 2014.

27. *Ibid*. This report cites the following seven countries as not having a stray population: Austria, Belgium, Denmark, Finland, Germany, the Netherlands, and Sweden. The eighth country is Luxembourg. See Docs4Dogs, "The Situation in Luxembourg," Europa Guantanamo For Strays. http://www.aerztefuertiere.de/index.php?option=com_content&view=article&id=122:luxembourg&catid=137&Itemid=587&showall=1&limitstart=&lang=en, accessed June 1, 2015. For estimate, see ESDAW (European Society for Dogs and Animal Welfare), "The Management of Strays—in Europe." http://www.esdaw/eu/the-management-of-strays.html, accessed June 1, 2015.
28. For Bucharest estimate, see Eva Voslářová and Annamaria Passantino, "Stray Dog and Cat Laws and Enforcement in Czech Republic and Italy," *Ann 1st Super Sanitá* 48:1 (2012): 98. For estimated population in Italy and UK, see "Statistics on Dogs," Carodog. http://www.carodog.eu/statistics-on-cats-and -dogs/, accessed June 11, 2018. For UK, also see Adam Withnall, "Haunting Images Lay Bare Britain's 'Invisible' Stray Dog Problem," *The Independent*, October 27, 2014.
29. On Detroit, see Mark Binelli, "City of Strays: Detroit's Epidemic of 50,000 Abandoned Dogs," *Rolling Stone*, March 20, 2012. http://www.rollingstone.com/culture/news/city-of-strays-detroits-epidemic-of-50-0000wild-dogs20120320, accessed September 16, 2014. Also see Poppy Harlow and Sheila Steffan, "Detroit Grapples with Stray Dog Epidemic," CNN, 29 August 2013. http://www.cnn.com/2013/08/29/us/michigan-detroit-stray-dogs, accessed September 16, 2014. An animal advocacy group, the World Animal Awareness Society launched the American Strays Project, which has used volunteers to gather data about the number of strays. Beginning with Detroit, it seeks to gain an accurate description of the free-roaming canine population. For its estimate, see its website: http://www.wa2s.org/american-strays.html, accessed September 16, 2014.
30. MaryAnn Mott, "U.S. Facing Feral-Dog Crisis," *National Geographic News*, August 21, 2003. http://news.nationalgeographic.com/news/2003/08/0821_030821_straydogs.html, accessed June 1, 2015.
31. On impossibility, see ASPCA, "Pet Statistics," http://www.aspca.org/about-us/faq/pet-statistics, accessed September 16, 2014.
32. See Will Doig, "The Secret Lives of Feral Dogs," *Salon*, January 14, 2012. http://www.salon.com/2012/01/14/the_secret_lives_of_feral_dogs/, accessed June 1, 2015.
33. Thomas Hobbes, Chapter XIII—"Of the Natural Condition of Mankind Concerning their Felicity and Misery," *Leviathan* (originally published 1651). http://www.bartleby.com/34/5/13.html, accessed June 15, 2015.
34. Tasker, on behalf of WSPA and RSPCA, "Report," 4.
35. Alan M. Beck, *The Ecology of Stray Dogs: A Study of Free-Ranging Urban Animals* (Purdue University Press, 1973), 35. http://docs.lib.purdue.edu/purduepress_ebooks/3, accessed June 1, 2015.
36. ESDAW, "The Management of Strays."
37. Doig, "Secret Lives."
38. Mott, "U.S. Facing Feral Dog Crisis."
39. Doig, "Secret Lives." On Romania, see BBC News Europe, "Romania Campaign to Kill Stray Dogs after Boy's Death," September 9, 2013. http://www.bbc.com/news/world-europe-24015166, accessed 16 September 2014. In Slovakia, one town mayor "caused

outrage by urging Romanies to help him deal with the stray dog problem—he said they were welcome to eat them free of charge." See Daniela Lazarová, "Czech Volunteers Help to Save Stray Dogs in Slovakia," Radio Praha, October 13, 2011. http://www.radio.cz/en/section/panorama/czech-volunteers-help-save-stray-dogs-in-slovakia, accessed September 17, 2014.

40. Angela K. Fournier and E. Scott Geller, "Behavior Analysis of Companion-Animal Overpopulation: A Conceptualization of the Problem and Suggestions for Intervention," *Behavior and Social Issues* 13:1 (Spring/Summer 2004): 53.
41. *Ibid.*
42. Francesca Mondelli, Emanuela Prato Previde, Marina Verga, and Paola Valsecchi, "The Bond that Never Developed: Adoption and Relinquishment of Dogs in a Rescue Shelter," *Journal of Applied Animal Welfare Science* 7:4 (February 2004): 253–266.
43. FEDIAF European Pet Food Industy, "Facts and Figures 2014." http://www.fediaf.org/facts-figures/, accessed August 26, 2016.
44. Andy Kiersz, "Here's the Official Map of Cat States vs. Dog States," *Business Insider*, July 11, 2014. http://www.businessinsider.com/cat-and-dog-ownership-maps-2014-7, accessed August 28, 2016.
45. RSPCA, "Welfare Indicator: The number of non-microchipped cats and dogs taken into RSPCA care," *Measuring Animal Welfare in the UK 2005–2009*, 70.
46. *Ibid.* Also see Tasker, on behalf of WSPA and RSPCA, "Report," 28.
47. Voslářová and Passantino, "Stray Dog and Cat Laws," 101.
48. For Germany, see "National Legislation," Carodog. http://carodog.eu/national-legislation, accessed June 2, 2015. On Estonia, see "Estonia has over hundred useless pet registers," *Postimees in English*, July 15, 2014. http://www.news.postimees.ee/2857815/estonia-has-over-hundred-useless-pet-registers, accessed June 2, 2015.
49. Hana Müllerová, "Animals Finally Above Objects and Stricter Criminalization of Cruelty: Some Insights in Czech Animal Legislation," *Derecho Animal Archive Papers*, March 20, 2012. http://papers.ssrn.com/so13/papers.cfm?abstract_id=2236441, accessed June 2, 2015.
50. ASPCA, "Pet Statistics."
51. Elizabeth A. Clancy and Andrew N. Rowan, "Companion Animal Demographics in the United States: A Historical Perspective," in Deborah J. Salem and Andrew N. Rowan, eds., *The State of the Animals II* (Washington, DC: Humane Society Press, 2003), 9.
52. The study was conducted by Linda Lord, et al. and was published in the Journal of the American Veterinary Medical Association in 2010. For more about the study and more statistics on microchips, see "Microchips Result in High Rate of Return of Shelter Animals to Owners," *Ohio State University Research News*. http://researchnews.osu.edu/archive/shelterchip.htm, accessed June 2, 2015.
53. Found Animals, "Microchip Policy Overview," May 2014. http://www.foundanimals.org/docs/pdfs/pet-microchipping-policy-2014.pdf, accessed June 2, 2015.
54. Dvm360.com staff, "More Pet Owners Choosing to Microchip their Pets," *Veterinary Economics*, November 9, 2011. The estimate is from the American Pet Products Association.
55. Clancy and Rowan, "Companion Animal Demographics," 14; and Rebecca J. Huss, "Rescue Me: Legislating Cooperation Between Animal Control Authorities and Rescue Organizations," *Connecticut Law Review* 39 (2007): 2068.

56. For discussion of the health effects of sterilization and review of the limited research in this area, see Martha Schindler Connors, "Spay/Neuter Alternatives: Weighing the Options of Sterilization," *The Bark* (Fall 2014). http://thebark.com/content/spayneuter-alternatives, accessed June 2, 2015.
57. Fournier and Geller, "Behavior Analysis," 51.
58. Sara C. White, Ellen Jefferson, and Julie Levy, "Impact of Publicly Sponsored Neutering Programs on Animal Population Dynamics at Animal Shelters: The New Hampshire and Austin Experiences," *Journal of Applied Animal Welfare Science* 13:3 (2010): 191–212.
59. Fournier and Geller, "Behavior Analysis," 53.
60. White, Jefferson, and Levy, "Impact of Publicly Sponsored."
61. Joshua Frank, "An Interactive Model of Human and Companion Animal Dynamics: The Ecology and Economics of Dog Overpopulation and the Human Costs of Addressing the Problem," *Human Ecology* 32:1 (February 2004): 107–130.
62. Antonio DiNardo, Luca Candeloro, Christine M. Burke, and Margaret R. Slater, "Modeling the Effect of Sterilization Rate on Owned Dog Population Size in Central Italy," *Preventive Veterinary Medicine* 82:3–4 (December 2007): 308–313.
63. M. V. Root Kustritz, "Effects of Surgical Sterilization on Canine and Feline Health and on Society," *Reproduction in Domestic Animals* 57:S4 (August 2012): 214–222.
64. Cynthia Hodges, "Quick Summary of State Spay and Neuter Laws," Animal Legal and Historical Center (Michigan State University College of Law, 2010). http://www.animallawinfo.com/intro/state-spay-and-neuter-laws, accessed September 16, 2014. For number of states, see HSUS, "Humane State Rankings" (2017). https://blog.humanesociety.org/wp-content/uploads/2018/01/State-Rank-2017-MT-WY-1.pdf and https://blog.humanesociety.org/wp-content/uploads/2018/01/State-Rank-2017-AL-MO-2.pdf, accessed May 29, 2018.
65. Jenifer Champ Wallis, "Why Some Southern Dogs are heading North: The Practical Effects of Animal Population Control Legislation," *American Bar Association Animal Law Committee Newsletter* (Fall 2008).
66. For states with pet-friendly license plates, see "Animal Friendly License Plates," Doris Day Animal League, 2007. http://www.dddal.org/licenseplates, accessed September 17, 2014. Also see "Pet Friendly License Plates Support Animals," Pet-Zet, October 7, 2013. http://pet.zet.com/news/item/pet-friendly-license-plates-support-animals1, accessed September 17, 2014; and United Spay Alliance, "State License Programs." https:://www.unitedspayalliance.org/faq/state-license-plate-program, accessed June 11, 2018. For other programs, see Best Friends Animal Society, "Public Funding for Spay/Neuter," (Kanab, Utah: Best Friends Animal Society, April 2014). http://apnm.org/programs/shelter_support/docs/public funding for spay neuter.pdf, accessed September 16, 2014.
67. C. D. Watson, "The Trouble with Mandatory Spay/Neuter Laws," *Pets Adviser*, 22 April 2013. http://www.petsadviser.com/animal-welfare/mandatory-spay-neuter-laws/, accessed October 28, 2014.
68. European Parliamentary Research Service, "Stray Dogs," January 13, 2014. http://epthinktank.eu/2014/01/13/stray-dogs-2/, accessed June 2, 2015.
69. Tasker, on behalf of WSPA and RSPCA, "Report," 21. For Austria, see "National Legislation," Carodog.

70. Tasker, on behalf of WSPA and RSPCA, "Report," 29. Another study reported that 99 percent of dogs were intact in Sweden. See Gretel Torres de la Riva, et al., "Neutering Dogs: Effects on Joint Disorders and Cancers in Golden Retrievers," *PLoS ONE* 8:2 (2013): e55937. doi:10.1371/journal.pone.0055937.
71. *Ibid.*
72. Tasker, on behalf of WSPA and RSPCA, "Report," 22.
73. On Warsaw program, see Michal Piotr Pregowski and Justyna Wlodarczyk, "Four Paws of the Third Republic of Poland: A Timeline," in Michal Piotr Pregowski and Justyna Wlodarczyk, eds., *Free Market Dogs: The Human-Canine Bond in Post-Communist Poland* (West Lafayette, Indiana: Purdue University Press, 2016), xxiii. On campaigns in rural areas, see Michal Piotr Pregowski and Justyna Wlodarczyk, "Researching the Human-Canine Relationship in Democratic Poland," in Michal Piotr Pregowski and Justyna Wlodarczyk, eds., *Free Market Dogs*, 26.
74. Tasker, on behalf of WSPA and RSPCA, "Report," 22. In Poland, the central government plays a role.
75. Československý Kastračný Program, "About Us." http://www.cskp.eu/onas_en.html, accessed June 2, 2015.
76. Madlen Vasileva, "Stray Animal Situation and Management in Bulgaria," Task Force Rabies Subgroup Meeting (Plovdiv, Bulgaria: March 2011). http://ec.europa.eu/food/animal/diseases/eradication/14150320l1_Presentation%202_Stray%20animal%20situation%20and%20management%20in%20Bulgaria.pdf, accessed June 2, 2015. For discussion of effectiveness of this approach and reference to studies, see "The Catch, Neuter and Release Approach," Carodog. http://www.carodog.eu/the-catch-neuter-and-release-approach/, accessed June 2, 2015.
77. "Dog Ownership and Canine Overpopulation: A General Introduction on Implications, Effects, Problem Definition," Carodog. http://www.carodog.eu/?p=3, accessed September 16, 2014.
78. ASPCA, "Pet Statistics."
79. On early problems, see Voslářová and Passantino, "Stray Dog and Cat Laws," 100. On protocol, see "Shelters," Carodog. http://www.carodog.eu/dog-population-management-2/shelters/, accessed June 3, 2015.
80. Voslářová and Passantino, "Stray Dog and Cat Laws," 102.
81. Lazarová, "Czech Volunteers Help to Save Stray Dogs."
82. *Ibid.*
83. Carmen Arsene, *Stray Dog Situation in Romania* (National Federation for Animal Protection, August 2011). http://www.fnpa.ro/imagini/2011/09/Stray-dog-situation-in-Romania.-Animal-cruelty.pdf, accessed June 3, 2015. The original report was updated in July 2014 and the situation continues to be very poor for dogs in shelters. For the update, see https://serbiananimalsvoice.files.wordpress.com/2014/07/stray-dog-situation-in-romania-c-arsene-july-2014-english-version-1.pdf, accessed June 3, 2015.
84. *Ibid.*
85. Research and Information Support Center (RISC), U.S. Department of State, "Mitigating the Dangers of Dog Attacks in Eastern Europe," January 23, 2013. http://photos.state.gov/libraries/bulgaria/231771/PDFs/130118-OSAC straydogs.pdf, accessed June 3, 2015.

86. Pregowski and Wlodarczyk, "Researching the Human-Canine Relationship," 21–22.
87. PAWS (Protecting Animals Without Shelter), "Cyprus Stray Problem." http://www.pawscy.com/index.php/en/cyprus-stray-problem, accessed September 4, 2014.
88. RSPCA, "Welfare Indicator: The Number of Healthy Dogs being Euthanized due to Irresponsible Pet Ownership," *Measuring Animal Welfare in the UK 2005–2009*.
89. Article 11- "Killing," European Convention for the Protection of Pet Animals.
90. Arsene, "Stray Dog Situation."
91. Stray Animal Foundation, "Animal Welfare in Spain." http://www.stray-afp.org/wp-content/uploads/2012/06/Animal-welfare-in-Spain.pdf, accessed June 3, 2015.
92. Vier Pfoten, "Killing of Healthy Dogs in Europe: Legal Research" (Brussels: European Policy Office, 2014).
93. Huss, "Rescue Me," 2090.
94. American Veterinary Medical Association, "State Laws Governing Euthanasia," May 2015. https://www.avma.org/Advocacy/StateAndLocal/Documents/Euthanasia_Laws.pdf, accessed June 3, 2015.
95. On reduction in deaths, see ASPCA, "Pet Statistics;" and Peter Marsh, *Replacing Myth with Math: Using Evidence-Based Programs to Eradicate Shelter Overpopulation* (Town and Country Reprographics, 2010). On concerted efforts, see Huss, "Rescue Me," 2074–5.
96. David Grimm, *Citizen Canine: Our Evolving Relationship with Cats and Dogs* (New York: Public Affairs, 2014), 269.

Bibliography

Beck, Alan M. *The Ecology of Stray Dogs: A Study of Free-Ranging Urban Animals*. West Lafayette, Indiana: Purdue University Press, 1973.

Coe, J. B., et al. "A Scoping Review of Published Research on the Relinquishment of Companion Animals." *Journal of Applied Animal Welfare Science* 17:3 (2014): 253–273.

Diesel, G., D. Brodfelt, and D. U. Pfeiffer. "Characteristics of Relinquished Dogs and their Owners at 14 Rehoming Centers in the United Kingdom." *Journal of Applied Animal Welfare Science* 13:1 (2010): 15–30.

DiNardo, Antonio, Luca Candeloro, Christine M. Burke, and Margaret R. Slater. "Modeling the Effect of Sterilization Rate on Owned Dog Population Size in Central Italy." *Preventive Veterinary Medicine* 82: 3–4 (December 2007): 308–313.

Fournier, Angela K. and E. Scott Geller. "Behavior Analysis of Companion-Animal Overpopulation: A Conceptualization of the Problem and Suggestions for Intervention." *Behavior and Social Issues* 13:1 (Spring/Summer 2004): 51–69.

Frank, Joshua. "An Interactive Model of Human and Companion Animal Dynamics: The Ecology and Economics of Dog Overpopulation and the Human Costs of Addressing the Problem." *Human Ecology* (February 2004): 107–130.

Grimm, David. *Citizen Canine: Our Evolving Relationship with Cats and Dogs*. New York: Public Affairs, 2014.

Hodges, Cynthia. "Quick Summary of State Spay and Neuter Laws." Animal Legal and Historical Center, Michigan State University College of Law (2010). http://www.animallawinfo.com/intro/state-spay-and-neuter-laws, accessed September 16, 2014.

Hunter, Susan and Richard A. Brisbin, Jr. *Pet Politics: The Political and Legal Lives of Cats, Dogs, and Horses in Canada and the United States*. West Lafayette, Indiana: Purdue University Press, 2016.

Huss, Rebecca J. "Rescue Me: Legislating Cooperation Between Animal Control Authorities and Rescue Organizations." *Connecticut Law Review* 39 (2007): 2059–2106.

Kavin, Kim. *The Dog Merchants: Inside the Big Business of Breeders, Pet Stores, and Rescuers*. New York: Pegasus Books, 2016.

Kustritz, M. V. Root. "Effects of Surgical Sterilization on Canine and Feline Health and On Society." *Reproduction in Domestic Animals* 57:S4 (August 2012): 214–222.

Kwan, J. and M. Bain. "Owner Attachment and Problem Behaviors Related to Relinquishment and Training Techniques of Dogs." *Journal of Applied Animal Welfare Science* 16:2 (2013): 168–183.

Mondelli, Francesca, et al. "The Bond that Never Developed: Adoption and Relinquishment of Dogs in a Rescue Shelter. *Journal of Applied Animal Welfare Science* 7:4 (February 2004): 253–266.

Mott, MaryAnn. "U.S. Facing Feral-Dog Crisis." *National Geographic News* (August 21, 2003). http://news.nationalgeographic.com/news/2003/08/0821_030821_straydogs.html, accessed June 1, 2015.

Pregowski, Michal Piotr and Justyna Wlodarczyk, eds. *Free Market Dogs: The Human-Canine Bond in Post-Communist Poland*. West Lafayette, Indiana: Purdue University Press, 2016.

Salem, Deborah J. and Andrew N. Rowan, eds. *The State of the Animals II*. Washington, DC: Humane Society Press, 2003.

Serpell, James, ed. *Domestic Dog: Its Evolution, Behavior and Interactions with People*. New York: Cambridge University Press, 1995.

Shor, E. R., C. L. Petersen, and D. K. Douglas. "Moving as a Reason for Pet Relinquishment: A Closer Look." *Journal of Applied Animal Welfare Science* 6:1 (2003): 39–52.

Tasker, Louisa, on behalf of the World Society for the Protection of Animals (WSPA) and the Royal Society for the Prevention of Cruelty to Animals (RSPCA), "Report—Stray Animal Control Practices (Europe): An Investigation of Stray Dog and Cat Practices across Europe." (March 2007). http://www.fao.org/fileadmin/user_upload/animalwelfare/WSPA_RSPCA International Stray Control Practices in Europe 2006_2007.pdf, accessed September 17, 2014.

Voslářová, Eva and Annamaria Passantino. "Stray Dog and Cat Laws and Enforcement in Czech Republic and Italy." *Ann 1st Super Sanitá* 48:1 (2012): 98.

White, Sara C., Ellen Jefferson, and Julie Levy. "Impact of Publicly Sponsored Neutering Programs on Animal Population Dynamics at Animal Shelters: The New Hampshire and Austin Experiences." *Journal of Applied Animal Welfare Science* 13:3 (2010): 191–212.

Wisch, Rebecca F. "Detailed Discussion of State Dog Impound Laws." Animal Legal and Historical Center, Michigan State University College of Law (2003). http://www.animallaw.info/article/detaile-discussion-state-dog-impound-laws, accessed September 16, 2014.

· 4 ·

BETRAYAL OF TRUST

Public Policies to Prevent Common Cruelties

Although humans can betray the trust of canines in many ways, certain activities are notorious for their abuse and banality. Commercial greyhound racing, unnecessary surgeries for cosmetic reasons, and many forms of scientific experimentation are such activities and are prevalent to varying degrees in the US and EU. While comprehensive anti-cruelty statutes might apply to aspects of these activities or perhaps even to their entirety, such general statutes often exclude "accepted" uses of animals, such as experimentation, from their purview and limit themselves to "deviant" behavior. In such "accepted" areas, targeted legislation is therefore essential to protect dogs from cruelty. Otherwise, abusive and cruel acts can fall through the proverbial "legal cracks."

Given the American propensity toward laissez-faire policies, it is anticipated that commercial greyhound racing and unnecessary surgeries for cosmetic reasons will be legal. Similarly, the US government and American states are not expected to forbid scientific experiments on dogs and instead are hypothesized to have lax regulations over such experiments. In contrast, it is considered likely that the EU and its member states will prohibit commercial greyhound racing and unnecessary surgeries for cosmetic reasons and will either ban the use of dogs in scientific experiments or heavily regulate their use for the animals' benefit. These expectations will essentially be met in all areas for the EU and in the areas of experimentation and unnecessary surgeries for the US. In the area of commercial greyhound racing, however, policies in the US will not accord with these expectations.

Dogfighting is one of the most egregious betrayals of trust. Because it is a deviant and not socially accepted activity, it is legally forbidden throughout the US and EU. However, there is much variation in the specificity and comprehensiveness of statutes, the enforcement of such statutes, the penalties for their violation, and the prevalence of the activity. Given the illegal and underground nature of dogfighting, only estimates of its pervasiveness are available. A cursory review of US and EU policies is provided in this area to differentiate the treatment of a "deviant" from "accepted" use of canines and to complement the portrait of canine welfare in the US and EU.

Commercial Greyhound Racing

Greyhound racing, once a popular spectator activity, arguably is cruel and subjects its canine participants to "entire lives of pain and abuse."[1] Fortunately, the popularity of this "sport" has substantially declined in the US and EU. It is not extinct, however. Commercial tracks, with betting, remain in operation in Ireland, the UK, and the US. Although such commercial tracks have closed in Spain, greyhound racing continues in some areas and is tied into gambling.

According to Atkinson and Young, racing greyhounds confront four major types of violence: breeding, training, housing, and disposal.[2] If puppies are unsuitable for racing, they are killed or abandoned in many cases, as are the retired dogs. There are myriad examples of mass killings. In a particularly egregious case in the UK, "more than 10,000 healthy greyhounds" were "shot and buried in a mass grave in County Durham over a period of 15 years." The *Sunday Times* of London broke this story in 2006.[3] The remains of between 1,000 and 3,000 greyhounds were discovered in 2002 on the Alabama property of a former security guard for a Florida racetrack. These dogs had also been shot.[4] In a formal report, the League Against Cruel Sports estimated that approximately 1,000 greyhounds who are retired from racing each year, or about 12.5 percent of total retirees, are not re-homed and "missing." Some of these dogs are sold to university laboratories where they are "slaughtered and used ... to teach anatomy to veterinary students." The University College of Dublin admitted to purchasing 33 dogs for this purpose in 2013 and the Report asserts that approximately 550 greyhounds have been sold to laboratories in the UK for dissection since 2006.[5] Once the greyhounds are no longer fit for racing, they are discarded similarly to trash.

During their short racing lives, generally about two to three years, the dogs are treated as "expendable commodities."[6] They are fed sub-standard and cheap foods. As Atkinson and Young explain, "some low budget tracks utilize what has been termed '4-D' (dead, dying, downed, diseased) meat to minimally sustain the greyhounds' nutritional requirements and athletic bodies."[7] This food is of such a poor quality that it may lead to a skin condition of open lesions and ulcers, dubbed "Alabama rot," or "an intestinal problem referred to as 'blow-out,'" characterized by chronic vomiting and diarrhea. Approximately 15–20 percent of racing greyhounds in the US have consumed this type of meat.[8] They are also not given sufficient quantities of food. To that point, in yet another case of egregious cruelty, 37 racing dogs were more recently found dead from starvation in Florida.[9] Racing dogs are also routinely given steroids and other performance-enhancing drugs, including cocaine. Females are additionally given testosterone to block their cycles.[10]

When these dogs are not racing, they are confined 95 percent of the time or more, often in stacked cages with poor sanitary conditions. According to Schaffner, the housing is "as inhumane as" that for "chickens in factory farms."[11] When the cages are stacked, those dogs on the bottom rows "are showered with the waste of others" given the lack of proper flooring.[12] Such unsanitary conditions lead to disease and vermin. This arrangement additionally deprives the dogs of social interaction with members of their own species. The physical health of racing dogs is jeopardized on poorly maintained tracks as well. With declining revenue in this industry, poor conditions on tracks are increasingly common, leading to serious injuries, such as broken legs and other fractures. These wounded dogs are euthanized 16 percent of the time, a fact recognized by the Retired Greyhound Trust in the UK, which includes a check-off on its retirement form for "'injury not treated on economic grounds' as a reason to euthanize a dog."[13] To understate the matter greatly, these dogs are not treated as sentient beings but are instead subjected to a life of physical and psychological abuse.

Trending Illegal, but Not Quite There

Consistent with the American model, it was anticipated that the US government and American states would not prohibit commercial greyhound racing. In the case of the US government, that is true. There is no national prohibition against the commercial racing of dogs. Nor is there any specific legislation to protect racing dogs. However, the hypothesis is not valid at the state level, as 40/50 states prohibit the activity. In four additional states, Connecticut, Kansas, Oregon, and Washington, all racing tracks are closed but there has not yet been a prohibitory statute. Greyhound racing continues in only six states, Alabama, Arkansas, Florida, Iowa, Texas, and West Virginia, with 18 tracks in operation. However, citizens in Florida voted to make the activity illegal in November 2018. As a result, two-thirds of the tracks currently in operation will shut down and the number of racing dogs will be substantially reduced. Florida, by far, had the biggest industry, with 12 tracks.[14] In that state alone, there were an estimated 7,000 dogs housed in track kennel compounds. There were 9,488 dogs registered to race in the US in 2016. That number is down from 27,142 in 2002.[15] Iowa's lone track is also facing an uncertain future. Despite these holdouts, 90 percent of American states or 45, with the addition of Florida, do not conform with the American model in this area. As a result, hypothesis # 5, *the US Government and American states will not prohibit greyhound racing*, is not validated.

Given the European persuasion, it was expected that the EU, to the extent it has jurisdiction, and its member states would prohibit commercial greyhound racing. The legality of this activity is left up to member states. Consistent with expectations, 26/28 EU member states prohibit commercial greyhound racing. The hypothesis is thus confirmed. Only the UK and Ireland have commercial dog racing. There are 29 tracks currently in operation in the UK, 22 of which are licensed at the national level, two in Northern Ireland which are regulated by the Irish Coursing Club, and nine "flappers" or independent tracks. The latter are under local jurisdictions only. Over the last several years, at least 14 tracks have closed operations in the UK and revenue is down 43 percent since 2009. There were approximately 7,520 dogs racing on the licensed tracks in 2013.[16] In Ireland, where the industry receives government subsidies, there are 16 tracks in operation with approximately 4,280 dogs in the racing pool.[17]

Although these two EU member states have failed to prohibit commercial dog racing, both have passed some legislation with the intention to protect greyhounds. In England, statutory regulations were instituted in 2010. However, the regulations are "limited in scope," do "very little to improve dog welfare," and "leave the industry to regulate itself." To be sure, these regulations introduced some improvements, such as the microchipping of all dogs and the collection of injury data, but they failed to address critical issues, such as over-breeding, placement of retired dogs, and the publication of injury data.[18] There are no specific laws in Northern Ireland, which has two tracks. In the Republic of Ireland, the government passed in 2011 the Welfare of Greyhounds Act, which established standards for breeding, operations, and general welfare requirements for housing, transport and record-keeping. However, the semi-state body, the Irish Greyhound Board, is responsible for *both* regulating and promoting the industry, a dual charge that can result in weak enforcement.[19] The enactment of legislation and regulations to protect greyhounds is consistent with the European model, but the leniency of this legislation gives it a strong "American" flavor.

It should be noted as well that greyhound racing, though not the commercial variety, is practiced in other EU member states. There is a significant problem in Spain, where thousands of Galgos or Spanish greyhounds, are bred for hunting and to win the national coursing championship. These dogs are kept in extremely poor conditions, in many cases worse ones than those of the commercially-raced dogs, and are discarded at the end of the coursing season. It is estimated that approximately 30,000 Galgos are killed each year.[20] In other EU member states, such as Germany and the Netherlands, clubs race dogs, but with no wagering. Absent the commercial element and with no wagering, there is much less risk of systematic abuse. The financial incentives are more likely to lead to the objectification of the dogs. Some member states, such as Croatia, nonetheless stipulate in law that dogs cannot be raced on hard surfaces. Such regulations serve to protect all dogs who are required to partake in this activity. The overwhelming majority of EU member states have policies and practices consistent with the European model on this matter, but the exceptions, though small in number, are significant. Still, hypothesis #12, *The EU, to the extent it has jurisdiction, and its member states will prohibit commercial greyhound racing*, is validated.

Scientific Experimentation

The American and European models are anticipated to yield vastly different policies about the use of canines in scientific research. It was hypothesized that the US government and American states will not prohibit scientific experiments on dogs and will have lax regulations over any such experiments, while the EU and its member states will either ban the use of dogs in scientific experiments or heavily regulate their use for the animals' benefit. The evidence supports these hypotheses. While the EU does not prohibit experiments on dogs, it has much tougher regulations than the US does. Although dogs comprise a small percentage of the total animals used in testing, the whole numbers are not insignificant. In 2016, nearly 61,000 dogs lived in medical and scientific research facilities in the US and according to the European Commission, 17,896 dogs were used for scientific experimentation in the EU from 2009 to 2013.[21] Statistics for Europe were previously published every three years, but under the requirements of the new Directive, they will not be reported again until November 2019. Among EU member states, for the last period reported, France, Germany, and the UK used the greatest number of animals, including dogs.[22]

Historically, as Cunniff and Osenkowski detail, "Dogs have been used extensively in many areas of research, including the cardiovascular, respiratory, and circulatory systems; emphysema; … the gastrointestinal system and the effects of radiation; diabetes; and testing for toxicity levels of pharmaceutical drugs. Dogs are also favored as experimental subjects in the study of trauma and shock, including post-shock infections, and in research on the skeletal system, such as repairing fractured bones, re-attaching limbs, and developing artificial limbs."[23] In layman's terms, as the Animal Legal Defense Fund highlights, dogs have been subjected to "burning, poisoning, starving, forced smoking, mutilating, blinding, electrocuting, drowning, and dissecting without painkillers" for decades.[24] Clearly, regulation over the use of dogs in scientific experimentation is necessary to minimize pain, injury, fear, distress, and discomfort and to ensure that dogs have the opportunity to express natural behaviors.

Short of a prohibition on the use of dogs, which neither the US nor the EU has, what regulations would be protective of the animals? Just as for commercial breeders, explicit standards of care that address the housing, health, nutritional, exercise, and social needs of dogs are essential. Protective regulations would also have strict protocols in place to ensure that experiments are conducted only when absolutely necessary and for the purposes of an important health need. If an alternative means to achieve the scientific objective exists, then permission for the experiment would be denied. Subjecting dogs to tests for cosmetics, weaponry, or convenience products would be prohibited. In addition, a strong regulatory framework would include requirements for the use of anesthetics for surgeries and place limitations on the number of times any given animal had to be subjected to such painful procedures. Veterinary supervision and approval would obviously be included in the regulatory mandates as well. Because it is considered especially egregious to subject former companion animals to scientific experimentation, protective policies would prevent that outcome. All dogs used in research would be specifically bred for that purpose. Protective legislation would promote or mandate the placement of these dogs in homes after the completion of their service in laboratories provided that they are in good health and pose no risk to the public.

EU Law: Centralization and Uniform Standards

All EU member states must comply with *supra*-national guidelines for scientific experimentation on animals. In Directive #63 of 2010, which came into full effect on January 1, 2013, the Council of the EU and Parliament updated requirements in this area. Prior to this update, the EU, as a signatory to the European Convention for the Protection of Vertebrate Animals Used for Experimental and Other Scientific Purposes, agreed to the guidelines therein for all member states. The updated Directive built upon the framework established in the Convention, strengthening the protections in many areas but arguably weakening them in a few others. In the Directive's Preamble or justification, it highlights the significant disparities that existed among member states in this area, with some providing "high" levels of protection for animals and others ensuring only "the minimum" required under the European Convention. The Directive seeks to rectify that situation with uniform standards.

In most EU member states, the Directive strengthens regulations for animal testing. Member states had to incorporate the new standards into national law by the end of 2012. In some cases, such as that of Poland, the requisite new law, even if a bit late in coming, introduced significant improvements for the plight of laboratory animals. However, the Directive, in its quest for uniformity, forbids member states from enacting regulations that are more protective of animals unless they were already in place in 2010. In the UK, advocates of animals expressed concern that the Directive might entice lawmakers to dilute standards in areas such as cage sizes and the use of feral animals.[25] Because the UK had stricter regulations in place in 2010, its Parliament has the choice to retain those protections or amend them to comply with the new standards.

Such a choice might not be possible in Italy. In that country, lawmakers passed stringent regulations on the use of laboratory animals after the publication of the 2010 Directive. The Italian law banned the breeding of cats and dogs for laboratory use and forbade testing them unless mandatory for new drugs to be approved or aimed at improving human health. The regulations also require the use of anesthesia in all experiments causing pain to the animal. Since these regulations were not in place in 2010, their legality is in dispute and the subject of fierce debate.[26] In 2017, the European Commission had sent a reasoned opinion to Italy requiring the member state to change its law to comply with the Directive. If the Italian authorities fail to act within two months, the case will most likely be referred to the EU Court of Justice.[27] Advocates of the Italian regulations stress the effective date of the Directive, January 1, 2013, not the date of its publication in 2010. The Italian regulations had been legislated before 2013. Whatever the outcome of the dispute about their legality, it is clear that member states will not be able to strengthen their legal protections of laboratory animals after January 1, 2013. In essence, the Directive creates both a "floor," below which standards cannot go, *and* a "ceiling," which caps the available protections for animals in the name of uniformity.

This Directive, then, establishes the guidelines in this area for all EU member states. Grounded in the three R's, replacement, reduction and refinement, it seeks to reduce the number of animals used in research. To that end, the Directive specifically lists the purposes for which animals can be used. The list is rather comprehensive, though, as it includes "basic research," "forensic inquiries," some educational purposes, and broad wording for the avoidance, diagnosis, and treatment of disease including related drugs, foods, and products. Importantly, it omits cosmetics testing, which is banned in the EU, and military weapons testing, which several EU member states explicitly prohibit in national legislation.[28]

If alternative means exist to achieve an experiment's goals, they are to be invoked with the animals spared. The Directive stresses the need for competent authorities to enforce this principle, which was also included in the European Convention. Despite its inclusion in that earlier agreement, there has not been universal adherence to this critical requirement. For example, in the UK, as Creamer explains, there was no "workable framework and mechanism" in law "to ensure that animal tests" were "replaced by non-animal alternatives."[29] The new Directive compels the UK to remedy this situation. It also demands that the least number of animals necessary be used in research and more specifically, that those used have the lowest capacity to experience pain and suffering.[30] As a result, the EU regulations are protective in their call for replacements to animal experimentation if possible and at least have some restrictions on their purposes.

For those animals used in experiments, the Directive details requirements to ensure that animals are provided with sanitary accommodation and care appropriate to health and well-being. For all animals, there is to be provision of sufficient space so as to ensure the "expression of a wide range" of normal behavior. Animals are to have some control and choice over their environment to reduce stress and there are to be "enrichment techniques in place," such as physical exercise.[31] When possible, dogs are to be provided with outside runs and are not to be single-housed for more than four hours at a time. Space allocations are tailored to beagles, with the stipulation that larger breeds be given more room. Based on their weight, dogs are given between one-half and four square meters per animal (or 19.5 square inches and 4.33 square yards). Nursing dogs must have sufficient space to remove themselves from their pups. Although the minimum enclosures are by no means spacious, they ensure some freedom of movement. Importantly, the Directive mandates that member states conduct inspections, an "appropriate portion" of which are surprise ones, to ensure compliance. Here again, the EU directive is imposing regulations for the benefit of the animals.

Additionally, the Directive requires the use of anesthesia and pain killers for the performance of procedures unless "inappropriate." While anesthesia can be deemed inappropriate if "incompatible with the purposes of the procedure," there is arguably some limitation on this exception. In Article 14, the Directive unequivocally states, "Procedures that involve serious injuries that may cause severe pain shall not be carried out without anesthesia."[32] Hence, exceptions for incompatibility apply only to less painful experiments. There is no such unequivocal statement made in the European Convention.[33] At the conclusion of the experiment, a veterinarian is to decide if the animal will remain in moderate or severe pain, suffering or distress, or sustain lasting harm. In those cases, the animal is to be euthanized. Otherwise, the animal is to receive care and accommodation appropriate to ensure health. Some animals may be "re-used," but only if their health has been restored, the severity of previous and further procedures was not and will not be greater in intensity than "moderate," and a veterinarian consents in light of the lifetime experience of the animal.[34] There is also an option to re-home laboratory animals, who are in good health, provided that there is no risk to the public. However, such a practice is not mandatory. According to a British Union for the Abolition of Vivisection (BUAV) investigation in 2013, one laboratory in the UK killed beagle puppies and dogs "because it was easier than finding them homes" despite the EU Directive. Many of the dogs killed were never even used in experiments, but were deemed "surplus."[35]

Only those dogs specifically bred for experimentation and research are to be used in laboratories. Stray and feral animals are not to be used unless there is "an essential need for studies concerning the health and welfare of the animals or serious threats to the environment or to human or animal health" AND "there is scientific justification to the effect that the purpose of the procedure can be achieved only by the use of a stray or feral animal."[36] Because the European Convention does not allow exceptions for the use of stray dogs and cats, the BUAV expressed concerns and lobbied for an unconditional ban on the use of strays in the UK. A spokesman for the Home Office considered such legislation unnecessary, noting that "the possibility of exemption is extremely narrow and unlikely."[37] Those dogs bred for research, laboratory dogs, are to be marked when weaned and records are to be maintained for each individual dog. Only those dogs are to be used for experimentation. While there are concerns that the EU Directive does not go far enough to prevent experimentation on dogs, it unquestionably provides stronger protection than that found in the US and is protective enough to validate hypothesis #13 that *the EU and its member states will either ban the use of dogs in scientific experiments or will heavily regulate their use for the animals' benefit.*

US Law: Minimal Protection

In the US, the principal source of regulation for animals used in research is the AWA. When passed in 1966, its main goals were "(1) to ensure humane care and treatment of animals in facilities; (2) to ensure humane treatment of animals while in transport; [and] (3) to address pet theft and black market sales of animals to research facilities."[38] Unlike the EU Directive, this law does not impose any meaningful restrictions on the purposes of experiments. There is no national ban on the use of dogs and other animals in cosmetics or weapons testing, though some cosmetic companies have stopped using them. Additionally, only four states, California, New Jersey, New York, and Virginia, ban animal testing for cosmetics when an alternative exists.[39]

To understate the matter greatly, the AWA's humane care and treatment requirement is weak. Researchers are required under the law to "minimize" pain to animals, not eliminate it. As Favre highlights, the definition of "minimize" is elusive and therefore not a strong source of protection.[40] The statute mandates recovery time for animals who have undergone surgery and the use of anesthetics and other painkillers, but creates an exception if doing so would impede the objectives of the scientific experiment.[41] Those objectives take precedence over the animal's suffering. The law dictates that alternatives to animal experimentation be considered, but, unlike the EU Directive, does not demand their adoption if available. In these areas, the AWA provides lax protections and very few states have placed additional limitations on the purposes of experiments.

In the case of dogs, the AWA affords some meagre additional protections, but fails to deliver them given loopholes and poor enforcement. More specifically, the AWA instructs the USDA to issue minimum exercise requirements, but the USDA has delegated this task to oversight committees at research facilities and created a ready loophole for them. "If dogs who are housed in a group where the enclosure is large enough to provide a single dog with the required exercise area as determined by a veterinarian, the enclosure is deemed sufficient without additional exercise opportunities for dogs."[42] Clarifying the implications of this loophole, Wagman and Liebman explain, "In the case of a dog two feet in length, the research facility would need to provide him only 6.25 square feet…of space, in order to avoid having to provide him with 'additional' exercise."[43] Similar to the EU, the US regulations ensure that there is "sufficient space to allow each dog and cat to turn about freely, to stand, sit, and lie in a comfortable, normal position and to walk in a normal manner;…."[44] They do not, however, satisfy the exercise needs of most dogs. Nor does the US law authorize the USDA to prescribe these minimally humane housing standards "during actual research."[45] It is also common practice to remove the vocal chords of dogs for the comfort of the staff.[46] Although all states have anti-cruelty statutes, they routinely contain exceptions for the "most common commercial and recreational uses of animals," including scientific experimentation.[47] According to the National Anti-Vivesection Society, eight states imply or affirm that cruelty statutes can apply to research facilities for the ways animals are treated when they are not partaking in a sanctioned research protocol[48] (see Table 4.1). Such cases, however, are difficult to bring and rare. In sum, the US government has fairly lax standards of care given the loopholes and states have not supplemented them.

Table 4.1: US States with Rules Applying to Animal Research.

	Prohibits Pound Seizure	Prohibits Cosmetics Tests on Animals	Requires Re-homing	Cruelty Laws Apply When Not in Research Protocol
California	yes	yes	yes	
Connecticut	yes		yes	
Delaware	yes		yes	
Hawaii	yes			
Illinois	yes		yes	
Iowa				yes
Kentucky				yes
Maine	yes			
Maryland	yes		yes	yes
Massachusetts	yes			
Minnesota	yes		yes	
New Hampshire	yes			
New Jersey	yes	yes		
New Mexico				yes
Nevada			yes	
New York	yes	yes	yes	
Pennsylvania	yes			
Rhode Island	yes			
South Carolina	yes			
Tennessee				yes
Vermont	yes			yes
Virginia	yes	yes		yes
West Virginia	yes			
Wisconsin				yes

Sources: National Anti-Vivisection Society, "State Cruelty Laws Concerning Research Animals," and "State Laws." https://www.navs.org/what-we-do/keep-you-informed/legal-arena/research/state-cruelty-laws-concerning-research-animals/, and https://www.navs.org/what-we-do/keep-you-informed/legal-arena/product-testing/state-laws/, accessed June 19, 2018; see American Anti-Vivisection Society, "Pound Seizure Laws." http://aavs.org/animals-science/laws/pound-seizure-laws/, accessed June 19, 2018; and Adam Edelman, "Lab Dog to Lap Dog: Research Animals get New Lease on Life," *NBC News*, May 12, 2018. https://www.nbcnews.com/politics/politics-news/lab-dog-lap-dog-research-animals-get-new-lease-life-n873391, accessed June 19, 2018.

After use in a "major operative experiment from which…allowed to recover," an animal is not to be used in such an experiment again. However, there are exceptions for "scientific necessity" and "other special circumstances," and unlike the EU, no outright prohibition on subjecting the same animal to experiments causing severe pain.[49] Here again, the AWA is lax in its protection of animals. Additionally, the US government does not prohibit the routine euthanasia of dogs when they are no longer needed for experiments. Indeed, "most dogs end up euthanized" after their service.[50] However, eight states now require research facilities to offer dogs for adoption prior to euthanasia if they are in good health and present no danger to the public[51] (see Table 4.1). There are now groups, such as the Beagle Freedom Project, which work with cooperative laboratories in an attempt to re-home these retired dogs as well. While the trend among states is in favor of protective legislation in this area, 42 states do not yet mandate placement of these retired dogs.

Beagles, specifically bred for laboratory use, are by far the most commonly used for research in the US. However, there is a much higher risk in the US than EU of former companion animals finding themselves in laboratories. There are some legal safeguards to prevent the theft of companion animals for sale to laboratories. In fact, the American public demanded legislative action from Congress after the much publicized and tragic story of the companion Dalmatian Pepper who was stolen and sold to a research laboratory, where she died.[52] In 1966, Congress responded with the AWA. This law prohibits research facilities from obtaining animals from anyone other than licensed dealers, both Class A breeders and Class B wholesalers, which are also required to be licensed. As animals proceed through the sales chain, a record-keeping trail is required. There is also a five-day mandatory holding period when a dog or cat enters the chain, the purpose of which is to allow time for a stolen animal to be traced. Although these provisions have substantially reduced the number of *stolen* pets going to research facilities, they have not addressed the use of *former* pets or those at shelters and pounds. Class B dealers can sell such dogs obtained from dubious sources to research facilities legally. In 2011, the National Institute of Health implemented a pilot project to reduce the number of dogs in laboratories obtained from Class B dealers, but that project is "not likely to have an effect on animals taken directly from shelters."[53]

To combat this problem, 18 states have passed legislation banning research facilities from obtaining pets from animal shelters (see Table 4.1). Almost all of these states do not have large shelter populations. In the South, where shelters are overcrowded, there are just a couple of states with such a prohibition. What is more, Oklahoma requires pound seizure of animals in government-run facilities unless prohibited by a municipality. Many local governments in other states either require that pounds surrender dogs unclaimed for a specified period, which must be at least five days per US law, to laboratories or give the pounds and shelters the option to do so. Because these facilities are paid for animals surrendered to laboratories, they have a financial incentive to take advantage of that option when provided.[54] Unlike the EU, which requires the use of animals specifically bred for the lab with very limited exceptions, the US has no national law against pound seizure or the use of former companion animals in laboratories. Although any dog, whether bred for experimentation or not, suffers in a laboratory, it is considered a particularly egregious betrayal of trust in the case of former companion animals. In sum, hypothesis #6, which states the *US Government and American states will not prohibit scientific experiments on dogs and will have lax regulations over any such experiments*, is validated.

A More Protective but Not Perfect EU

US policy in the area of experimentation conforms to expectations, as the regulatory scheme is lax and dependent upon self-monitoring. The animals are used for human purposes, with little attention given to their capacity to suffer. The AWA conceptualizes dogs and other companion animals as property, with safeguards against their theft to prevent the distress of human caretakers. For those companion animals no longer wanted or specifically bred for the laboratory, there is minimal protection. It is worth noting that the AWA, as the reader may recall, offers no protection at all to mice, rats, and birds or over 90 percent of the animals used in laboratories![55] At the state level, there is some divergence from the American model, as 18 states forbid pound seizure, four require alternatives to animal testing when available for cosmetics testing, and eight require laboratories to rehome animals when no longer used for experimentation. The majority of states do not diverge from the American model though and the national government is primarily responsible for legislation in this area. Similarly, there is now less variation from the European model in the EU given the homogenizing effect of the 2010 Directive. That Directive is consistent with the European model, as it recognizes the sentience of animals and seeks to reduce their use in experiments and to minimize pain to them.

With that said, in both the US and EU, it is legal to experiment upon dogs and therefore subject them to pain, fear, and distress. Compared with the use of other animals, the aggregate numbers are not large but the fate is nonetheless grim for human's "best friends" unlucky enough to find themselves in laboratories. There is much debate about the ethics of using animals in experiments, or for that matter, humans. Utilitarians argue that the greater good of the majority justifies the sacrifice of a small number. However, more sophisticated utilitarian theorists insist upon equal consideration of interests and an absolute need to impose pain on some, such as the need to discover a cure for pancreatic cancer and not yet another variety of shampoo. Even when there is an absolute need, the pain imposed on anyone should be minimized. For those who presume that animals have rights, there is no justification for their sacrifice to science. There are also those who give weight to the capacities of particular species and might be inclined to defend the use of some species but not others.[56] The current use of dogs in both the US and EU, despite the limited numbers, would not satisfy any of these ethical positions.

Unnecessary Surgeries

The freedom from pain, injury, and disease should surely preclude unnecessary surgeries, such as ear cropping and tail docking, for cosmetic purposes. "Tail docking refers to the amputation of all, or part of an animal's tail…," while ear cropping is "the practice of reshaping a dog's ears by surgically removing the pinna, or 'floppy part' of the ear."[57] Typically performed when the puppy is between six and twelve weeks old, ear cropping requires a large incision with several sutures and the dog's ears are taped up for a few weeks. In contrast, tail docking is usually done when the puppy is under five days old. Frequently, the tail is either cut or a rubber ligature is used to restrict the blood flow to the tail. With the latter method, the tail typically falls off within 24–96 hours. While tail docking was and still sometimes is defended for working dogs, tail injuries are "generally rare." According to the AVMA, "routine tail docking has not been shown to produce demonstrable benefits for most dogs." Likewise, there is "no evidence" that ear cropping prevents infections, but it does have "potential negative outcomes for the animal."[58] Devocalization is another unnecessary procedure done for human convenience, though it is far less common.

Despite their potential harm to dogs, both tail docking and ear cropping have nonetheless been part of breed standards for select kennel clubs. According to Gina Spadafori, many breeders in the US "would happily stop doing" these procedures "if they thought they could still win in the ring."[59] Among veterinarians and in society at large, there is a growing consensus on both the needlessness of these procedures and the reality of the pain caused to animals because of them. According to the AVMA, across a range of countries, 83–92 percent of veterinarians and 68–88 percent of the general public consider these procedures unacceptable.[60]

Given the European concern for the well-being of animals, it was hypothesized that *the EU, to the extent it has jurisdiction, and its member states will prohibit unnecessary surgeries, such as tail docking and ear cropping, done for the sake of appearance or human preference*. The data validate this hypothesis (#14), as 27/28 member states ban ear cropping and devocalization when done for non-curative purposes. Spain leaves the decision to its autonomous communities, almost all of which ban these two procedures. Only 6/28 member states allow tail docking and one of those mandates that the procedure be performed by a veterinarian. Sixteen ban the procedure outright, while six others prohibit it but have exceptions for certain hunting and working breeds (see Table 4.2). The ECPPA, ratified by 17 of 28 EU member states, specifically lists the docking of tails, cropping of ears, devocalization, and declawing and defanging as examples of prohibited surgical operations when done for non-curative purposes.[61] Importantly, the Kennel Clubs in the EU almost universally do not allow such altered dogs to compete in shows. As a result, there is no incentive for breeders to perform these procedures. The member states of the EU overwhelmingly ban these procedures in light of the negative impact on animals and as a result, are true to their declarations of concern for sentient beings.

Table 4.2: EU Member States and Unnecessary Surgeries.

	Bans Tail Docking	Bans Ear Cropping	Bans Devocalization
Austria*	yes	yes	yes
Belgium*	yes	yes	yes
Bulgaria*	yes	yes	yes
Croatia	yes	yes	yes
Cyprus*	yes	yes	yes
Czech Republic**	no	yes	yes
Denmark**	yes, with exceptions	yes	yes
Estonia	yes	yes	yes

	Bans Tail Docking	Bans Ear Cropping	Bans Devocalization
Finland*	yes	yes	yes
France**	no	yes	yes
Germany**	yes, with exceptions	yes	yes
Greece*	yes	yes	yes
Hungary	no	yes	yes
Ireland	yes, with exceptions	yes	yes
Italy*	yes, with exceptions	yes	yes
Latvia**	yes, with exceptions	yes	yes
Lithuania*	yes	yes	yes
Luxembourg*	yes	yes	yes
Malta	yes	yes	yes
Netherlands	yes	yes	yes
Poland	yes	yes	yes
Portugal**	no, but vet must do	yes	yes
Romania*	yes	yes	yes
Slovakia	no	yes	yes
Slovenia	yes	yes	yes
Spain***	no	no	no
Sweden*	yes	yes	yes
UK	yes, with exceptions	yes	yes

*Signed and ratified ECPPA, which stipulates these procedures should be banned.
**Signed and ratified ECPPA but with exceptions for tail docking.
***It is up to Spain's autonomous communities to decide these issues.

Sources: "National Legislation and Standards," Carodog. http://wwwcarodog.eu/?p=3&s=5, accessed September 17, 2014; Anti-Docking Alliance, "World Legislation." http://anti-dockingalliance.com/page_10.htm, accessed September 17, 2014; European Enforcement Network of Animal Welfare Lawyers and Commissioners, "National Animal Welfare Legislation." http://lawyersforanimalprotection.eu/national-animal-welfare-legislation/, accessed September 17, 2014; and EU Dog & Cat Alliance, "The welfare of dogs and cats involved in commercial practices: a review of the legislation across EU countries," (London, 2017). https://s3-eu-west-1.amazonaws.com/assets.dogandcatwelfare.eu/live/media/publicationtemp/all.pdf, accessed June 15, 2018.

Contrarily, it was hypothesized that *the US government and American states will not prohibit unnecessary surgeries, such as ear cropping and tail docking, on dogs*. In law, the data overwhelmingly support that hypothesis (#7). Ear cropping and tail docking are legal throughout the US, albeit subject to some regulation in select states. Only two states, Maryland and Pennsylvania, regulate tail docking. Maryland law stipulates that a veterinarian must perform the procedure and only when "appropriate," and Pennsylvania law prohibits tail docking for puppies over five days old but allows veterinarians to perform the procedure under anesthesia when the dog is at least twelve weeks old. In all other states, breeders can perform this procedure without oversight. This practice, done inappropriately by a non-veterinarian, can lead to pain. In one example, a breeder, using the rubber ligature method to dock tails, applied the bands so tightly that they became embedded in the puppies' tails.

Nine states regulate ear cropping, with eight requiring that the procedure be performed by a licensed veterinarian and five of those eight stipulating that anesthesia be used. The state of Washington prohibits the procedure unless it is a "customary husbandry practice"[62] (see Table 4.3). Only three states, Maryland, Massachusetts, and New Jersey, prohibit devocalization unless medically necessary. Pennsylvania requires that a veterinarian perform the procedure using anesthesia, while California and Rhode Island make it unlawful to require devocalization as a condition for real estate occupancy.[63] Public policy provides little protection of canines, then, from unnecessary procedures if caretakers opt for them.

Table 4.3: US States that Regulate Ear Cropping.

	Licensed Vet Required	**Anesthesia Required**
Connecticut	yes	yes
Maine	yes	
Maryland	yes	yes
Massachusetts	yes	
New Hampshire	yes	yes
New York	yes	yes
Illinois	yes	
Pennsylvania	yes	yes

Source: AVMA, "State Summary Report: State Laws Governing Elective Surgical Procedures," (April 2018). https://www.avma.org/Advocacy/StateAndLocal/Pages/sr-elective-procedures.aspx, accessed June 19, 2018.

However, in practice, there is a burgeoning recognition of the needlessness of these surgeries in the US. In 2009, Banfield Pet Hospitals, the largest network of animal hospitals in the US at the time, announced that they would no longer crop ears or dock tails for cosmetic purposes.[64] The AVMA passed a resolution in 2008, which states that it "opposes ear cropping and tail docking of dogs when done solely for cosmetic purposes. The AVMA encourages the elimination of ear cropping and tail docking from breed standards." This statement was re-affirmed in 2012.[65] It has become less common for people to get dogs' ears cropped. However, tail docking remains pervasive for several breeds. Because tails are docked within days of birth, breeders routinely do it. Since ears are often cropped after the puppy is purchased or adopted at eight weeks, caretakers can opt out and increasingly do so.[66] The AKC has been a major obstacle in attempts to eliminate these practices. Indeed, it requires that dogs of certain breeds have their tails docked in order to compete in shows. While the AKC does not require ear cropping or devocalization, it does not disqualify dogs who have had these procedures.[67] What is more, the organization has successfully lobbied against attempts to outlaw tail docking and ear cropping in Illinois, New York, and Vermont.[68] Although a very small percentage of dogs are shown at AKC events, commercial and other breeders dock all dogs' tails so as to leave that option available for caretakers. While ear cropping is less common than it once was, American practices are nonetheless consistent with expectations.

Dogfighting: Universal Condemnation but Stubborn Persistence

There is universal consensus among policymakers in the US and EU that dogfighting is illegal and socially deviant behavior. This consensus is not surprising given that dogfighting is among the worst of cruelties perpetrated against canines. For most of the dogs made to participate in fights, the abuse is life-long. To predispose the dogs to violence, they are beaten as puppies, chained and prodded with sticks and electrocution, fed hot peppers and gunpowder, isolated in darkness and starved. They are forced to run on treadmills for several hours a day, wear weights around their necks, and take steroids and other drugs, including cocaine, to prepare for the fights. They are also forced to practice on "bait" animals, which are often themselves other dogs. These "bait" dogs are typically stolen pets, passive pups from fighting-breed litters, or strays. In parts of Europe, stray animals are at high risk for such "use." The snouts of bait dogs are either broken or wrapped to prevent any self-defense. If the bait dogs do not die from the "training" session, they are either given to the fighting dog or the human criminals. In either case, they are cruelly killed. The fighting dogs face similar physical abuse in their "fights," which are "bloody battles to the death." The dogs have their flesh torn apart. If not killed, the dogs experience horrific injuries, such as "lacerations, ripped ears, puncture wounds and broken bones" that go untreated. Worse, losing dogs who survive are "punished" via more torture and execution by drowning, hanging, gunshot, or incineration.[69] It is the epitome of animal cruelty.

The most common canine victims of dogfighting are "pitbulls."[70] As Gibson explains, "the great majority of the American fighting dogs that are referred to as pitbulls tend to be an amalgamation of ...various breeds," such as American Staffordshire terriers and others. In some areas, "super-breeds," namely Bullmastiffs and Presa Canarios, "that are much larger than pitbulls" have been bred with the latter to make "larger and more ferocious fighting dogs."[71] In Europe, dog fighters use similar breeds and amalgamation of breeds. Because these breeds are intensely loyal, they tend to endure the abuse without becoming aggressive toward the human handlers, who of course exploit that loyalty.

While there is variation in how comprehensive the statutes are and penalties differ, dogfighting is illegal throughout the US and EU. In the US, all 50 states have established felony penalties for the crime of dogfighting, and with the lone exception of Montana, all states ban attendance at dogfights.[72] In addition to these state laws, national law makes dogfighting illegal. The AWA was amended in 1976 to prohibit certain forms of animal fighting, including dogfighting. Specifically, Section 26 of that law makes it a crime both to knowingly sell, buy, transport, deliver or receive animals for fighting via inter-state or foreign commerce and knowingly to sponsor or exhibit animals in any animal fighting venture to which the animal was moved in interstate or foreign commerce. In 2008, Congress enhanced the penalties for violation of this law from three to possibly five years in prison and added "prohibitions on possession and training as well as advertising animals or sharp instruments for use in animal fighting."[73] In 2014, President Obama signed into a law a farm bill, which made attendance at an animal fight a federal crime and imposed additional penalties for bringing a minor to an animal fight.[74] Such federal laws are critical to fill the proverbial gap when state laws or enforcement are wanting.

Dogfighting is illegal throughout the EU as well. In almost every member state, the law specifically prohibits animal fights and/or the organization of such fights. Similarly to US states, EU countries exhibit variety in the details of their dogfighting prohibitions. Some, such as the UK, have comprehensive statutes explicitly forbidding not just dogfighting, but all of its supporting activities, while others, such as Malta, make succinct and general declarations about its illegality. At least half of the member states specifically forbid the training of dogs for aggression against other animals. In Bulgaria, for example, the law forbids the promotion of "aggressive behavior in animals through selection or training in aggressive behaviors towards other animals and humans."[75] Such wording is typical, but some member states, such as Greece, more broadly ban "education/training and use of animals for any kind of fights."[76] Others, including Bulgaria, additionally list and forbid commonly-used methods in the training of fighting dogs. For instance, Croatia prohibits the use of chemicals and stimulants as well as technological devices to punish dogs.[77] At least nine member states in the EU, or just shy of one-third, explicitly forbid participation and/or attendance at animal fights. Four expressly stipulate that the promotion and advertisement of fights are illegal, while two, Greece and the UK, ban depictions of animal fighting.[78] As the reader may recall, EU member states, to the dismay of animal welfare groups, are also more likely to ban certain dog breeds, commonly used in fighting, place restrictions on them, and/or prohibit their reproduction.

Throughout the EU, the trend has been toward increasing penalties for dogfighting and other egregious forms of animal cruelty. Fines are now steeper and the crime carries the possibility of a prison sentence of up to two or three years in many member states.[79] However, there is a problem with enforcement.[80] In Hungary, for instance, one observer noted that no one has yet been sent to prison for cruelty despite the possibility of a three-year sentence and in Spain, as another example, offenders are "hardly punished."[81] A few member states, such as Sweden, have the authority to bar those convicted of animal cruelty from caring for an animal again as well.[82] Yet compared to the US, criminal penalties for dogfighting in the EU are less severe. The "American" approach is more punitive for criminal offenders than the "European" one and that holds in this area. Given that dogfighting is deviant behavior, both the national and state governments in the US not only punish it more harshly than EU member states but explicitly and uniformly prohibit it and its supporting activities. However, as EU member states update laws, the trend is toward the incorporation of more specific prohibitions in this area. The more specific and comprehensive the laws against dogfighting, the better the chances for police to apprehend offenders. Since the activity is universally illegal, though, the challenge is in the area of enforcement.

Crimes are more likely to be deterred by the certainty of sanctions than by their severity. Unfortunately, even with strong legislation, it is extremely difficult for law enforcement to catch dogfighters and thereby ensure the application of sanctions. According to the RSPCA, there are several factors that account for the difficulties in the enforcement of dogfighting prohibitions. Those involved in this crime go to great lengths to avoid detection, traveling long distances, and crossing geographical and police boundaries. This fact requires timely communication and cooperation among authorities. Fighting venues are changed at the last minute and communicated to participants in secure ways. Indeed, dogfighters operate in a clandestine world, closed to outsiders and therefore challenging for law enforcement officers to penetrate. Nor do these criminals take the dogs to veterinarians, who could report the telltale signs of fighting to police, but instead they "treat" or kill the dogs themselves. As a result, even in places with some commitment to the enforcement of comprehensive legislation against dogfighting, the problem persists. Absent that commitment and strong prohibitions, it is likely to operate on a greater scale.

Despite the strength of laws in the US, the HSUS, per Ortiz, "estimates that at least 40,000 people engage in high-stakes dogfighting, with at least another 100,000 participating at the street level…."[83] In one year alone, highlights Gibson, the city of Chicago responded to 1,093 complaints of animal fighting.[84] There were over one thousand *arrests* for dogfighting from 2003–2014 in the US.[85] According to Shafer, dogfighting is "a multi-billion dollar industry," with an average fight netting around 10,000 dollars but with top fights paying 100,000 dollars or more.[86] There are three classifications of dogfighters, professionals, hobbyists or mid-level fighters, and street fighters. Operating on a national or international level, the professionals publish underground trade journals, breed dogs, and engage in high-stakes gambling. These criminals tend to be wealthy and are quite successful at evading law enforcement. The mid-level fighters operate on a regional level and typically do not breed fighting dogs. Found in both urban and rural areas, they tend to return to "predetermined fight venues." Finally, "street fighters," based in urban areas, engage in lower-stakes gambling but much violence. The dogfights, for this group, become part of a gang culture and are integrally related to gambling and drug trafficking.[87] Some studies have identified similarities among dogfighters. More specifically, they are said to "engage in dogfighting as a show of masculinity,...have criminal tendencies, and...rationalize their behavior by anthropomorphizing the dogs."[88] Otherwise, dogfighters in the US are a diverse lot, hailing from rural and urban areas and representing all races and ethnicities.

Since the notoriety of the Michael Vick case in 2007, in which this professional football player served time in prison for dogfighting, there has been more public awareness of the abusive nature of this crime and greater attention from law enforcement. In 2013, the second largest dogfighting ring in US history was cracked, with 367 dogs rescued during raids in Alabama and Georgia. While eight people were sent to jail, one defendant was given a sentence of eight years in prison, "the longest...ever handed down for a federal dogfighting case." What is more, the judge in this case noted that the federal sentencing guidelines were too lenient given the gravity of this crime.[89] Although dogfighting continues in the US, then, authorities are beginning to take it seriously.

Unfortunately, dogfighting is prevalent throughout the EU as well. Because the activity is illegal, as in the US, it is possible only to estimate the scope of the problem. There are similar categories of dogfighters in the EU, with "street fighters" especially on the rise and indications of increased involvement of organized crime in "professional" fights. According to the ESDAW, thousands of dogs are victimized by this crime, with fights "constantly being organized."[90] Like in the US, there is no geographical section of the EU that is immune from this crime. In the UK and Ireland, street fighters, often linked to gangs, present a growing problem. According to the Irish Society for the Prevention of Cruelty to Animals (ISPCA), people are "just putting two dogs together that they think will fight."[91] Similarly, the RSPCA reports "more impromptu dog fights."[92] Supporting these concerns, the RSPCA highlights a "massive increase in the number of dogs seized in London under the Dangerous Dogs Act" and the Battersea Dog Home noted that 50 percent of the 6,125 dogs accepted in 2011 were "bull breeds" and "many" exhibited signs of involvement in dogfighting.[93] Since 2007, complaints about dogfighting to the RSPCA have decreased from 358 that year to 204 in 2009, but "the incidence of young people fighting dogs has increased."[94] Of course, the complaints and convictions for dogfighting, the latter of which numbered 63 in the UK in 2009, do not capture the full scale of what the RSPCA deems an "ongoing problem." Indeed, dog theft is the "fastest growing crime in the UK," motivated in part to "supply animals for illegal dogfights."[95] These stolen companion animals serve as "bait" for training the fighting dogs.

In southern Europe, there are problems with both amateur and professional dogfighters. In Spain, "illicit dogfighting," sponsored by hobbyists, "continues to be a problem." Similarly to the UK, dogs, especially large family ones, are stolen to be used as bait.[96] Strays are also at risk for this fate. In Italy, per Manzini, dogfighting is a "major problem." Criminal organizations, dubbed "zoomafia" when involving animals, operate "underground fights where huge sums of money are bet on the outcome." According to one estimate, dogfighting grosses nearly 500 million dollars a year. Stray animals in shelters are "now regularly sold for dogfighting throughout Italy."[97] Likewise, organized crime, in the form of the Russian Mafia and others, operates dogfighting rings in eastern Europe. In fact, the activity has become "quite popular" in eastern Europe, where it was legal in some places not all that long ago.[98] According to an RSPCA official, the Baltic region, which includes Latvia, Estonia and Lithuania, is "probably the fastest growing area of organized dog fighting in the world." Fighting dogs, bred larger than usual, have been illegally imported to the UK from this region as well.[99] In Hungary, Poland, and other eastern member states, dogfighting is also a persistent problem. In Poland, the *first* raid on a dogfighting ring took place as recently as 2009. After officials raided a dogfighting ring in Hungary in 2013, they seized only 37 of 83 dogs and claimed the others were not in "bad enough physical condition to warrant seizing." In states with no toleration for dogfighting, all dogs would have been seized.[100] Nor are the northern and western member states of continental Europe free from this crime. For example, dogfighting persists in the Netherlands, where the "police are not effectively dealing with it, mostly because of the difficulty of catching dogfighters in the act."[101] In short, dogfighting continues to be a major problem in the EU. Its persistent presence in both the US and EU attests to a minority mindset that conceptualizes dogs as objects.

Conclusion

In both the areas of unnecessary surgeries and experimentation, the US and EU legislate in accord with expectations. Almost all member states in the EU prohibit unnecessary surgeries and the *supra*-national government has imposed uniform and comprehensive guidelines for experimentation. In contrast, the US has notoriously weak protection for laboratory animals, no guarantee that companion animals will not transition to laboratory ones, and no outright prohibitions on unnecessary surgeries. Without any value on the lives of sentient animals in national law, the US government is unlikely to impose constraints on the research community, which is both politically and economically powerful. Since scientific experiments are conducted out of the public eye, there is little pressure to do so. The "property" status of companion animals helps as well to prevent any constraints on "owners" from altering "their" animals as desired. The philosophical recognition of the sentient nature of dogs and other animals provides the EU and its member states better opportunity to impose restrictions on how they are treated.

Commercial greyhound racing, which is a public activity, is treated differently than experimentation in the US. No longer deemed an "acceptable use" of animals in most parts of both the US and EU, the activity has not only declined in popularity but has been prohibited in law in most places. As a result, the EU legislates in accord with expectations on this matter, but the US does not. The replacement of dog racing with other forms of legalized gambling in the US has weakened the industry's clout at the state level and made it more economically palatable to prohibit it. Even with that dynamic, referendums, not legislative votes, have outlawed the activity in some states. Rarely in the US will lawmakers prioritize the interests of animals over industry, however that particular industry defines "accepted uses" of animals. Because dogfighting is a "socially deviant" use of animals, the US criminalizes and punishes the behavior.

The challenge in these areas of common betrayal of canines is to convince people of their unacceptable nature. The battle has been won at the legislative level for dogfighting in both the EU and US, though cultural acceptance persists in minority pockets of the public. Enforcement of law in this area continues therefore to be imperative to stop the abuse. There is near victory in the area of commercial racing in both the US and EU and in the EU only, in the area of unnecessary surgeries. On the latter issue, there has been some cultural, if not legal, change in the US on ear cropping only. With respect to experimentation, there is acceptance of the use of dogs in the EU and US but a much greater level of protection for such dogs in the EU. Indeed, the EU considers it unacceptable for a companion animal to become a laboratory one, while the US does not. In general, a dog is more protected from common and culturally accepted uses, such as experimentation and unnecessary surgeries, in the EU.

Notes

1. Michael Atkinson and Kevin Young, "Reservoir Dogs: Greyhound Racing, Mimesis and Sports-Related Violence," *International Review for the Sociology of Sport* 40 (2005): 346.
2. *Ibid.*, 347.
3. Rosamund Urwin, "The Mystery of the 1,000 Greyhounds Who Retire and Then Vanish," *The Independent*, October 26, 2014. http://www.independent.co.uk/news/uk/home-news/the-mystery-of-the-1000-greyhounds-who-retire-and-then-vanish-9818554.html, accessed December 3, 2014.
4. David M. Halbfinger, "Dismal End for Race Dogs, Alabama Authorities Say," *New York Times*, May 23, 2002. See also People for the Ethical Treatment of Animals, "Greyhound Racing: Death in the Fast Lane." http://www.peta.org/issues/animals-in-entertainment/animals-used-entertainment-factsheets/greyhound-racing-death-fast-lane/, accessed December 3, 2014. The latter source puts the number at 3000. Robert L. Rhodes was charged with three counts of animal cruelty in this case.
5. For quote, see Urwin, "The Mystery." For findings, see The League Against Cruel Sports and Grey2K USA/Worldwide, *The State of Greyhound Racing in Great Britain: A Mandate for Change* (League Against Cruel Sports, 2014), 28–30. http://www.league.org.uk/~/media/Files/LACS/Publications/Greyhound-Report-2014.pdf, accessed December 3, 2014.
6. Atkinson and Young, "Reservoir Dogs," 347.
7. *Ibid.*, 348.
8. *Ibid.*, 348–349.
9. Tom McLaughlin, "A Bad Bet? Future of Greyhound Racing at Stake," *NWF Daily News*, March 1, 2014. http://www.nwfdailynews.com/local/a-bad-bet-future-of-greyhound-racing-at-stake-documents-1.285000, accessed December 3, 2014. The trainer, Ronnie Williams, was sentenced to five years in prison for felony animal cruelty in this case. The autopsies revealed that the dogs died from starvation and lack of water. See also People for the Ethical Treatment of Animals, "Greyhound Racing."
10. The League Against Cruel Sports and Grey2K USA/Worldwide, *The State of Greyhound Racing*, 24–26; and also Atkinson and Young, "Reservoir Dogs," 349.
11. Joan E. Schaffner, *An Introduction to Animals and the Law* (New York: Palgrave Macmillan), 37.
12. Atkinson and Young, "Reservoir Dogs," 350.
13. For quote, see Urwin, "The Mystery." For statistic and types of injuries, see The League Against Cruel Sports and Grey2K USA/Worldwide, *The State of Greyhound Racing*, 20–22.
14. Grey2K USA/Worldwide, "Greyhound Racing in the United States." https://www.grey2kusa.org/about/states.php, accessed June 19, 2018.
15. For breeders and number of total dogs, see Grey2K USA/Worldwide, "Fact Sheet—Greyhound Racing in the United States," (2018): 3 and 8, respectively. https://www.grey2kusa.org/pdf/GREY2KUSANationalFactSheet.pdf, accessed June 18, 2018.
16. See The League Against Cruel Sports and Grey2K USA/Worldwide, *The State of Greyhound Racing* 14; and Urwin, "The Mystery." For number of tracks, see Grey2KUSA/Worldwide, "Greyhound Racing in the UK." https://www.grey2kusa.org/about/worldwide/uk.php, accessed June 20, 2018.

17. Grey2K USA/Worldwide, "Greyhound Racing in Ireland." https://www.grey2kusa.org/about/worldwide/ireland.php, accessed June 20, 2018.
18. League Against Cruel Sports and Grey2K USA/Worldwide, *The State of Greyhound Racing*, 13.
19. Grey2K USA/Worldwide, "Ireland—Summary." For the law, see Office of the Attorney General, Ireland, Welfare of Greyhounds Act 2011, *Irish Statute Book*. http://www.irishstatutebook.ie/2011/en/act/pub/0029/index.html, accessed December 3, 2014.
20. See Greyhound Compassion. http://www.greyhoundcompassion.com, accessed December 3, 2014. Other estimates are higher, with one putting the number at 50,000. See Nick Snelling, "Animal Cruelty in Spain," *Culture Spain*, July 19, 2011. http://www.culturespain.com/2011/07/19/animal-cruelty-in-spain, accessed November 30, 2014.
21. Estimates range from 61,000 to 75,000 in the US. For high end, see People for the Ethical Treatment of Animals (PETA), "Dogs in Laboratories." http://www.peta.org/issues/animals-used-for-experimentation/dogs-laboratories/, accessed October 14, 2014. For lower estimates, see Adam Edelman, "Lab Dog to Lap Dog: Research Animals get New Lease on Life," *NBC News*, May 12, 2018. https://www.nbcnews.com/politics/politics-news/lab-dog-lap-dog-research-animals-get-new-lease-life-n873391, accessed June 19, 2018; and Richard Dool, "Group Receives Beagles from Labs," *Headline News*, November 15, 2013. http://www.hlntv.com/video/2013/11/15/group-rescues-beagles-labs, accessed October 14, 2014. For EU numbers, see EU Commission Staff Working Document Accompanying Document to the "Report from the Commission to the Council and European Parliament—Seventh Report on the Number of Animals Used for Experimental and Other Scientific Purposes in the Member States of the European Union, 2013." http://eur-lex.europa.eu/legal-content/EN/TXT/?uri=CELEX:52013SC0497, accessed December 22, 2014.
22. *Ibid.*; and Ted Jeory Whitehall, "Test Drugs on Pets, Says EU," *Express*, June 19, 2011. http://www.express.co.uk/news/uk/253655/Test-drugs-on-pets-says-EU, accessed December 22, 2014.
23. Peggy Cunniff and Pamela Osenkowski, "Animals Used in Research," in Andrea Linzey, ed., *The Global Guide to Animal Protection* (University of Illinois Press), 180.
24. Animal Legal Defense Fund, "Animal Testing and the Law." http://aldf.org/resources/when-you-witness-animal-cruelty/animal-testing-and-the-law/, accessed October 14, 2014; and Judith Reitman, "From the Leash to the Laboratory," *The Atlantic Monthly*, July 2000. https://www.theatlantic.com/past/docs/issues/2000/07/reitman.htm, accessed October 14, 2014.
25. On poor conditions prior to Directive, see BUAV, "Stray Cats and Dogs in EU Labs—The Result." http://www.buav.org/undercover-investigations/straycatsanddogs/theresult, accessed December 22, 2014. Regarding concerns about feral animals, see Tim Iredale, "MPs want to keep laboratory ban on stray cats and dogs," *BBC News England*, June 28, 2012. http://www.bbc.com/news/uk-england-18617561, accessed December 22, 2014; and Whitehall, "Test Drugs on Pets."
26. See Marta Paterlini, "Strict Limits on Animal Research Stun Italian Scientists," *Science Insider*, August 2, 2013. http://news.sciencemag.org/2013/08/strict-limits-animal-research-stun-italian-scientists, accessed December 22, 2014. Marta Paterlini, "E.U. May Punish

Italy for Stalemate on Animal Research," *Science News*, January 27, 2014. http://www.salvalasperimentazioneanimale.it/slsa/wp-content/uploads/2014/01/E.U.-May-Punish-Italy-for-Stalemate-on-Animal-Research.pdf, accessed December 22, 2014.

27. European Animal Research Association, "Commission announces infringement procedure against restrictive Italian animal research law," updated November 2017. http://eara.eu/en/commission-announces-infringement-procedure-against-restrictive-italian-animal-research-law/, accessed June 18, 2018.
28. Article 5—"Purposes of Procedures," "Directive 2010/63/EU of the European Parliament and of the Council on the Protection of Animals Used for Scientific Purposes," September 22, 2010. http://eur-lex.europa.eu/legal-content/EN/TXT/?uri=CELEX:32010L0063, accessed December 22, 2014.
29. Jan Creamer, "Freedom of Information," in Linzey, ed., *The Global Guide to Animal Protection*, 187.
30. Article 13—"Choice of Methods," Directive 2010/63/EU.
31. Annex III—"Requirements for Establishments and for Care and Accommodation of Animals," Section 3—"Housing and Enrichment," Directive 2010/63/EU.
32. Article 14—"Anaesthesia," Directive 2010/63/EU.
33. See Council of Europe, Article 8, "European Convention for the Protection of Vertebrate Animals Used for Experimental and Other Scientific Purposes," No. 123, (Strasbourg, 1986). https://rm.coe.int/168007a67b, accessed June 20, 2018.
34. See Article 16—"Re-Use," Directive 2010/63/EU.
35. "British Stars Unite To Support Campaign for Dogs in Laboratories," *Look to the Stars: The World of Celebrity Giving*, September 26, 2014. https://www.looktothestars.org/news/12637-british-stars-unite-to-support-campaign-for-dogs-in-laboratories, accessed December 22, 2014.
36. Article 11—"Stray and Feral Animals of Domestic Species," Directive 2010/63/EU.
37. Iredale, "MPs want to keep Laboratory Ban."
38. Pamela D. Frasch, Katherine M. Hessler, Sarah M. Kutil, and Sonia S. Waisman, *Animal Law in a Nutshell* (West, Thomas Reuters, 2011), 328, 331.
39. Animal Legal Defense Fund, "Animal Testing and the Law;" and National Anti-Vivisection Society, "State Laws." https://www.navs.org/what-we-do/keep-you-informed/legal-arena/product-testing/state-laws/, accessed June 19, 2018.
40. David Favre, "Overview of U.S. Animal Welfare Act," Animal Legal and Historical Center (Michigan State University College of Law, 2002). https://www.animallaw.info/article/overview-us-animal-welfare-act, accessed October 14, 2014. Also see Frasch, et al., *Animal Law*, 335.
41. *Ibid.*; and Henry Cohen, "The Animal Welfare Act," *Journal of Animal Law* 2 (2006). https://www.animallaw.info/article/animal-welfare-act, accessed October 14, 2014.
42. Frasch, et al., *Animal Law*, 335.
43. Bruce A. Wagman and Matthew Liebman, *A Worldview of Animal Law* (Durham, North Carolina: Carolina Academic Press, 2011), 198.
44. USDA,"Animal Welfare Act and Animal Welfare Regulations," November 2013, 64. http://www.aphis.usda.gov/animal_welfare/downloads/animal-care-blue-book-2013–final.pdf, accessed December 19, 2014.

45. 89th U.S. Congress, Public Law 89–544, Animal Welfare Act, Section 13, August 24, 1966. http://awic.nal.usda.gov/public-law-89-544-act-august-24-1966, accessed December 22, 2014.
46. "Dog Testing: The Beagle Freedom Project," *Huffington Post*, July 14, 2011. http://www.huffingtonpost.com/2011/07/14/dog-testing-the-beagle-fr_n__898513.html, accessed October 14, 2014.
47. Wagman and Liebman, *A Worldview*, 39.
48. National Anti-Vivisection Society, "State Cruelty Laws Concerning Research Animals." https://www.navs.org/what-we-do/keep-you-informed/legal-arena/research/state-cruelty-laws-concerning-research-animals/, accessed June 18, 2018.
49. Favre, "Overview of U.S. Animal Welfare Act."
50. Betty Yu, "Beagles Rescued from Labs in Bay Area, Nation after being used for Chemical Testing," *CBS San Francisco*, November 4, 2014. http://sanfrancisco.cbslocal.com/2014/11/04/beagles-rescued-from-labs-in-bay-area-nation-after-being-used-for-chemical-testing-medicine-pharmaceutical-dogs-emeryville-hercules-menlo-park-san-carlos-peta-beagle-freedom-project/, accessed December 22, 2014.
51. Edelman, "Lab Dog to Lap Dog." *NBC News*, May 12, 2018.
52. Wagman and Liebman, *A Worldview*, 196.
53. Peggy Kuniff, Marcia Kramer and Alexandra Bernstein, "Pound Seizure," in ed. Linzey, *The Global Guide to Animal Protection*, 154.
54. *Ibid*. For current number of states prohibiting the practice, see American Anti-Vivisection Society, "Pound Seizure Laws." http://aavs.org/animals-science/laws/pound-seizure-laws/, accessed June 19, 2018.
55. Wagman and Liebman, *A Worldview*, 38.
56. For utilitarian view, see Peter Singer, "Animal Liberation or Animal Rights," in Linda Kalof and Amy Fitzgerald, eds., *The Animals Reader: The Essential Classic and Contemporary Writings* (New York: Berg, 2007), 14–22. For example of rights view, see Tom Regan, "The Rights of Humans and Other Animals," in Linda Kalof and Amy Fitzgerald, eds., *The Animals Reader*, 23–29. For the view about the capacities of animals, see Martha Nussbaum, "The Moral Status of Animals," in Linda Kalof and Amy Fitzgerald, eds., *The Animals Reader*, 30–36.
57. Amy L. Broughton, "Cropping and Docking: A Discussion of the Controversy and the Role of Law in Preventing Unnecessary Cosmetic Surgery on Dogs," Animal Legal and Historical Center (Michigan State University College of Law, 2003). http://www.animallaw.info/article/cropping-and-docking-discussion-controversy-and-role-law-preventing-unnecessary-cosmetic, accessed September 16, 2014.
58. American Veterinary Medical Association (AVMA), "Ear Cropping and Tail Docking." https://www.avma.org/KB/Policies/Pages/Ear-cropping-and-tail-docking-of-dogs.aspx, accessed June 7, 2015.
59. Quoted in Elizabeth Weise, "Banfield Pet Hospitals ban Tail Docking, Ear Cropping on Dogs," *USA Today*, August 12, 2009. http://www.usatoday30.usatoday.com/news/nation/2009-07-30-dog-tails_n.htm, accessed June 4, 2015.
60. AVMA, "Ear Cropping and Tail Docking."

61. Article 10—"Surgical Operations," European Convention for the Protection of Pet Animals, Council of Europe (effective date 1 May 1992). http://conventions.coe.int/treaty/en/treaties/html/125.htm, accessed September 17, 2014. The following member states signed with reservations for docking tails: Czech Republic, Denmark, France, Germany, Latvia and Portugal. Latvia also claimed exemption for ear cropping as well, but prohibits the practice. See "List of Declarations made with respect for Treaty No. 125," European Convention for the Protection of Pet Animals, as of September 17, 2014, Council of Europe Treaty Office. http://conventions.coe.int/treaty/commun/listedeclarations.asp?nt=125&cm=&df=&cl=ENG&vl=1, accessed September 17, 2014.
62. AVMA, "State Summary Report: State Laws Governing Elective Surgical Procedures," (April 2018). https://www.avma.org/Advocacy/StateAndLocal/Pages/sr-elective-procedures.aspx, accessed June 19, 2018.
63. *Ibid.* For more information about legislative initiatives, see United Against Devocalization: A Campaign of Coalition to Protect and Rescue Pets. http://stopdevocalizing.weebly.com, accessed September 16, 2014.
64. Weise, "Banfield Pet Hospitals."
65. AVMA, "Ear Cropping and Tail Docking."
66. Weise, "Banfield Pet Hospitals."
67. See American Kennel Club, "Canine Legislation Position Statement—Ear Cropping, Tail Docking and Dewclaw Removal." https://images.akc.org/pdf/canine_legislation/position_statements/ear_cropping_tail_docking_and_dewclaw_removal.pdf, accessed September 19, 2014. Also see American Kennel Club, "Frequently Asked Conformation Questions." https://akc.org/events/conformation/faqs.cfm, accessed September 19, 2014.
68. Weise, "Banfield Pet Hospitals."
69. Counsel for the Humane Society of the United States, "Brief of *Amicus Curiae* The Humane Society of the United States in support of Petitioner in the Supreme Court of the United States, United States of America, Petitioner v. Robert J. Stevens, Respondent," 5–6; and Counsel for the American Society for the Prevention of Cruelty to Animals, "Brief of *Amicus Curiae* The American Society for the Prevention of Cruelty to Animals in Support of Petitioner in the Supreme Court of the United States," *United States of America, Petitioner v. Robert J. Stevens, Respondent*, June 15, 2009, 29–30. For more on violence to dogs, see Meredith L. Shafer, "Casenote: Perplexing Precedent: *United States v. Stevens* Confounds a Century of Supreme Court Conventionalism and Redefines the Limit of 'Entertainment,'" *Villanova Sports and Entertainment Law Journal* 19 (2012): 305–309; and Hanna Gibson, "Detailed Discussion of Dogfighting," Animal Legal and Historical Center (Michigan State University College of Law, 2005). http://www.animallaw.info/article/detailed-discussion-dog-fighting, accessed October 14, 2014.
70. Shafer, "Casenote: Perplexing Precedent," 306.
71. Gibson, "Detailed Discussion of Dogfighting."
72. HSUS, "Humane State Ranking 2017," https://blog.humanesociety.org/wp-content/uploads/2018/01/State-Rank-2017-MT-WY-1.pdf, and https://blog.humanesociety.org/wp-content/uploads/2018/01/State-Rank-2017-AL-MO-2.pdf, accessed June 19, 2018.
73. U.S. Congress, Public Law 110–246—Food, Conservation, and Energy Act of 2008 (Farm Bill). Text obtained at United States Department of Agriculture, National Agricultural

Library, Animal Welfare Information Center. http://awic.nal.usda.gov/public-law-110-246-food-conservation-and-energy-act-2008, accessed October 28, 2014.

74. ASPCA, "ASPCA Declares April 8 'National Dog Fighting Awareness Day'" April 8, 2014. http://www.aspca.org/about-us/press-releases/aspca-declares-april-8-national-dog-fighting-awareness-day, accessed October 14, 2014.
75. Bulgaria Legislature, Article 7, Chapter 1—"General Provisions," Animal Protection Act (13/8.02.2008), available at European Enforcement Network, "Country Profile Regarding Animal Welfare." http://www.lawyersforanimalprotection.eu/country-profile/, accessed June 20, 2018.
76. President of the Greek Republic, Line 3, Article 12—"Ban of use of any animal to every kind of entertaining shows, events and other relevant activities," Law 4039, available at European Enforcement Network, "National Animal Welfare Legislation."
77. Croatian Parliament, Line 10, Article 4—"Procedures Prohibited for the Purpose of Protecting Animals," Animal Protection Act (December 2006). http://www.prijatelji-zivotinja.hr/index.en.php?id-470, accessed November 2, 2014.
78. The nine states that explicitly criminalize attendance/participation are Bulgaria, Croatia, Hungary, Ireland, Italy, Latvia, Netherlands, Romania and the UK. Those explicitly banning promotion/advertising are Bulgaria, Croatia, Slovenia and the UK.
79. For examples of member states with possible prison sentence of two years, see President of the Greek Republic, Line 3, Article 20—"Penalties," Law 4039; Chapter 11—"Penal Regulations," Polish Animal Protection Act, available at Animal Legal and Historical Center (Michigan State University College of Law), https://www.animallaw.info/statute/poland-cruelty-polish-animal-protection-law, accessed November 30, 2014; and Paul Hosford, "ISPCA warns that casual dogfighting is on the rise," *The Journal.ie* , July 18, 2014. https://uk.news.yahoo.com/ispca-warns-casual-dog-fighting-rise-121133864.html#71G1S18, accessed November 30, 2014. Poland's penalty applies to cases of egregious cruelty to animals, which dogfighting would be.
80. Gibson, "Detailed Discussion of Dogfighting."
81. For Hungary, see Toth J. Zoltan, "Animal Protection and Animal Rights in Hungary," *Jogelmeleti Szemle* 13:4 (2012). http://jesz.ajk.elte.hu/2012_4.html, accessed November 19, 2014. For Spain, see Stray Animal Foundation, "Animal Welfare in Spain," 2012. http://www.stray-afp.org/wp-content/uploads/2012/06/Animal-welfare-in-spain.pdf, accessed June 3, 2015.
82. Ministry of Agriculture, Sweden, Section 29—"Prohibition against having animals in care," Animal Welfare Act (1988:534, as last amended by SFS 2009:303), available at European Enforcement Network, "Country Profile." Other member states that can opt to prevent ownership of animals after convictions for animal cruelty include Estonia, Latvia and the UK.
83. Francesca Ortiz, "Making the Dogmen Heel: Recommendations for Improving the Effectiveness of Dogfighting Laws," *Stanford Journal of Animal Law and Policy* 3 (2010): 4. Also see Shafer, "Casenote: Perplexing Precedent," 305; and Gibson, "Detailed Discussion of Dogfighting." Estimates are based on fight reports in underground publications and the number of animals entering shelters with evidence of fighting.
84. *Ibid.*

85. "Database of Criminal Animal Cruelty Cases," Pet-Abuse.com. http://www.pet-abuse.com/pages/cruelty_database.php, accessed October 28, 2014. Cases include those for all dogfighting arrests, pitbulls and non-pitbulls, and the statuses vary from conviction to acquittal (though only four cases resulted in acquittal).
86. Shafer, "Casenote: Perplexing Precedent," 305.
87. Gibson, "Detailed Discussion of Dogfighting;" and Ortiz, "Making the Dogmen Heel," 14–17.
88. *Ibid.*, 11. Also see Rhonda Evans, Deann Kalich (Gauthier) and Craig J. Forsyth, "Dogfighting: Symbolic Expression and Validation of Masculinity," in Kalof and Fitzgerald, eds., *The Animals Reader*, 209–218.
89. Melissa Cronin, "FBI Case Results in Harshest Dogfighting Penalty Ever," *The Dodo*, November 12, 2014. https://www.thedodo.com/historic-dog-fighting-ruling-815434314.html, accessed November 30, 2014.
90. ESDAW, "Dogfighting." http://www.esdaw.eu/dogfighting1.html, accessed November 30, 2014.
91. Hosford, "ISPCA Warns."
92. RSPCA, "The Number of Organised Animal Fights in the UK," *Five Years Measuring Animal Welfare in the UK, 2005–2009* (2010): 84–87. For link to report, see https://science.rspca.org.uk/sciencegroup/companionanimals/reportsandresources/details/-/articleName/CAD_ReportsAndResourcesPets, accessed June 20, 2018.
93. *Ibid.*, and for Battersea, see Chloe Combi, "A Terrifying Encounter with the Brutal World of Dog-fighting," *The Independent*, November 18, 2013. http://www.independent.co.uk/life-style/health-and-families/features/a-terrifying-encounter-with-the-brutal-world-of-dogfighting-8947853.html, accessed October 31, 2014.
94. RSPCA, "The Number of Organised Animal Fights."
95. On number of convictions, see *Ibid*. For quotes, see Katherine Albro Houpt, et al., "Proceedings of a Workshop to Identify Dog Welfare Issues in the U.S, Czech Republic, Spain and the United Kingdom," *Applied Animal Behavior Science* 106 (2007): 230.
96. Snelling, "Animal Cruelty in Spain."
97. For quotes, see Bruno Manzini, "Stray Animals," in Andrea Linzey, ed., *The Global Guide to Animal Protection* (University of Illinois Press, 2013), 158. For dollar estimate, see Gibson, "Detailed Discussion of Dogfighting." On this issue, also see Adolfo Sansolini, "Italian Mafia Finds New Cash Cow—Fighting Dogs," *San Francisco Chronicle*, September 15, 2000. https://www.sfgate.com/news/article/EUROPE-Italian-Mafia-Finds-a-New-Cash-Cow-2738841.php, accessed June 20, 2018.
98. Gibson, "Detailed Discussion of Dogfighting."
99. Anonymous, "Super-size European pitbulls terrorize UK," *Daily Star*, September 8, 2013. http://www.dailystar.co.uk/news/latest-news/337272/Super-size-European-pitbulls-terrorize-UK, accessed December 1, 2014. The quotation is from Mike Butcher, RSPCA Special Operations Chief Inspector.
100. Kenn Bell, "Polish Raid Dog Fight, 18 Men Detained," *Dogfiles*, September 26, 2009. http://www.thedogfiles.com/2009/09/26/polish-police-raid-dog-fight-18-men-detained/, accessed December 1, 2014. On Hungary, see April Remons, "Recent Raid on Dogfighting

Ring finds 83 dogs," *Examiner.com*, September 3, 2013. http://www.examiner.com/article/recent-raid-on-dogfighting-ring-finds-83-dogs, accessed November 30, 2014.

101. Alexandra Semyonova, "The 2011 Dutch 'Animal Police' Plan, Viewed in 2014," at Merritt Clifton, ed., *Animals 24–7* (March 2014). http://www.animals24-7.org/2014/03/14/the-2011-dutch-animal-police-plan-viewed-in-2014/, accessed December 1, 2014.

Bibliography

Atkinson, Michael and Kevin Young. "Reservoir Dogs: Greyhound Racing, Mimesis and Sports-Related Violence." *International Review for the Sociology of Sport* 40 (2005): 335–356.

Broughton, Amy L. "Cropping and Docking: A Discussion of the Controversy and the Role of Law in Preventing Unnecessary Cosmetic Surgery on Dogs." Animal Legal and Historical Center, Michigan State University College of Law, 2003. http://www.animallaw.info/article/cropping-and-docking-discussion-controversy-and-role-law-preventing-unnecessary-cosmetic, accessed September 16, 2014.

Cohen, Henry. "The Animal Welfare Act." *Journal of Animal Law* 2 (2006). https://www.animallaw.info/article/animal-welfare-act, accessed October 14, 2014.

Favre, David. "Overview of U.S. Animal Welfare Act." Animal Legal and Historical Center, Michigan State University College of Law, 2002. https://www.animallaw.info/article/overview-us-animal-welfare-act, accessed October 14, 2014.

Frasch, Pamela D., et al. *Animal Law in a Nutshell*. West, Thomas Reuters, 2011.

Gibson, Hanna. "Detailed Discussion of Dogfighting." Animal Legal and Historical Center, Michigan State University College of Law, 2005. http://www.animallaw.info/article/detailed-discussion-dog-fighting, accessed October 14, 2014.

Houpt, Katherine Albro, et al. "Proceedings of a Workshop to Identify Dog Welfare Issues in the U.S., Czech Republic, Spain, and United Kingdom." *Applied Animal Behavior Science* 106 (2007): 221–233.

Kalof, Linda and Amy Fitzgerald, eds. *The Animals Reader: The Essential Classic and Contemporary Writings*. New York: Berg, 2007.

Linzey, Andrea, ed. *The Global Guide to Animal Protection*. University of Illinois Press, 2013.

Ortiz, Francesca. "Making the Dogmen Heel: Recommendations for Improving the Effectiveness of Dogfighting Laws." *Stanford Journal of Animal Law and Policy* 3 (2010): 3–75.

Schaffner, Joan E. *An Introduction to Animals and the Law*. New York: Palgrave Macmillan, 2011.

Shafer, Meredith L. "Casenote: Perplexing Precedent: *United States v. Stevens* Confounds a Century of Supreme Court Conventionalism and Redefines the Limit of 'Entertainment'." *Villanova Sports and Entertainment Law Journal* 19 (2012): 281–342.

Wagman, Bruce A. and Matthew Liebman. *A Worldview of Animal Law*. Durham, North Carolina: Carolina Academic Press, 2011.

Zoltan, Toth J. "Animal Protection and Animal Rights in Hungary." *Jogelmeleti Szemle* 13:4 (2012). http://jesz.ajk.elte.hu/2012_4.html, accessed November 19, 2014.

· 5 ·

A DISCRIMINATING SEARCH FOR CANINE JUSTICE IN THE US AND EU

Because there are stronger legal protections for canines in the EU, it is more dog friendly than the US on paper. However, there are notable and significant exceptions to this pattern. What is more, there are places in the EU, especially in the South and East, where there is virtually no compliance with protective laws. In fact, there are outposts of canine hell, such as the "canine death camps" in Slovakia. Yet several eastern and southern EU member states have changed their laws to the advantage of canines and are now using those laws to prompt changes to practices. The EU itself is a driver of this process, proclaiming the sentience of animals and insisting upon better treatment of animals in many cases. In the US, dog-friendly practices have emerged despite poor protection of all animals in national law. Many advocacy groups are working to change state laws to provide better protection of canines and they can claim success in many instances. As a result, there are pockets where canines are protected in the US. Laws, at the *supra*-national and increasingly national levels, in the EU assist in the effort to create dog-friendly practices. In the US, advocacy groups and a sympathetic public are working to mold the laws to reflect dog-friendly values.

Law: Head to the EU?

The EU: A Protective Approach

In those policy areas for which hypotheses were tested, the EU and its member states did a better job protecting canines than did the US national government and its states. Indeed, the EU conforms to expectations for six of the seven policies: codes of caretakers' responsibility, mandatory identification, regulation of commercial breeders, regulation of scientific experimentation, and the prohibition of commercial greyhound racing and unnecessary surgeries. Almost all EU member states are inclined to codify the duties of canine caretakers in law and to do so affirmatively. In substance, the duties themselves are not so dramatically different from those found in American anti-cruelty statutes, but the language puts caretakers on notice of their responsibilities. Virtually all EU member states prohibit ear cropping and devocalization when done for non-curative purposes. Only Spain is an exception and that country leaves the decision up to its autonomous communities. In addition, only 6/28 member states allow tail docking without restrictions. Likewise, 21/28 member states require the permanent marking of companion animals via microchips. The EU demands the latter for any dog crossing national boundaries. In the area of scientific experimentation, the EU has much more protective legislation than the US and prohibits the use of animals in certain areas, such as testing cosmetics or weapons. Dogs are not exempted, however, from laboratory use in the EU, but it is highly unlikely that any former companion animal will be surrendered to scientific research. Only two EU member states, Ireland and the UK, allow commercial greyhound racing in law and even in those two states, its popularity is in decline. In these five areas, the exceptions are minor. Overwhelmingly, EU member states legislate in accord with expectations.

In the area of commercial breeding, the EU member states met expectations, but the exceptions were greater in number and more significant. Importantly, there is no effective *supra*-national legislation to date regulating commercial breeders. As the reader may recall, more than half of EU member states had strong regulations for licensing and inspections, but almost 40 percent or 11/28 defied expectations with lax regulations. Almost half had prohibitions against breeding defects, which in turn means more than half did not. Though the hypothesis was validated, there are several member states clustering toward the American approach.

The only refuted hypothesis was that the EU and its member states would prohibit the euthanasia of healthy dogs. Only 9/28 member states and one autonomous community in Spain do so. However, there are four additional states that have virtually no stray or "unwanted" population and therefore the practice is rare in those places. Still, that leaves a slim majority of member states that routinely euthanize healthy dogs and in some cases, the scale is staggering. This glaring exception to the European model results from the fallout of poor management of canine population, especially in eastern and southern member states. In some of those member states with large stray populations, there is experimentation with spay/neuter-release programs so as to minimize the numbers of healthy dogs killed. Nonetheless, the euthanasia of healthy dogs is widely and legally used in the EU.

The US: Laissez-Faire Alive but Not Unchallenged

In the US, the American model was clearly evident in five of the seven hypothesized areas, namely, codes of caretakers' responsibilities, mandatory identification, the prohibition of the euthanasia of healthy dogs, regulations for scientific experimentation, and the prohibition of unnecessary surgeries. The overwhelming majority of US states do not employ affirmative language in their animal cruelty laws. While close to a majority mandate a minimal level of veterinary care, only six states require comprehensive medical care for dogs. Also consistent with the American model, no state requires the permanent microchipping of dogs. *Public* policies about the euthanasia of healthy dogs also remain overwhelmingly consistent with the American model. Just two of 50 states buck this tide and none makes the practice illegal. In the area of experimentation, the US conforms fully to expectations as well with weak protections for laboratory animals, including dogs. Indeed, a majority of states do not protect former companion animals from finding themselves in laboratories, a practice considered egregious in the EU. Finally, there are very few states that regulate unnecessary surgeries, and none that outrightly prohibits either tail docking or ear cropping.

The hypothesis that the US government and American states will have lax regulations on commercial breeders for the benefit of consumers only was validated, but just barely. Almost half of the states require licensing and inspection of breeders with coverage that is comprehensive or that does not exclude medium-sized breeding establishments. In this area, then, there is a large minority of states clustering toward the European model. However, other factors, such as prohibitions on the breeding of defects, training requirements for commercial breeders, and restrictions on the number of times and frequency that females can be bred, were either wholly absent or rare. The trend at the state level though is toward regulation. That is not the case with the national government, which is currently proposing a weakening of enforcement with third parties allowed to conduct inspections. Finally, the hypothesis about greyhound racing was refuted. Contrary to expectations, only six states continue to host commercial greyhound racing and the "sport" is declining in popularity even in those places.

Law in the US and EU

The review of these seven policies offers confirmation of distinct European and American approaches. As hypothesized, American states and certainly the US government cluster toward the American approach and the EU and its member states gravitate toward the European one. The findings thus contribute quite clearly to one side of the academic debate in comparative politics. Yet the review also exposes a lack of universality, as there are states in both the US and EU that defy these approaches on a number of policies. More importantly, the findings do not fully answer the question about the more just place for dogs. Even in these policy areas, the substantive differences are not always striking. Commercial greyhound racing is as rare in the US as it is in the EU, the euthanasia of healthy dogs is done in both places, and the duties of caretakers and for that matter, commercial breeders are not all that different in their particulars. To conclude as to the more dog-friendly place, practices, which do not lend themselves to the same level of accurate analysis, must also be considered.

Compliance and Enforcement Equal Complexity

When adherence to law, both in letter and spirit, is taken into account, the search for canine justice becomes more complex. There are strong indicators, in the forms of dollars spent on food and veterinary medicine as well as opinion surveys, that people take good care of their dogs throughout the US and EU. Yet there are also troubling signs in the forms of abandoned and relinquished dogs that highlight poor ethics of responsibility. There are places where hunting dogs are treated like objects, tortured, and discarded. In the

EU, there is more of a problem with irresponsible care in eastern and southern member states, while the US has higher shelter populations in the south and problematic practices in the plains. However, in all of these areas, there have been significant improvements reflected in more protective laws and changing attitudes.

A critical indicator of the welfare of canines is the size of the stray and/or "unwanted" population. In those places where such numbers are high, there is more likely to be crowded shelters, routine euthanasia, abandonment, relinquishment, and a lower value on canine life. There is a major problem with the management of the canine population in the EU. The national governments are not doing enough to persuade people to sterilize dogs in member states with less-than-perfect ethics of care. Without full adherence to such ethics of highly responsible care, low rates of sterilization lead to increases in the canine population. To be sure, some states are experimenting with spay/neuter/release and also stepping up efforts to educate the public. Yet there are multiple states, especially in the South and East, with large "unwanted" populations that are treated poorly. Indeed, in those places where the euthanasia of healthy dogs is legal in the EU, it is used much more in the eastern and southern member states, where there is a large stray population. In addition, there is serious doubt as to the compliance with the prohibition in the Czech Republic. Given legal requirements in the EU, the permanent identification of dogs, however, is becoming more commonplace. That practice is expected to help in the deterrence of abandonment, which contributes to an increasing stray population.

To manage canine population, many US states have legislated incentives for people to sterilize dogs as well as creative funding mechanisms for this purpose. There are crowded shelters, especially in the South, but there are also efforts to relocate as many dogs as possible to areas where they are likely to be adopted. Nonetheless, the euthanasia of healthy dogs is done on a larger scale where shelters are full. The US has more of a problem with relinquishment than abandonment, but the permanent identification of dogs can still be helpful in returning lost dogs and managing the canine population. Despite a lack of legal mandates, the practice of permanently identifying dogs is becoming more common.

While a majority of states in both the US and EU have regulatory frameworks in place for commercial breeders, the lack of strong regulations at the central level allows puppy mills to continue operations on both continents. Failing central regulations, abusive breeders can flock to those states with poor regulations and market the pups to other states. While added regulations have helped, there continue to be stories of abusive conditions in this industry on both sides of the Atlantic. Relative to the canine population, the numbers involved in commercial racing and scientific experimentation are small. For those unlucky few, however, the fate is a grim one. In the US, there are few legal protections and loopholes at the ready to avoid even those. The EU has better protections on paper but it has yet to be seen how well they will be enforced. For example, previous policies requiring that animals not be used in experiments if alternative means to the same objective existed were not strictly enforced.

Despite a lack of prohibitions, fewer Americans are cropping their dogs' ears, but tail docking remains the norm for many breeds. In the EU, these unnecessary surgeries are increasingly rare given that clubs expel such altered dogs from shows. There is no incentive for breeders to dock tails even if it was legal. Finally, as the reader may recall, dogfighting is illegal throughout the US and EU. Despite that fact, it is prevalent in both places. In the US, there has been a trend toward more enforcement and stiffer penalties at both national and state levels. Parts of the EU, especially the Baltic region in the East but others as well, confront an epidemic of this cruelty. Given this harsh reality, such areas are not as dog-friendly as protective policies might indicate. Laws are useless unless they are enforced.

Where Is the More Dog-Friendly Place?

There are member states in the EU, particularly in the North-Central region, where both protective laws and widespread compliance yield ideal conditions for dogs. Yet also in the EU are member states with lax regulations and poor ethics of care. Conditions for some dogs in Slovakia and Romania, for example, are grim given uninspected breeding facilities, poor conditions in shelters, and the widespread use of euthanasia. In between these extremes are many member states with less-than-perfect ethics of care and some protective legislation. It is additionally clear that there is variation in the welfare of canines *within* member states. For example, in urban areas of eastern and southern Europe, there is evidence of "pet humanization" or treating dogs as members of the family. In some rural areas in these same states, there are problems with abandonment of hunting dogs and poor supervision, with intact dogs allowed to roam. To be sure, this rural-urban split is evident only in aggregate indicators. For example, dogfighting is a major problem in urban areas, while many dogs find loving homes in rural ones. To improve conditions for dogs, the EU and many of its member states are using laws to change human practices. At this point, however, the location within the EU matters greatly in determining the presence of canine justice and welfare.

Despite its comparatively lax regulations, the US can claim lots of places that are more dog-friendly than parts of the EU. There is also a growing number of states that are passing protective legislation for canines. The West Coast is well known for its dog-friendliness, with parks and amenities for dogs. Yet in cities across the country, including Southern and Midwestern ones, dog parks have become very popular and attest to caretakers' awareness of the need to socialize and exercise dogs. Nonetheless southern and rural states in the plains are more likely to have negative indicators, such as large shelter populations and high rates of euthanasia. Four of those five states with commercial greyhound racing are southern and the fifth is Iowa, an agricultural state. However, as in the EU, there are abusive practices, such as dogfighting, in cities, and dog-friendly rural areas. Nowadays, in most southern states of both the EU and US, it is a shrinking minority that views dogs as objects and more and more who consider them family members. Indeed, the legislative trend in the South is toward more canine protection and better management of population.

Canine justice is not similar in all places in the US, though there is not the same level of extremes of protective and neglectful care as found in the EU. Like in the EU, there is a trend toward homogenization in the US, but its sources are more from internal migration and media socialization than national law. In both the US and EU, the status of the dog also impacts canine justice. For those canines without human families, there are decidedly unfriendly places in both the US and EU. In contrast, *companions* are generally more welcome in the EU than US. Most EU member states are inclined to welcome such dogs in public places, including restaurants and parks. The US is less welcoming, but there are more and more dog parks and many businesses, including hotels and outdoor restaurants, that have come to recognize the financial benefits of canine-friendly policies. In sum, there is just too much variation, especially in the EU but in the US as well, to declare one entity more dog friendly than the other. Specific locations matter!

Explaining the Differences: Thoughts for Future Research

What accounts for the variations in dog-friendliness? While this study does not provide evidence to answer that question, it yields suggestions for further research. Several variables could be postulated as having a relationship with protective canine legislation, including the wealth of the state, the strength of democratic institutions, the degree of religiosity, patriarchal attitudes, and population density.

The poor conditions for dogs in parts of eastern EU member states are arguably the result of the very different history in that region in comparison to the rest of the EU. As former satellites of the old USSR, these member states lacked democratic institutions and consumer-oriented economies until the 1990s. They are much poorer than the western states. Additionally, they have historically been governed by corrupt regimes. When there is no security for human individuals, in terms of economic well-being and civil rights, there is not likely to be much concern for other species. With the fall of the USSR and now the inclusion of eastern member states in the EU, there have already been tremendous strides to improve the lot of animals, including dogs. Indeed, the pet industry is growing in these states and there are discernible trends of pet "humanization" and demand for premium products among a growing minority. However, the differential in both law and practice currently in place between many of these member states and those in the west could lead researchers to consider the impact of wealth and stable democratic institutions on the strength of protective legislation for canines.

In both the US and EU, southern states have more problematic cultures for canines. However, in both cases, there have been significant improvements reflected in more protective laws and changing attitudes. As the reader may recall, it is increasingly customary for pets to be considered family members in Spain, Portugal, and Italy. Yet there are stubborn pockets of resistance. There are several possible explanations for the slower path to canine friendliness in southern states of the US and EU. Southern cultures, in both places, tend to be both more masculine and hierarchical. In such cultures, compassion toward animals is labeled "feminine" and avoided, particularly by insecure men. As the reader may recall, one study found the dog-fighting world to be one where the dogs become surrogates for men to prove their masculinity. The need to do so is stronger in cultures that devalue feminine virtues and respect only masculine ones. It follows that lines in these subcultures are clear, with more traditional gender roles and sharp distinctions between humans and other animals. One's standing is elevated via the reduction of the status of others. In this hierarchy, animals are at the bottom, with little compassion shown to them. The cultures are inherently conservative, with change deemed threatening. As a result, any objection to the treatment of animals is likely to be strongly discouraged. Future studies could compare attitudes about gender roles and/or ideology with the presence of protective legislation for canines. Once again, the wealth of a state might also be an important determinant, as many of these southern states are not as wealthy as northern neighbors.

It is not just southern areas but rural ones that view animals, including dogs, with less sentimentality. In the US and EU, the combination of these two factors, southern and rural, combines to create less hospitable places for canines. There is a world of difference, for example, between metro Atlanta and rural areas. It is not just southern cultures that can be problematic either. According to Bulliet, those cultures that practice animal husbandry, which he calls domestic societies, have a very different view of animals than those that are not regularly exposed to farm animals. In domestic cultures, there is a sharp differentiation made between humans and other animals. People come into "daily contact with domestic animals (other than pets) and witness the slaughter of animals." Thinking of these animals as "other," they are more likely to become hardened to their suffering. As Bulliet explains, "domestic societies take for granted the killing of animals and experience few moral qualms in consuming animal products."[1] For the most part, dogs and cats in such cultures are placed alongside other domestic animals in status. Though they are not slaughtered for food, they are valued more for their use to humans. Any assignment of sentience to dogs and cats would pose a threat to the sharp demarcation between humans and other animals. Certain religious denominations prevalent in rural areas tend to reinforce this demarcation as well, with some of these rural areas in the US still resisting the theory of evolution, for example. In contrast, post-domestic societies, or those where "people live far away, both physically and psychologically, from animals that produce the food, fiber, and hides they depend on,…" maintain "very close relationships with companion animals—pets—often relating to them as if they were human."[2] There is not the same psychological need to differentiate humans from other animals. This theory invites consideration of the impact of population density, the presence of animal husbandry, and religious beliefs on protective laws for canines. In short, there is much fodder here for quantitative works identifying correlations and/or qualitative ones perhaps doing an in-depth case study of one state with rural and urban areas.

Spreading Justice—the Way Forward

In the southern regions of both the US and EU, there has been considerable change in laws and attitudes. The EU is helping to bring about legal change in the East, with its protocol on experiments as one example. The challenges are greater in some of the eastern member states, but the economic benefits of membership in the EU should help to jumpstart change to some degree. Since many easterners migrate to the West and then return home for visits or extended stays, there is likely to be some convergence in attitudes over time. The role of European public opinion should not be understated as a force of change either, as people in the East want to be a part of Europe and not a differentiated and isolated enclave. According to Risse, that desire to be a part of Europe influenced Germans and Spaniards on other issues.[3] However, there are also problematic signs for animals in parts of the east, such as Hungary and Poland, where non-democratic forces are gaining strength. Given the role the EU has played in improving the legal treatment of animals in that region, a retreat from its values would be a loss for animals.

If the plight of canines is to improve, the EU most certainly needs to regulate commercial breeding. At a minimum, it must set humane conditions for kennels throughout the EU and ensure humane transport of puppies across borders. Because some western member states have very high standards for breeding, the EU must be careful to allow such standards to remain law but also to insist on a better "floor" for other places. Ideally, there would be included in the regulations meaningful sanctions for offenders. As the reader may recall, some criminals have switched from smuggling drugs to puppies in light of the lenient treatment if caught. In addition, the EU must develop a comprehensive strategy to manage the canine population, spreading the practice of spay-neuter-release programs in regions with large stray populations, encouraging sterilization in those member states with less-than-perfect ethics of caretaking, and helping to facilitate the re-location of dogs from states with high shelter populations to those with minimal shelter populations. There are other issues, especially in the East and parts of the South, that merit immediate attention. However, these are the most pressing matters for the EU to tackle. If population was better managed, other concerns, such as the mass euthanasia of healthy animals, would become less of such a gargantuan challenge.

In the US, the national government needs to improve its regulatory scheme over commercial breeders and it is long past time to update its laws on experimentation. These goals are of course not easily accomplished. However, over 60 percent of the American public, per recent survey results, support a ban on animal research for non-medical commercial purposes, a ban on animal research when an alternative exists, and the extension of cruelty legislation to protect research animals. What is more, almost 90 percent of Americans support licensing and inspections for commercial breeders.[4] In light of those views, canine advocates could begin a conversation that might bring pressure to bear upon lawmakers. Avoiding the demonization of all breeders, advocates could highlight good ones on both small and large scales as models on which to base reasonable regulations. Likewise, a discussion of experimentation can reference the European model to demonstrate that steps can be taken to improve the lives of laboratory animals without dooming science. At a bare minimum, the public could insist upon a ban on the use of all former companion animals in the laboratory. With the AVMA now on record against unnecessary surgeries, the AKC needs to be shamed on this point. The inhumane means by which some commercial breeders dock tails must be exposed. Again, advocates can take advantage of the European comparison. There are still dog shows in the EU and the kennel clubs have re-written their standards to exclude any dogs with docked tails or cropped ears. Why won't the AKC?

It is less likely that mandatory identification of dogs with permanent markers, such as microchips, will be accepted in the US, but their benefits can be advertised as a good option for the caretakers of companion animals. Nor are states likely to ban euthanasia soon, but the success of the No-Kill movement can serve as evidence that such laws are possible in the future. The major challenge in the US and to some extent in the EU is to overcome the cognitive dissonance and to see all dogs as one species. When that is accomplished, there will be less tolerance for puppy mills, laboratory dogs, and the mass euthanasia of healthy and abandoned dogs.

Notes

1. For both quotations, see Richard W. Bulliet, *Hunters, Herders, and Hamburgers: The Past and Future of Human-Animal Relationships* (New York: Columbia University Press, 2005), 3.
2. *Ibid.*
3. Thomas Risse, *A Community of Europeans? Transnational Identities and Public Spheres* (Ithaca: Cornell University Press, 2010), 52, 65–71.

4. Susan Hunter and Richard A. Brisbin, Jr. *Pet Politics: The Political and Legal Lives of Cats, Dogs, and Horses in Canada and the United States* (West Lafayette, Indiana: Purdue University Press, 2016), 104.

Bibliography

Bulliet, Richard W. *Hunters, Herders, and Hamburgers: The Past and Future of Human-Animal Relationships*. New York: Columbia University Press, 2005.

Hunter, Susan and Richard A. Brisbin, Jr. *Pet Politics: The Political and Legal Lives of Cats, Dogs, and Horses in Canada and the United States*. West Lafayette, Indiana: Purdue University Press, 2016.

Risse, Thomas. *A Community of Europeans? Transnational Identities and Public Spheres*. Ithaca: Cornell University Press, 2010.

INDEX

A

B

C

D

E

F

G

T

U

V

W

www.ingramcontent.com/pod-product-compliance
Ingram Content Group UK Ltd.
Pitfield, Milton Keynes, MK11 3LW, UK
UKHW021827100926
8556IPUK00003B/207

9 781433 159015